BOSTON ON GUNS & COURAGE

Proven Tools for Chronic Problems

by

Boston T. Party

Published by

JAVELIN PRESS

c/o 504 West 24th St., Suite 73E, Austin, Texas. (78705)
(Without any 4 USC §§ 105-110 *"Federal area"* or *"State."*)
www.javelinpress.com

First Printing: *March, 1998*
Printed in the united states of America,
without any 4 §§ 105-110 *"Federal area"* or *"State."*

10 9 8 7 6 5 4 3 2 1 / 05 04 03 02 01 00 99 98

Library of Congress Catalog Number 98-065085
ISBN 1-888766-04-2

ACKNOWLEDGMENTS

Huge appreciation goes to my proofreaders and editors-- you know who you are.

Special thanks to my friend "R.H." for his great help in polishing this book's material, even though he hates AR15s. (He *used* to hate Glocks, too, but now carries a G27, so perhaps there's "hope" for him...)

Kisses to my lioness "N.L." for her new passion for guns and liberty, and for her subsequent fine editing of my book. (She's got a G27 and now wants an AR15. Gee, I might have created a "monster." Good. I'm really enjoying her company.)

Finally, I thank all my distributors and readers who so enthusiastically supported my first four books, *Good-Bye April 15th!*, *You & The Police!*, *Bulletproof Privacy,* and, most notably, the controversial *Hologram of Liberty*. I'm grateful, *profoundly* grateful, for such a fine public.

DEDICATION

To the Massachusetts Militia Captain John Parker, and to his present and future successors.

To the late Glenn Wilburn and his wife Kathy of Oklahoma City who had the relentless courage to fully investigate the OKBOMB(s) on their own suspicions.

To Bill and Hillary Clinton, without whom this book would not have been possible, or necessary.

To the several dozen murdered souls who were brave enough to speak out on the Clintons' criminal enterprises.

Finally, to Bill and Hillary's pal, Vince Foster, who might be alive today if he'd only had a gun on 20 July 1993.

Other works by
Boston T. Party

Good-Bye April 15th!

Published November 1992. Crystal-clear and supremely readable, *Good-Bye April 15th!* is considered *the* "untax" classic. Unfortunately, we are currently out of stock but will reprint soon--details to follow on our Web Site--**http://www.javelinpress.com**

You & The Police!

Published January 1996. The definitive modern guide regarding your rights and tactics during police confrontations. Every gunowner needs a copy to avoid seizures under the *Gun Free School Zone Act* (repassed in 1996). Don't lose your freedom through ignorance!

128 pp. Available for Ø15 + Ø4 s&h (cash, please).

Bulletproof Privacy

How to Live Hidden, Happy, and Free! Published January 1997. Our book will explain precisely how to lay low and be left alone by the busy-bodies, snoops, and bureaucrats. Boston has "been there--done that" and shares many of his unique methods. Don't settle for old, fluffy, rip-off titles. Nothing we've seen compares to this book.

160 pp. Available for Ø16 + Ø4 s&h (cash, please).

Hologram of Liberty

The Constitution's Shocking Alliance with Big Government Published August 1997. A splash of cold water on our civic mythology and parchment worship. The Philadelphia Convention of 1787 and its Constitution was the most brilliant and subtle *coup d'état* in history. The federalist/nationalist framers *wanted* a strong central government, which they guaranteed through purposely ambiguous verbiage.

262 pp. Available for Ø20 + Ø4 s&h (cash, please).

a novel (yet untitled)

Due 1999. If you liked *Unintended Consequences* by John Ross or Ayn Rand's *Atlas Shrugged*, then Boston's novel will be a favorite. It dramatically outlines an innovative recipe for Liberty which neatly bypasses the bureaucracies, the courts and the Congress. A practical continuation of *Hologram of Liberty*, his unique plan *can actually work*, if a comparatively small number of Americans will do it. Boston says this is his most exciting work yet. Stay tuned to our Web Site!

TABLE OF CONTENTS

8   Battle Rifles

PREFACE

Arms are the only true badges of liberty. The possession of arms is the distinction of a free man from a slave.
-- Andrew Fletcher, *A Discourse of Government with relation to Militias* (1698), p. 47

My puny philosophical and political opponents will no doubt pigeonhole me as a *"gun nut."* True, I enjoy owning and shooting guns, and am an unabashed enthusiast--however, guns are more a means than an end. I am a *"freedom nut"* and guns (along with the responsibility, training and will to properly use them) are *"liberty's teeth"* (George Washington).

This book is not about hunting. There are already plenty of good hunting books, and yet another one is not direly needed right now. The 2nd Amendment is not *really* about hunting--it is about keeping politicians nervous, honest *servants.* An armed citizenry is the *ultimate* "check and balance" on government. When the ballot box and the jury box no longer work, then it's probably time for the cartridge box.

I can't speak for other nations, but *Americans* merely collectively *delegate* their individual sovereignties to servant government to operate on their *behalf.* When the servant grows haughty it should get corrected or fired. Since, however, the Constitution set up an *insular* arrangement of political correction (congressmen impeach and try *themselves*), and since voting out the congressional servants has proven to be nearly worthless, people are now contemplating sterner measures. We should no longer *"spare the rod and spoil the child."*

It's only because congressmen are *not* in fear of their jobs, their fortunes, or their lives that they have the *nerve* to propose repealing the 2nd Amendment, classifying vitamins as prescription drugs, or banning wood-burning stoves. Such D.C. ilk should have been dragged down the streets back in 1933 when they outlawed the private ownership of gold--which they blamed for the Depression!

The thugs who enforced such obscenity should have been strung up from the first day. Since they weren't, they *now* feel free to stomp family pets to death, shoot nursing mothers in the face, and pour helicopter gunfire through the roofs of homestead churches *with women, children and babies inside*.

Men that are above all fear, soon grow above all shame.
-- Trenchard and Gordon, *Cato's Letters* (1755), vol. I, p. 255

Our government, now fearless, has grown above all shame. We *could* have easily pulled these weeds when they first sprouted-- now they've Kevlar® vests, night vision, and silenced submachine guns. For us, the *Gun Control Act of 1968* was 1936 Rhineland and we blew it. The "Brady" bill was 1938 Sudentenland *Anschluss*, the "Crime" bill Czechoslovakia, and the "Terror" bill 1939 Poland.

Now we're probably going to have to fight "WWII." And we're not *ready*. (Thankfully, neither are *they*.) Oh, we've got the *guns*--we just don't have the courage. We are nearly perfectly gelded. Never before has such a well-armed people become so utterly apathetic to the preservation of their liberties, so lazy in their thinking, and so cowardly in their actions.

Our domestic gun-control Hitlers have successfully called our bluff too many times, and have grown too confident with their progress. A slap in their faces back in 1968 would have saved us incalculable bloodshed a generation later. If there is not a John Ross *Unintended Consequences* scenario *very soon*, then we're in for some extremely nasty business--Civil War 2.

I don't desire this, but if it's inevitable, then let it come. *"Is life so dear, or peace so sweet as to be purchased at the price of chains or slavery?"* No, it's not. It never *was*. **We have the badges of liberty, but not the *soul*. We're serfs with guns.** This unprecedented paradox *will* be resolved in one of only two ways: We'll either lose our serfdom, or we'll lose our guns.

If you *won't* fight for your Liberty, then sell your guns to us *now* before they're confiscated without compensation.

Or, read on.

Boston on Guns & Courage is about regaining the soul and polishing the badges.

❖ **1**

USING THIS BOOK

Boston on Guns & Courage is not meant to be the definitive guide to all, or even most, firearms matters. Many subjects worthy of complete books (e.g., ballistics, CQB tactics, law, gun history, reloading, shooting techniques, equipment, sniping, etc.) are only briefly covered, else this would have been a 500 page book not seen before 1999. We don't have that kind of time, and besides, excellent information on those subjects already exists. My goal is simply to dispel many potentially dangerous gun misconceptions, and illustrate what you *don't* know.

Why listen to *me*?

I do not claim to be a working professional in the shooting industry. I am not a Jeff Cooper, Clint Smith, Bill Rogers, or Chuck Taylor. I have neither the extensive military experience of these men, nor their years of instruction. I'm not even a cop.

So, *what*? Did you learn to drive from *Al Unser*? No, it was more likely your dad or your brother. My point is this: the personal instruction from bonafide experts is very expensive. It takes great commitment. Although not even 1% of gunowners will ever get to a shooting academy, there's no reason why much of that training cannot "trickle down" from civilian alumni.

Of all our prestigious shooting schools combined, probably less than 25,000 civilian Americans have enjoyed such training. That's 25,000 out of *75,000,000* gunowners--or one in 3,000. Most of them went to only one or two classes. I've been to more than six, for pistol, shotgun and rifle. I'd guess that only 2,500 civilians have been to at least six Ø750+ courses. That's one in only *30,000* gunowners.

I always shoot in the top 10% of my class, much to the dismay of the SWAT, SEAL and SF guys. At fifteen, with pimples and braces, I won a local pistol competition with my Colt Trooper .357 Magnum. (You can imagine how ecstatic the cops and highway patrolmen were.) Therefore, it seems fair to say that I'm a very highly-trained and practiced civilian and layman. Outside the military and police fraternities, few Americans have my firearms experience. I discuss all this, not to brag, but to back up my position of mild authority.

My dogma is fairly orthodox shooting doctrine. Shooting is more of a science than an art, and what has been so far discovered to work, *works.* If you learn and practice the basics, you'll get smooth, and with smoothness, comes speed.

I've eclectically collected (and rejected) bits from all the Masters. Thus, some of this book is just plain personal opinion and bias. Since guns are *personal* items, bias is to be expected. For example, although I'm somewhat of a "Glockaholic," if the 1911 or SIG or CZ "resonates" better with *you,* then by all means use one of those excellent pistols.

Boston on Guns & Courage is a catalog of one man's experience and opinions. I don't know everything, but I think you'll get your money's worth. I hope you will find this book a timely, useful, and informative work which stands out above the swill proffered by the misinformed to the ignorant.

ABBREVIATIONS & TERMINOLOGY

Every industry and hobby has its own nomenclature. I assume at least a *moderate* level of knowledge of shooting verbiage on your part. Here are some bits you might not know.

Ø   "Federal Reserve Notes" which are no longer redeemable in and masquerade as real $ dollars (gold/silver money). Ancient Chinese proverb (they're *all* ancient, aren't they?): *"The beginning of wisdom is to call things by their right name."* The inverse of that is to stop calling things by their wrong name, which is why I refuse to call FRNs "dollars."

George Orwell made the point that shoddy language results in shoddy politics. He was right. Calling dry "wet" and darkness "light" requires the simultaneous, purposeful mental suspension of truth--a 1/1000th second bit of insanity--and, in my opinion, evil. Once you begin

lying to yourself, you must also lie to others. Do this enough times (as did the Nazis and as do the Communists) and one's entire thinking (and thus actions) will become deranged and evil.
Make a firm habit of calling things by what they are, not by what sounds cute, kind, acceptable, "politically correct," or expedient.
§   **section.** You'll see this in law quotations.
5.56x45, 7.62x51, 12.7x99, etc. Metric designation of bullet diameter by case length. The above examples are our .223, .308, and .50BMG.
15 + 1, etc. Total gun capacity: mag capacity plus round in chamber.
AP   armor piercing. Usually designated with a painted black tip.
"assault rifles"   Military-style rifles which scare Congress.
bbl   barrel. Round into chamber; bullet out muzzle.
BC   ballistic coefficient. A rating system in decimal points of a bullet's "sleekness"--ability to retain velocity. The less a bullet sheds its velocity, the quicker it gets down range, and the less it drops.   Shape is everything for BC, and boattails help greatly.
BDC   bullet drop compensator. Sniper scopes (and some hunting ones) have BDC cams in them for certain loads (e.g., M118, etc.), so all the shooter has to do is dial in the distance and the reticle will be spot on.
BMG   Browning Machine Gun. As in .50BMG, which is very popular with civilians in long-distance (1000-1500yd) shooting matches.   The .50BMG throws a 700gr at 2950. *"Gee, willikers, Batman!"*
boattail   Bullets with tapered bases, designed for long-range.
BOL   bullet overall length. My own term. Same as bullet length.
Condition 1-4   Descriptions of a gun's loaded status. See Ch. 2.
CCW   concealed carry weapon permit. Today, some 31 states have approved a *"shall issue"* form of permit. Don't get too excited, however. If the states really supported your right to bear arms, they'd have simply removed any carry restrictions for nonfelon, sane adults (as in Vermont). Millions have rushed to obtain permits.   A permit means permission. Once Government knows the names, SSNs and fingerprints of all Americans with the nerve to conceal carry, these permits will be revoked through some future unilateral disarmament measure. My point is this: CCWs are merely a sneaky form of personal registration. Beware.
cheek weld   The consistent placement of cheek to buttstock. Precise and consistent mating is crucial to long-range accuracy.
clip   *Not* a magazine, but a stripper clip or revolver moon clip.
COL   cartridge overall length. A max COL describes the longest cartridge a magazine and/or chamber will accept and feed.
Commie   A Soviet Bloc caliber (7.62x25, 7.62x39, 9x18).
compound   The wood home of a dissident under federal siege.
concealment   Something which hides you from view (e.g., brush, curtain), but offers little or no protection from incoming fire (as does cover).

cover   Protective concealment, such as a brick wall, car, etc.

CQB   close quarters battle.

cup   Copper Units Pressure. A measure of chamber pressure. Guns in identical calibers (e.g., .45-70) differ in their chamber strength, especially antique vs. modern guns--so beware. Also, know an action's strength *before* rebarreling it. For example, the M96 Mausers from Spain and Chile are only 45,000cup actions, but were foolishly rebarreled for the 52,000cup .308.

DA   double action, which describes the first-shot cocking and dropping of the hammer by the trigger, instead of having to manually cock the hammer (which is a "single action" or SA).

DAO   double action only. Some DA pistols cannot be fired from SA, so as to make successive trigger pulls the same as the first.

DM   Dakota Magnum. Beltless Magnums formed from the .404 Jeffery case. DMs achieve Weatherby velocities without the belt (which sometimes gives feeding and reloading difficulties).

FFL   Federal Firearms Licensee. Gun manufacturers must sell their product through the 80,276 FFLs in America. FFLs must charge sales tax, perform background checks, keep those yellow BATF Form 4473s on file, etc. Increased licensing fees and BATF hassles have purposely reduced the number from 250,000 in 1994.

firepower   Hits per minute, not rounds (misses) per minute.

fps   foot per second. Bullet speed. 1067fps is Mach 1 at sea level. Ammo for silenced weapons is loaded subsonic, to avoid the *craaack*.

ft/lb   foot-pound. A unit of work; energy to lift 1 pound 1 foot.

ga   gauge. In shotguns, the bore size of a 12ga is a lead ball weighing 1/12th of a pound. The smaller the gauge, the larger the bore.

GCA   Gun Control Act of 1968. At least Congress had the honesty to accurately name this thing. It mandated the current FFL system, and the *NFA* registration of *"destructive devices"* like 20mm cannons.

gr   grains. Measure of bullet and powder weight. There are 7000gr per pound. 1lb of powder will fill 200 cases of 35gr powder loads.

HPBT   hollow point boattail. A great long-distance Sierra bullet.

ISW   inside waistband. A style of concealed-carry pistol holster.

KE   kinetic energy. Measured in ft/lbs.

locktime   The amount of time between the trigger's release of the sear and the firing pin's strike of the primer. Faster is better, as there's less movement of the shooter and target. The Remington 788 is renowned for its fast locktime, whereas the Mausers are much slower.

M80   U.S. .308 ball. Non-matchgrade (2½-3MOA) 147gr ammo. This is "spray & pray" stuff for M60 machine guns.

M96   Mauser 1896. The penultimate Mauser bolt-action design; much better than the M93 and M94 action. It is cock-on-closing and doesn't have the third locking lug of the M98. The Swedes used the M96 the most extensively with their 6.5x55. A good 45,000cup action, though not really suitable for .308 level pressure. They can be converted to cock-on-opening for about Ø25.

M98   **Mauser 1898.** The last, and best, German Mauser action.

M118   **U.S. .308 Match.** 173gr 1¼MOA ammo. Good stuff, though not the equal of the ¾MOA Fed 168gr Match (or comparable handloads).

M193   **U.S. 55gr .223 ball.** It's been replaced with 62gr M855.

M855   **U.S. 62gr .223 ball.** A copy of the Belgian SS109 ball.

magazine   A gun's ammo container. Detachable or not. Not a "clip."

malf   **malfunction.**

Magnum   A cartridge of greater case capacity (and thus power) than earlier standards in the same caliber. Manufacturers include Dakota, H&H, Imperial, Lapua, Norma, Remington, STW, Weatherby, and Winchester. The Imperial and Dakota mags are beltless.

ME   **muzzle energy.** The measure of ft/lbs at muzzle--distance 0.

militia   All adult male citizens of gun-bearing age (18-45y/o) who comprise the backbone of a nation's defense. The organized militia is the National Guard and the unorganized militia is the rest of us.

MOA   **Minute Of Angle**, which is exactly 1.047" at 100yds, though rounded down to 1". At 400yds 1MOA is 4", ½MOA is 2", etc.

MPBR   **maximum point blank range.** A hunter's system of zeroing his rifle to eliminate holdover/holdunder estimations. Since the heart/lungs vital zone area of a deer is about 10" in diameter, an MPBR zero is one in which a bullet will neither rise nor fall more than 5" at some maximum distance, to hit inside an 10" circle with a center hold. The higher the MV, the longer the MPBR. Most MPBRs are about 225-350yds. While the MPBR system is unsuitable for long distance work, it is good for those hunting within 350yds without BDC scopes and rangefinders.

MV   **muzzle velocity.** The measure of ft/sec at muzzle--distance 0.

ND   **negligent discharge.** Making a gun fire unintentionally.

NFA   ***National Firearms Act of 1934.*** The first serious federal gun law, passed by FDR's Congress. It mandated a national registry and taxation of automatic weapons and short rifles and shotguns. The camel's nose under the tent. Greatly expanded by *GCA68*.

NVD   **night vision device.** Soon to be outlawed for us. Get one *now*.

OEM   **original equipment manufactured.** Stock stuff.

overbore   A cartridge (usually Magnum) which gives high velocities through its inefficiently high powder charge (e.g., the .300 Phoenix). These calibers usually burn out their barrels very quickly (w/i 1,000rds).

parallax   The tendency for scope reticles to shift and change impact point if the shooter moves his head. Consistent cheekweld is vital with scopes above 10X.

Patriot An American who loves his/her country. Currently demonized.

QD   **quick detachable,** as in sling and scope mounts.

rd   **round.** One loaded cartridge. Can also mean a bullet enroute.

reticle The "crosshairs" in a rifle scope. Mil-Dot is the way to go.

RM   **Remington Magnum.** In .222, 6.5, 7, and 8mm, .350, and .44.

Rule 1-4 The classic, overlapping safety rules of Jeff Cooper.

SA   **single action.** A trigger pull merely releases the already-cocked hammer; it cannot (as in DA) cock the hammer first. The Colt 1911 is a SA semi-automatic.

SBT   **spitzer boattail.** A long-distance, lead-tipped hunting bullet (e.g., Sierra Game King). Regular spitzers have a flat base.

SD   **sectional density.** The ratio of a bullet's weight in pounds to the square of its diameter in inches. Bullets of the same shape but with higher SD retain their velocity and energy better.

"sniper rifle" Any rifle with a scope. The anti-gun pols are finally realizing the awesome capability of scoped, high-powered rifles, which make the AK47 look puny by comparison. Watch for this perjorative term to become a public buzzphrase (like "cult," "compound," "Saturday Night specials," "assault weapons" and "cop killer bullets") within 3 years.

STW   **Shooting Times Western.** An 8mmRM necked down to 7mm. It's the most powerful of the 7mm Magnums, throwing a 175gr at 3100+.

TANSTAAFL   *"There ain't no such thing as a free lunch."*
From Robert A. Heinlein's *The Moon Is A Harsh Mistress.* A catch phrase and motto of many hip Libertarians.

training The programming of subconscious muscle memory through physical exercise at the range. One trains by doing, not reading.

twist A bore's spiral grooves giving a bullet its spin, and thus directional stability and lift. Twist rate is described in turn/inches (1-9", etc.).

working   A caliber or gun primarily for hunting, pest control, etc.

WM   **Winchester Magnum.** In .240, .264, .300, .338, and .458.

zero   To sight in a gun at a specific distance (100, 200, 300, or MPBR).

NOTES ON READING THIS BOOK

Quotations are in this form. Any original emphasis is underlined. **Any added emphasis of mine is in boldface.** *When I supplement a quote, my nonitalicized comments are within ( ) or [ ]--(like this, for example).*

❖ 2

GUN HANDLING

THE FOUR SAFETY RULES

There only four basic safety rules. If you follow these perfectly, you'll never have a ND, or "negligent discharge." **There is no such thing as an "accidental discharge." Guns do not "go off" by themselves.** They must be chambered and fired by a human. When that human is untrained, unalert, and undisciplined--*then* occurs an ND.

Rule 1

All guns are always loaded. In your mind, there is no such thing as an "unloaded" gun. You *never* handle a gun differently because it's "unloaded." (Besides, guns *should* be loaded.)

Whenever you pick up a gun--even if you're alone and the only one handling it; even if you personally just disassembled it moments ago--*check the chamber.* Make this a perfect habit. You could have forgotten loading it, or somebody could have loaded/unloaded it without your knowledge. **Have firsthand knowledge of its condition *every* time you pick up a gun!**

Rule 2

Never let your muzzle cover anything you don't want to destroy. Do not wave your muzzle past people. If somebody can see even a *crescent* of your muzzle, then you're unsafe.

Rule 3

Keep your finger off the trigger until your sights are on the target. Resting your finger on the trigger is one of the hardest habits to break. Your trigger finger should feel "at home" indexed straight on the frame.

One of General Patton's principles was that mistakes should be *paid for* instantly. Does a hot stove ever postpone burning you? Similarly, gun safety violations should be safely "painful" before somebody gets killed. Make a pact with your family and shooting buddies that anybody catching you violate Rule 3 (or *any* Rule, for that matter) immediately gets a Ø20 bill. (I incorporate this plan in my classes. Never has anyone paid more than twice.) Mistakes and safety violations should be rarely made, and only in the initial training.

Rule 4
Be sure of your target and what's beyond it. A Houston father, untrained and nervous, blew away a suspected intruder hiding in the closet. The "intruder" was his 16 y/o stepdaughter, skipping school. This was no "accident"--this was *negligence*.

GUN SAFETY AND CHILDREN

Thanks to more and better safety programs like the NRA's Eddie Eagle, negligent fatal shootings of children have fallen from 550 in 1975 to 200 in 1995. Considering the tens of millions of gunowning households, 200/year is nearly zero (though even 1 is too many).

I believe in gunproofing children, *not* childproofing guns (which can't be reasonably done to readily accessible defensive guns). With proper safety education, guns are no more risky in your household than are gas stoves, solvents, or steak knives. The best family philosophy is as follows:

No toy guns allowed
Toy guns which are "safe" to point at others create very bad habits difficult to unlearn. Guns are serious tools requiring awesome responsibility, and toy versions will only dilute this vital issue. If you take your children shooting often enough, they'll never miss not having *toy* guns.

If a gun is unexpectedly found, don't touch it.
The child should know to leave it alone and tell an adult. Praise the child for doing this.

Family guns are *always* available for inspection
Eliminate the "forbidden fruit" syndrome of your guns. Face it, kids love to snoop around when parents are away. I did, and you did. (The hideous taste of that dictionary-sized bar of chocolate always perplexed me. I'll have to ask my mom about

that someday...) Therefore, let's make the desk drawer .38 and the closet shotgun no big deal.

You make an absolute promise to your children that, *with your supervision*, they may look at and handle *any* of the family guns *at any time, if they ask first.* You promise that you will drop what you're doing, day or night, and handle the gun together. **You will do this cheerfully, *without fail.*** Boston sez: Never break a promise to a child.

Once children are a little older and have proven their safe handling and responsibility, they may handle and/or shoot their guns without your supervision, but with prior permission.

Once they're in, say, junior high school, they may use their own guns as freely as their bicycles.

Once they're 18 y/o, take them to a good shooting school.

LEVELS OF ALERTNESS

White
Unalert and unaware. This is a separation of the conscious and subconscious mind (daydreaming). Drivers in car accidents often remark, *"He came out of nowhere."* This is White.

Yellow
Alert and aware--focused and conscious. *"I might have to shoot somebody today."*

Orange
Heightened Yellow. You now have a *specific* problem. *"I might have to shoot him in a few seconds!"*

Red
The fight begins. You *are* engaging and will do exactly as trained through subconscious action (viewing from above). If you have no training, then nothing is exactly what you will do.

Black
You're in the fight. Training and practice will decide the matter.

CONDITION OF WEAPON

Zero
Loaded chamber. Cocked hammer or striker. Safety *off.*

One
Loaded chamber. Cocked hammer or striker. Safety *on.*

Two
Loaded chamber. Hammer down. Safety off. (Pulling trigger overcomes safeties in Glocks and DAs.)

Three
Empty chamber. Loaded magazine.

Four
Empty chamber. No magazine.

RANGE COMMANDS

If you ever attend a shooting school or class, here are some common commands you'll hear at the range.

Index!	Straighten out trigger finger on frame.
Muzzle!	Adjust muzzle to safe direction.
Make Ready!	**From firing line only!:** load, chamber and engage safety: ready to fire.
Fire!	**From firing line only!:** Only on command. Draw or raise from Ready.
Front Sight!	You've lost the front sight. Reacquire focus.
Ready!	Keep muscle tension, down-hinge arms. Muzzle pointed 45° down. (Condition "Burnt Orange.")
Make Safe!	Reengage safety of loaded gun. Prepared to fire from Ready, or holster.
Unload!	**From firing line only!:** Drop magazine. Clear and check chamber.
Holster!	Preceded by *Make Ready!* or *Make Safe!* or *Unload!* command.
Sling!	Preceded by *Make Ready* or *Make Safe!* or *Unload!* command.
Ground 'em!	Engage safety and place rifle on ground, muzzle forward.
Range clear; Go Forward and Tape your targets.	Only on command.

TACTICS--AN OVERVIEW

As I mentioned in Chapter 1, I can't fully discuss tactics in this book. No book can train your muscle memory, anyway, so go to gun school and learn them firsthand. In the meantime, I'll cover the basics--not to teach, but to teach what you *don't* know.

Malfunctions

The firing cycle of a semi-auto weapon is: feed, fire, extract, and eject. Stoppages can occur at any phase of the cycle. Clearing malfs is a vital skill to ingrain in your subconscious where it is performed *automatically* without conscious thought.

Failure to feed (also called a Class 1 malfunction)

This is almost always the fault of either the magazine (empty, not fully seated, missing, or faulty) or the ammo (case deformed or too long). Sometimes it's just a dirty gun.

Usually the magazine was not fully seated. In tactically exigent situations, the first thing to attempt is the "tap-rack-bang." **Tap** forcefully the mag into the weapon to seat it fully. **Rack** the bolt or slide to charge a round into the chamber. **Bang** to fire the weapon. Tap-rack-bangs take less than a second with practice, and should be practiced with dummy rounds slyly mixed with your range ammo to surprise yourself.

Failure to fire

This is either an ammo or gun problem. Usually it's bad ammo (bad, high, inverted, or missing primer--or, no powder). When under fire, tap-rack-bang. When there's no hurry, eject the round after waiting out a potential hangfire for 30 seconds.

If an abnormal sound or sensation was felt upon the trigger pull, *cease firing* as it probably was a "squib" load. This is when a powderless round was nevertheless fired by the primer, lodging the bullet mid-barrel. Check your barrel!

Failure to extract (also called a Class 3 malfunction)

Sometimes a brass case sticks in the chamber; sometimes a case rim rips off or an extractor breaks; *usually* it's because of a double feed. A round remains in the chamber with a second round pressed hard from behind.

With all weapons but Glock pistols, you should "lock-drop-rack-rack-rack-tap-rack-bang." Meaning, lock back the action, drop the mag, rack vigorously 3X to clear the action and tap-rack-bang. Glocks need only a tap-rack-bang.

Failure to eject

These are called "stovepipes" because of the case being caught between the bolt face and the port. This usually happens because of a bolt/slide which failed to move all the way back to its stop before returning forward. Anything which diminishes recoil force (e.g., a too-lightly held gun, which occurs often with the light Glocks) or impedes bolt/slide movement (dirt, sludge, a rubbing thumb, etc.) can cause a stovepipe.

The solution is usually a tap-rack-bang.

Reloading your weapon

When under prolonged fire, you *will* shoot your gun dry. Ammo is only helpful when fired at hostile targets, and as long as they're hostile, you will fire. Fire long enough and you will run dry. This is no sin. Simply reload and continue fighting.

The speed reload

You're in a fight. Your bolt/slide locks back after your last round. *First*, grab your full mag. (*Never* dump your empty mag before having a grip on the full mag.) Next, dump your empty mag *while* you move your full mag up to the gun. Finally, insert (tap-tug) the mag, and release the bolt/slide. Chuck Taylor can speed reload his 1911 in one second. So can you with practice.

The tactical reload

When you're behind cover *and* there's a lull in the fight, a tactical reload is called for. *First*, grab your full mag. While holding on to the full mag with 2-3 fingers of your weak hand, pull out the less-full mag with the other fingers and replace it with the full mag--while still holding on to the less-full mag. (This will take some practice, and it varies from gun to gun.) Willem DaFoe in *Platoon* demonstrated a textbook tac reload of his M16. Do *not* put the less-full mag in your mag pouch--that's where *full* mags go. Put it in your pocket where you can retrieve it later since it still contains *some* ammo.

Tactics in low-light conditions

As 70% of lethal confrontations occur in conditions of low, altered, or failing light, you must have the proper equipment (night sights and a Sure-Fire flashlight) and training to effectively fight and win. There are techniques to tactilely discern your weapon's condition, hold your flashlight with your weak hand (Harries or Rogers technique), and shoot and move. The only way to learn all this is to attend gun school.

Transitioning from primary to secondary gun

If there's no time to clear or load your rifle in a fight, you must transition to your handgun. Since you don't want to drop your rifle on the ground and have it picked up by a hostile (who just *might* get it back into operation against you), you must somehow *retain* your rifle while drawing and firing your pistol.

There are two general ways to retain your rifle--by its sling, or by holding onto it with your weak hand. Simply clutching it by the forestock to your chest muzzle up is the quickest. If you need *both* hands free, then slinging it over your neck in the "scramble carry" is very quick. (Those with tactical slings can simply release the rifle.) Thunder Ranch teaches the sling dangle on the weak elbow crook, but the swinging rifle makes accurate pistol shot placement more difficult. *If you've got the time and cover*, sling your rifle on your back in a secure cross carry.

Clearing a building

You come home late at night and notice through the window an intruder inside. Call the police--that's what they're paid for. If calling or waiting for the police is not practical, then you'll have to clear your home alone. If clearing with a partner, *communicate*. One of you is the team leader; the other a subordinate member.

In a multistory building, work from the top-down, if possible. Lead with your muzzle--where your eyes are looking your muzzle is pointing. Make sure that your presence is not announced by sound and shadow. Clear as you go, leaving no uncleared areas behind you. You look in closets, behind doors and furniture, under beds--*everywhere* a potential threat could be hiding. Negotiating corners is the main task. Standing as far from a corner as possible (so that an intruder cannot easily grab your gun), you "pie slice" your way around, 20° at a time. At the *final* slice, *very* quickly peek (fire if necessary), and duck back. Use different heights to increase surprise.

If you discover an intruder, don't look at the face--look at the *hands*. **Hands, hands, hands.** Only hands can hurt you. An intruder hand with a weapon, even if not pointed at you, is a target. If the intruder even so much as *moves* his hands in a manner consistent with reaching for a weapon, shoot him. He needn't have been actually armed--the law only requires that a reasonable person would have *believed* that he was armed and therefore posed an imminent threat.

If you can't see his hands, *command him* to turn around, and raise his hands. Then, *command him* to slowly lie on the floor stomach-first, and place his arms behind his back, palms outward. Your commands must be clear and forceful, giving him no time to think tactically. He must comply immediately or be shot. *Do it, now!* He's unlawfully in your home and *you're* in control. *Never* retreat from this high moral and tactical ground. His actions must *diminish* his tactical position, or you are justified in shooting him. Stalling, moving closer, pleading, hiding his hands or inching them towards his coat--all of these are danger signals to you. If he is not obeying you, then he's planning to overcome you. *Do it now or I'll shoot!*

If he speaks, *command him* to shut up. At this moment, you don't care *what* he has to *say*, only what he is able to *do*. When he's safely in custody (preferably handcuffed), then you can listen to his "wrong house" story, if you want to.

WHEN, WHY, & HOW TO SHOOT

Lethal force is valid *only* against a *reasonably* perceived imminent and grievous threat. The jury must agree that your assailant had the opportunity, capability, and motivation to imminently cause you at least grievous bodily harm. You shoot to *stop--not* to kill. Any kill is *incidental.*

Front sight! Press! Front sight!

Front sight is *everything.* In Condition Black, nothing else in the universe exists but your front sight. Lose your front sight, and you'll likely lose the fight. You're going to be scared shitless--*so what?* Anybody would be. Focus on that front sight, press the trigger, and pick up your front sight again.

The Plan "A" Response--2 shots to the torso

The torso is the center of mass and the quickest to hit. The torso contains the *energy* center of the threat. While accurate, powerful rounds to the body will *usually* stop the fight, you're not interested in *probabilities*--you are concentrating on what *is* or is *not* stopping him. *Always* change a *losing* game.

The Plan "B" Response--the headshot

Shots to the body did not work. Maybe he's got a bullet-proof vest. Maybe he's high on PCP. Maybe your caliber and bullets don't impress him. *Whatever.* It doesn't *matter!* **Just recognize that *"B" isn't working.* Always change a *losing* game.** Move to the *control* center--the head. Front sight at the base of his nose, press, front sight. Make this shot count.

The Plan "C" Response--shots to the pelvis

Body and headshots missed and/or did not work. You will be stunned and amazed--this is natural. **Don't analyze *why,* just change your game plan and *keep fighting.*** Attack the *mobility* center, the pelvis. Anchor him to stop his advance, then deal with him while he's on the ground. Many shootings by police ended only after a Plan "C" response.

After the smoke clears...

You've just properly and successfully defended yourself with a gun. The Bad Guy is down. Be very careful now. While the physical peril may be over, the legal peril is just beginning.

Keeping him behind your front sight, disarm the assailant

Even if he's clearly dead, disarm him. If the weapon is still in his hand, step *hard* on both wrists and disarm him. If the weapon is on the floor, kick it away from him and behind you. Leave it behind you, and don't touch it, if possible. If you can safely do so, cuff or tape his hands behind his back.

Keeping him behind your front sight, call 911

You only wanted to stop his aggressive actions, not kill him. Now that the fight's over, get him medical help. Call 911, and say, *"I need an ambulance at____. An armed intruder has just been shot in self-defense. I'm the homeowner, and I'm wearing a ____ shirt and ____ pants."* That it, nothing more. You should sound reasonably upset, yet not hysterical. No "iceman" tone, please--it'll freak out the jury later.

Keeping him behind your front sight, call your lawyer

Tell him *exactly* what happened. Most likely he will instruct you to respectfully remain silent until he arrives. Hopefully, he can come over right away. If he can't, then call a best friend to be with you. Take pictures before the police arrive.

Keeping him behind your front sight, wait for the police

The police will be very edgy when they arrive. Watch your muzzle! Once they are in a position to take over, lower your muzzle and ask them to cover and frisk the assailant while you safely place your gun down.

They will naturally ask you what happened, and you will naturally want to talk about it. ***Don't!*** Simply say that you were in fear of your life, and your lawyer is on his way.

Do *not:* brag about your marksmanship and the effectiveness of your defensive loads, gloat on how his chest cavity looks like goo, complain how law-abiding citizens are sick of scumbag criminals, or marvel at how calm you feel and that only wimps go through that "post-operational-trauma" stuff.

You were *terrified* for your own life, you were *forced* to defend yourself, you didn't *want* to shoot him, and you're *very upset* over having taken another's life. That's your attitude. Let your lawyer do all the talking for you.

After police have left, write down exactly what happened

This is for your *own* records. Details will float into your memory over the next days and weeks. Revise your notes. I'd enter it in an encrypted computer file.

Don't discuss the incident until the legal matter is over

If it was a righteous shooting and you were lawfully in possession of the gun, then you're probably home free. Don't blow it by throwing a party, or mouthing off to the reporters.

If the DA wants to prosecute, don't fool around

Get the best defense attorney you can find. If the prosecution seems especially petty and vicious, contact the NRA and GOA for legal help. Just in case they later search your home, I'd clear it of most guns, and *all* gun-related receipts, magazines, etc. If it seems likely that you'll be convicted of a felony, then *sell* your guns as they'll be taken away from you, anyway.

Massad Ayoob of the Lethal Force Institute is a widely acclaimed expert witness. His description of a jury is good to contemplate, *"A jury is a twelve-headed creature with an I.Q. of at least 1,200 and as much as 500 years of experience, with 12 simultaneous bullshit detectors in operation."*

Everything you do must seem prudent and reasonable to a jury later. Think through how your life and actions may come across to them. Above all, keep your mouth shut!

❖ 3

GUN CONTROL LAWS

Don't look to the courts to strike down modern gun control legislation. They've had dozens of chances, but denied *certiorari* every time since 1939. This is no accident:

> *I cannot help but suspect that the best explanation for the absence of the Second Amendment from the legal consciousness of the elite bar, including that component found in the legal academy, is derived from a mixture of sheer opposition to the idea of private ownership of guns and the perhaps subconscious fear that altogether plausible, perhaps even "winning," interpretations of the Second Amendment would present real hurdles to those of us supporting prohibitory regulation. ...[T]he Amendment may be profoundly embarrassing to many who both support such regulation and view themselves as committed to zealous adherence to the Bill of Rights (such as most members of the ACLU).*
>
> -- Stanford Levinson, *The Embarrassing Second Amendment*, sourced from *Safeguarding Liberty*

Meanwhile, become educated.

The best digest is *Gun Laws of America* by Alan Korwin (ISBN 0-9621958-8-X; www.bloomfieldpress.com). It covers *all* federal gun laws, and although I resent the fact that I must pay Ø20 for a book on federal gun laws (because there shouldn't *be* any), this book is a must. The summaries alone are invaluable.

The novel *Unintended Consequences* by John Ross also contains excellent narratives on gun control laws.

I'll cover the main laws which affect us generally. For wider or deeper detail, you'll have to dive in yourself.

1934 NATIONAL FIREARMS ACT

Until 1933, you could order a new .45 Thompson submachinegun from the Sears catalog for Ø125, *with leather case.* You could own a BAR or an M1919A4. Silencers (or, more accurately, gun *mufflers*) were sold at the hardware store for under Ø10. You could even have $20 gold pieces in your pocket. The *only* federal gun restriction was a 1920 law which prohibited the mailing of handguns (although long guns could be mailed until 1968). What a great time to be a gunowner!

Since Prohibition had been ended by the 22nd Amendment in 1933, thousands of Treasury agents were idle by 1934 and, golly, they needed *some* kind of work. So, create a new class of criminals. (What else is new?)

The *NFA34* was our first serious federal gun law. Unless you have paid a Ø200 BATF tax stamp, you cannot legally own an automatic weapon, or any long gun less than 26" overall or with a barrel less than 18" (this was amended to 16" for rifles in 1958), or a silencer. Privately-owned gold had been outlawed just one year earlier. (Good thing that alcoholic beverages were decriminalized--*I'd* sure want a drink after Congress passed the *National Banking Act* and *National Firearms Act!*)

Not generally known is that the *original* language would have included *all handguns*, but women made such a proper and righteous stink that the handgun inclusion was stricken.

The phony rationale for *NFA34*

It was the Valentine's Day Massacre of 1929 and other similar gangster machine gunnings, but these infrequent incidents had all but ceased with Prohibition's end a year earlier.

So, what was the *real* reason?

The National Firearms Act fit in perfectly with the systematic creation of government programs and deficit spending that Franklin Roosevelt immediately began to institute the instant he took office. The NFA was a model vehicle for the continued expansion of government power: It was arbitrary (i.e., the 18-inch rule); it gave the government sweeping authority over something very common; it focused on inanimate objects rather than criminal behavior; it levied draconian taxes on these objects; and most certainly, it created millions of criminals with the stroke of a pen, just as Prohibition had.

-- John Ross, *Unintended Consequences* (1996), p. 356

There are nearly 200,000 *NFA34* weapons on record. Not *one* has ever been used to commit a crime, according to the BATF. Nevertheless, the feds will eventually try to confiscate these weapons *without compensation* just as they did in 1994 with the Striker and Street Sweeper shotguns.

1968 GUN CONTROL ACT

*The Congress hereby declares that the purpose of this title is to provide support for Federal, State, and local law enforcement officials in their fight against crime and violence, **and it is not the purpose of this title to place any undue or unnecessary Federal restrictions or burdens on law-abiding citizens** with respect to the acquisition, possession, or use of firearms appropriate to the purpose of hunting, trapshooting, targetshooting, personal protection, or other lawful activity, **and that this title is not intended to discourage or eliminate the private ownership or use of firearms by law-abiding citizens for lawful purposes,** or provide for the imposition by Federal regulations of any procedures or requirements other than those reasonably necessary to implement and effectuate the provisions of this title.*

-- 1968 Gun Control Act preamble

Bullshit. *Unbelievable* bullshit. This preamble reminds me of the FBI at Waco on 19 April 1993 shouting through their tanks' bullhorns *"This is not an assault!"* (The Davidians should have fired back, shouting, *"These are not bullets!"*)

Senator Dodd remembered Hitler's 1938 gun control legislation from the post-WWII Nuremberg trials and requested that it be translated into English for his study. Just a few months later Congress passed a virtual clone of Hitler's gun registration scheme (designed to prohibit guns to Jews and other minorities). The Nazi phrase *"sporting purpose"* was used verbatim in *GCA68*. Aaron Zelman's Jews For The Preservation of Firearm Ownership (JPFO) proved this absolutely in their *Gateway To Tyranny* with their side-by-side comparison of both laws.

Zelman sent a copy of *Gateway* to every Congressman and Supreme Court Justice, to all the media. Silence. Not even the *conservative* and *libertarian* press dared to touch this bombshell issue. First, Nazi gun regulation. Soon, the camps. There are guys in Montana, *right now*, welding shackles to the insides of railroad boxcars. (I spoke to the brother of one the welders, so this isn't rumor.) Folks, do the math.

Using the *"interstate / foreign commerce"* clause for the second time in gun regulation, *GCA68* prohibited the mail-order receipt of firearms, the importation of foreign weapons *"unsuitable for sporting purposes,"* and the ownership of unregistered *"destructive devices"* (e.g., mortars, bazookas, smokeless powder weapons with a bore in excess of ½").

It mandated the new BATF Form 4473 and prohibits the sale or transfer of firearms and ammunition to certain persons.

The phony rationale for *GCA68*

The murders of JFK, RFK, and MLK.

So, what was the *real* reason?

To create the beginnings of a national firearm registry, the means to a confiscation end.

The prohibited possessor list--18 USC §922(d)

(d) it shall be unlawful for any person to sell or otherwise dispose of any firearm or ammunition to any person knowing or having reasonable cause to believe that such person--

(1) is under indictment for, or has been convicted in any court of, a crime punishable by imprisonment for a term exceeding one year;

(2) is a fugitive from justice (BTP note: This means, according to §921(15), having *"fled any State to avoid prosecution for a crime or to avoid giving testimony in any criminal proceeding."*--so remaining in hiding within your State is O.K.?);

(3) is an unlawful user of or addicted to any controlled substance (as defined in section 102 of the Controlled Substances Act (21 U.S.C. 802));

(4) has been adjudicated as a mental defective or has been committed to any mental institution (political dissidents beware of Soviet-style psychiatric sentences);

(5) who, being an alien, is illegally or unlawfully in the United States;

(6) who has been discharged from the Armed Forces under dishonorable conditions;

(7) who, having, been a citizen of the United States, has renounced his citizenship (word your untaxation and rescission affidavits very carefully), *or;*

(8) is subject to a court order that restrains such person from harassing, stalking, or threatening an intimate partner of such person or child of such intimate partner or person, or engaging in other conduct that would place an intimate partner in reasonable fear of bodily injury to the partner or child, except that this paragraph shall only apply to a court order that--

(A) was issued after a hearing of which such person received actual notice, and at which such person had the opportunity to participate; and
(B)(i)   includes a finding that such person represents a credible threat to the physical safety of such intimate partner or child; or
(ii) by its terms explicitly prohibits the use, attempted use, or threatened use of physical force against such intimate partner or child that would reasonably be expected to cause bodily injury.

The "Lautenberg Amendment"

§658 was snuck in the 1997 *Department of Defense Appropriations Act.* This ugly bit added the prohibited possessor list anybody convicted of a **misdemeanor** *"crime of domestic violence"* involving the use or attempted use of physical force, or the threatened use of a deadly weapon, among family members (spouse, parent, guardian, cohabiter, or similar). Spouses slapping each other, or spanking their child, can be such a *"crime."* I'm not making light of actual wife *battering*, but to ban somebody from owning guns because they threw a cereal bowl at their spouse is going to ridiculous extremes.

Never **before has a** *misdemeanor* **offense, and an** *ex post facto* **one at that, been grounds for denial of the constitutional right to own and carry guns.** According to Korwin, *"It is as if a former speeding ticket were now grounds for felony arrest if you own a car or a gasoline."* It denies *"due process"* (felony accountability without Grand Jury indictment; dispossession of lawful private property without *"just compensation"*; equal protection of the law, right to accusation, counsel, trial, and jury; among many others).

THE "BRADY BILL"

Signed into law on 30 November 1993 and found at 18 USC §922(s&t), *The Brady Handgun Violence Prevention Act* mandated (for states without an instant-check system) waiting-period provisions for dealer handgun purchases after 28 February 1994. (These expire on 27 February 1999.) It contains extremely tortuous language. One sentence has *532* words.

Brady attempted to require the states to enforce Federal law at the states' expense, and the Supreme Court struck this portion of *Brady* down 5-4 on 27 June 1997 (***Printz v. U.S.***) as an improper use of the *"interstate commerce"* regulatory power. This is no huge setback for the feds, as they'll have their *National Instant Criminal Background Check* (NICBC) system up by 30 November 1998. This NICBC will predictably auger in a national ID with biometric numbering of your thumbprint.

The phony rationale of "Brady"
The attempted assassination by John Hinckley, Jr. of President Reagan and the wounding of James Brady.

So, what's the *real* reason?
To infringe more on your 2nd Amendment rights.

LAWS ON "ASSAULT WEAPONS"

18 USC §922(r)
*It shall be unlawful for any person to assemble **from imported parts** any semiautomatic rifle or shotgun which is identical to any rifle or shotgun prohibited from importation under section 925(d)(3) of this chapter as **not being particularly suitable for or readily adaptable to sporting purposes**...*

§925(d)(3) long guns are 26 USC §5845(a) *1934 National Firearms Act* weapons (machine guns, <18"bbl shotguns, etc.) and surplus military firearms. Non-*NFA* and nonmilitary firearms which are *"particularly suitable for or readily adaptable to sporting purposes"* may be customized.

Can I trick out my SKS with a folding stock, flash-suppressor, etc? Yes, if it was imported *before* 30 November 1990.

Customizing *post*-11/90 surplus military firearms
The *"from imported parts"* is intriguing. Can you add an *American*-made folding stock or flash suppressor to your SKS? Technically yes, if you're careful.

A rifle assembled or configured to *10 or less* of the imported parts listed in 27 CFR §178.39(c) is not subject to 18 USC §922(r). **These imported parts are:** frames, receivers; receiver castings/forgings/stampings; barrels; barrel extensions; mounting blocks (trunions); muzzle attachments; bolts; bolt carriers; operating rods; gas piston; trigger housings; triggers; hammers; sears; disconnectors; buttstocks; pistol grips; forearms; handguards; magazine bodies/followers/floorplates.

What's the point of all this? By substituting some of the original imported parts with American-made parts, *the total imported parts count of §178.39(c) can be reduced to 10 or less*, and you can legally add a separate pistol grip and buttstock.

First Son Enterprises (770-497-0204) sells an FAL American-made parts kit for Ø225 to allow a pistol-grip reversion of the Ø400 Canadian/British FAL hybrids. Clever, but perhaps ultimately fruitless as the feds will likely soon outlaw ownership of all mag-fed semi-auto rifles.

Also, if the rifle was imported *after 9/94* the "Crime Bill" says it cannot have *both* a pistol grip *and* a flash suppressor. One or the other, but not both.

So, what to do about your post-9/94 rifle?

If you've got a car trunk **SKS**, keep it utterly stock with 10rd fixed mag--no folders, no pistol grip, no bayonet (I'd grind off the barrel mount), no muzzle attachments (even though a compensator is permissible)--and you should be O.K. (for *now*).

If you've got a **"sporter" AK** variant, First Son also makes American parts for that, however, spending Ø225 on a Ø275 rifle just to add a legal pistol grip stock seems a bit silly.

If you've got a **post-11/90 FAL**, should you swap out some of the imported parts to achieve the pistol grip? It's probably not worth it, since DSA Inc. makes a tolerable replacement "sporter" stock for Ø75. (Or, "sporterize" it yourself by adding a 1" strip of flat material from the pistol grip to the buttstock.) Thread the muzzle for an *American-made* vortex flash suppressor and you'll remain in compliance with the Crime Bill. You can always add a pistol grip stock later, when the gloves are off.

If you've got an American-made **post-9/94 AR15** without flash suppressor, you can simply get a pre-ban threaded barrel or upper and install it at the "appropriate" time.

The "Crime Bill"

The Orwellian title is *The 1994 Public Safety and Recreational Firearms Use Protection Act.* This law (found at 18 USC §922(v&w)) allows us to possess nasty looking "assault weapons" and their accessories only if they were made *prior* to 13 September 1994. The act expires on 13 September 2004, but it'll be renewed, or replaced with something even *worse.*

Semi-automatic rifles (18 USC §921(30)(B))

Congress wet their panties over the military-style rifles. So, after 13 September 1994, the following rifle can no longer be imported, manufactured, or converted:

> [A] *semiautomatic* rifle that has an ability to accept a **detachable magazine and** *has at least 2* (e.g., no more than <u>one</u>) *of--*

(i) a folding or telescoping stock;
(ii) a pistol grip that protrudes conspicuously beneath the action
of the weapon (oooh!--how <u>scary</u>!)*;*
(iii) a bayonet mount; (!!)
(iv) a flash suppressor or threaded barrel designed to accom-
modate a flash suppressor; and
(v) a grenade launcher; (!!!)

It is because of this that all post 9/94 mag fed semi-auto rifles must have that stupid "sporter" stock. Reverting a post-ban rifle to full pre-ban condition is a felony--conviction of which cancels your 2nd Amendment rights. *Cuidado.* A semi-auto with a sporter stock *could* have *one* (but not two) of the above alterations, such as a flash suppressor.

Semi-auto rifles which *cannot* take a detachable mag of more than five rounds are excluded (e.g., Browning BAR, Remington 740, etc.).

Semi-automatic pistols (18 USC §921(30)(C))

Congress wet their panties over the TEC-9 gangsta 9mms, so, after 13 September 1994, the following pistols can no longer be imported, manufactured, or converted:

a semiautomatic pistol that has an ability to accept a detachable
magazine **and** *has at least 2 of--*
(i) an ammunition magazine that attaches to the pistol outside
of the pistol grip;
(ii) a threaded barrel capable of accepting a barrel extender,
flash suppressor, forward handgrip, or silencer;
(iii) a shroud that is attached to, or partially or completely encir-
cles, the barrel and that permits the shooter to hold the firearm with
the nontrigger hand without being burned;
(iv) a manufactured weight of 50 ounces or more when the pis-
tol is unloaded; and
(v) a semiautomatic version of an automatic firearm;

Semi-automatic shotguns (18 USC §921(30)(D))

Not only did the SecTreas *retroactively* outlaw the Street Sweeper and Striker 12 revolver shotguns, and the USAS-12 AR15-style shotgun, Congress outlawed these future shotguns:

a **semiautomatic** *shotgun that has* **at least 2 of**--
(i) a folding or telescoping stock;
(ii) a pistol grip that protrudes conspicuously beneath the action
of the weapon;
(iii) a fixed magazine capacity in excess of 5 rounds; and
(iv) an ability to accept a detachable magazine.

Don't put a mag tube extension and folding stock on your post-9/94 Remington 1100. (Bayonets, apparently, are O.K. for now.) *Pump* shotguns can have extended mags, folding stocks with pistol grip, etc., and I'd stock up on these parts *now*.

Plus 10rd mags (18 USC §921(31)(A&B))

Now, *this* is irksome. While I had already purchased all the nasty "assault weapons" I needed (though not all I *wanted*), you can never have enough mags.

> The term "large capacity ammunition feeding device"--
> (A) means a magazine, belt, drum, feed strip, or similar device manufactured after [13 September 1994] that has a capacity of, or that can be readily (whatever that means) restored or converted to accept, more than 10 rounds of ammunition; but
> (B) does not include an attached tubular device designed to accept, and capable of operating only with, .22 caliber rimfire ammunition.

Warning: it is illegal to put a 10+rd mag in a post-9/94 weapon. This also applies to *fixed* mags, so you SKS owners make *sure* that your rifles are pre-9/94 before you install a 10+rd mag.

If a 10+rd mag does *not* have an 18 USC §923(i) post-ban serial number or date of manufacture, then the owner can assert under 18 USC §922(w)(4) that lack of such *"shall be a presumption that the large capacity ammunition feeding device is not subject to the prohibition of possession in paragraph (1)* [of 18 USC §922(w)]." This is a handy bit of info to know.

"armor piercing ammunition" (18 USC §921(17)(B))

> (B) The term "armor piercing ammunition" means--
> (i) a projectile or projectile core which may be used in a handgun and which is constructed entirely (excluding the presence of traces of other substances) from one or a combination of tungsten alloys, steel, iron, brass, bronze, beryllium copper, or depleted uranium; or
> (ii) a full jacketed projectile larger than .22 caliber designed and intended for use in a handgun and whose jacket has a weight of more than 25 percent of the total weight of the projectile.

Congress cannot document a *single* case of police homicide from these so-called *"cop killer bullets"*--but, *so what*?

Enforcing the Crime Bill

All post-9/94 self-loading rifles have something like "Sporter" stamped or engraved on the receiver. Having a pistol grip or folding stock, flash suppressor, 10+rd mag, etc. on a "Sporter" is asking for trouble. Be discreet. Don't take your reverted post-ban rifle to gun shows or to the range. In fact, you shouldn't even keep it any known address (home, office, storage, etc.) Save this rifle for that rainy decade.

The phony rationale of the "Crime" bill

Taking *gansta* weapons off the streets, just like the *NFA34* did to the mob. L.A., NYC, and Chicago are now safe.

So, what's the *real* reason?

To relieve certain Congressmen from their nightmares in which they were attacked by irate Citizens with military-style weapons. This legislative sedative hasn't worked, so expect a future outright *ban* on all *existing* nasty *"assault weapons."*

GUN-FREE SCHOOL ZONES

The *Gun-Free School Zones Act of 1991* (which was found at 18 USC §922(q)) prohibited the knowing possession of a firearm on or within 1,000 feet of a school. America had 121,855 schools as of 1994, and their 1,000' zones covered just about anywhere a gunowner would typically drive or travel. This was no accident. It's already illegal in every state to use a gun recklessly on school property, so Congress *didn't* have children's safety in mind. Since concealed-carry permit holders were exempted, it was an obvious ploy to herd all the other gunowners into the artificial CCW corral (to be eliminated within 10 years).

In *Hologram of Liberty* I thoroughly covered the Supreme Court's reversal (1995 ***U.S. v. Lopez***) of this act. Undeterred, Congress simply repassed the struck down act in §657 of the 2,000 page DoD Appropriations Act of 1997. Congressmen voted for this Act without even having read the thing. Typical.

The only difference in this new version is that the phrase *"that has moved in or that otherwise affects interstate or foreign commerce"* was added in two places. Since this new language alone would not seem to affect the Supreme Court's ***Lopez*** 5-4 decision, I suspect that Rehnquist and/or O'Connor have been privately dealt with and that a 5-4 or 6-3 reversal of ***Lopez*** can be expected. Even if the 5 Justice ***Lopez*** majority holds fast, Congress will nevertheless enjoy 2-4 years of "free" enforcement and many innocent people will become convicted felons.

To avoid a needless felony arrest over this, you *must* get my book *You & The Police!* for its invaluable info and tips on car travel while armed.

IS THE 2nd AMENDMENT AN INDIVIDUAL OR COLLECTIVE RIGHT?

[Textual exegesis] *suggests that "the people" protected by the Fourth Amendment, and by the First **and Second** Amendments, and to whom rights and powers are reserved under the Ninth and Tenth Amendments, refers to a class of persons who are part of a national community or who have developed sufficient connection with this country to be considered part of that community.*
-- *U.S. v. Verdugo-Urquidez,* 110 S.Ct. 1056, 1060 (1990)

It would...be strange to find in the midst of a catalog of the rights of individuals a provision securing to the states the right to maintain a designated "Militia." **Dispassionate scholarship suggests quite strongly that the right of the people to keep and bear arms meant just that.** *There is no need to deceive ourselves as to what the Second Amendment said and meant.*
-- Justice Antonin Scalia, *A Matter of Interpretation: Federal Courts and the Law* (Princeton University Press)

As poorly as the 2nd Amendment was written, the *"People"* of the 2nd are the same *"People"* as in the 1st, 4th, 9th, and 10th. Any intellectually honest scholar will agree.

Was the 2nd Amendment deliberately sabotaged with imprecise language?

I touched on this in *Hologram of Liberty*. While the thought is unpleasant, please at least hear me out.

Save for a few, the 55 Philadelphia delegates did not *want* a Bill of Rights in the Constitution. Not only did they exclude such from the document, they fought against adding one before the Constitution was ratified by the States. Hamilton in *Federalist* #84 insisted that *"bills of rights,...are not only unnecessary in the proposed Constitution but would even be dangerous."*

Only when five of the 13 States made ratification contingent (though unenforceably so) upon a Bill of Rights did Representative Madison convince Congress of the matter's political necessity. Grudgingly, and with much more haste than concern for our rights, did Congress finally pass 12 *very* scrappy proposals to the states. (Read pages 4/1-5 of *Hologram of Liberty*.)

When five of the ratifying states urged amendments of rights to the Constitution, *all* of them included the right to bear arms, whereas only *three* mentioned freedom of speech--which would suggest that private armament was constitutionally more important than even free speech. The New York version was basically copied by the other four states:

> *That the people have a right to keep and bear arms; that a well-regulated militia, including the body of the people capable of bearing arms, is the proper, natural, and safe defense of a free state.*

Madison's original proposal to the House was:

> *The right of the people to keep and bear arms shall not be infringed; a well-armed and well-regulated* (well-trained, well-disciplined) *militia being the best security of a free country; but no person religiously scrupulous of bearing arms shall be compelled to render military service in person.*

Because the semicolon after *"keep and bear arms"* is grammatically the equal of a period, the individual right is not even *theoretically* conditional upon the rest of the sentence. It was the federalist, big-government Senate which altered the syntax to:

> *A well-regulated militia, being necessary to the security of a free state, the right of the people to keep and bear arms shall not be infringed.*

Even though contemporaries of the First Congress (e.g., St. George Tucker and William Rawle), along with the populace at large correctly viewed the 2nd Amendment as an *individual* right, the germ of ambiguous syntax was set for eternity.

That change of sentence structure was crucial. No longer was the right *"to keep and bear arms"* listed first and independent. By vaguely couching the right within the duty of a common militia, the 2nd Amendment can be theoretically read to mean that people may only keep and bear arms *for militia purposes only and no others.* The Senate of 1789 likely *knew* that the 2nd Amendment was slightly ambiguous, giving future courts an excuse to sanctify federal infringement of that right.

The courts have done precisely that. In the 1939 case of **U.S. v. Miller,** 307 US 175, the Supreme Court unanimously held that a short-barreled shotgun (controlled by the *NFA34*) was *not* a weapon suitable for militia purposes and therefore *no* right to possess such a shotgun existed. Gun ownership was declared to be conditional on militia practices.

The Congress of 1789 knew how to write the 2nd Amendment to set in stone our right to keep and bear arms, *period*--but they didn't choose to write it that way. Heck, even *I* could have written a sabotage-proof 2nd Amendment:

> *Neither Congress, nor the President, nor any State shall deny, infringe, regulate, or tax the absolute right of the people, in both their individual and collective militia capacities, to own, carry, and use weapons. Any congressional act, executive order, or State legislative act which would, under any guise or pretense, deny, infringe, regulate, or tax this cornerstone right is null and void at moment of passage, and may lawfully be, without risk of prosecution, ignored, or, if deemed necessary, forcibly resisted.*

Now *that's* a *real* 2nd Amendment!

Given the federalists' desire and plan for a supreme, unchallengeable central government and an armed citizenry's opposition to such a future government, I believe that the 2nd Amendment was *intentionally* "watered down" to make possible the gradual judicial whittling away our right of private armament. **Has this not happened *exactly*?**

Now that the common militia has unlawfully been usurped by the *select* militia of the National Guard, militia-type weapons such as the full-auto M16A2 are no longer judicially warranted. And, since the 30rd semi-auto AR15 with flash suppressor is not *"suitable for sporting purposes"*--there's no longer any legal rationale for owning one of these, either. The next step will be to outlaw hunting, target-shooting, etc. to eliminate the *"sporting purpose"* application, and thus ban all remaining guns (bolt-action rifles, shotguns, pistols--*everything*).

All this was made possible by the deliberately wimpy verbiage of the 2nd Amendment. It left an "out" for the feds. On purpose. Had it been as strongly written as the states' version or as Madison's version, I'd be shooting a Ø600 BAR right now.

SO, WHAT RIGHTS ARE *LEFT?*

Not many, and they exist mainly in certain southern and western states. The feds do not yet regulate the private, *intra*state transfer between non-licensed adults.

Buying ammo privately

Until 1986, you had to fill out a form to buy ammo, but no longer. You can even order the stuff by the case from out of state and have it UPSd to your door (although I'd order it under an alias and receive it at a Mail Boxes Etc. for Ø3). Stock up *now* on affordable, quality, anonymous ammo--while we can.

Transferring firearms privately, without an FFL

As long as the buyer or recipient is not an 18 USC §922(d) prohibited person, *and* the nonlicensed transfer is legal in your home state and city, you may privately buy/sell used firearms as you can used books or clothing. You may sell from classified ads, garage sales, flea markets, and gun shows.

The buyer must also be from your home state, to avoid the applicability of *"interstate commerce"* federal gun laws.

Do not expect this right to last much longer. The gun haters are beside themselves that in 24 states no record of sale is required to be reported to the state or local government. (As of June, 1996, these states are: Alaska, Arizona, Arkansas, Colorado, Delaware, Florida, Georgia, Idaho, Kansas, Kentucky, Louisiana, Maine, Mississippi, Montana, Nebraska, Nevada, New Mexico, Oklahoma, Texas, Utah, Vermont, West Virginia, and Wyoming.) Since most of these states will *never* ban record-free private sales, the feds will, some day.

Out-of-state transfers

You'll need to go through a local FFL and fill out a BATF Form 4473 to legally send or receive (even as gifts) firearms from out-of-state. The only exception to this is a temporary loan or rental of firearm for lawful sporting purposes.

If you visit a non-recordkeeping state, you can get away with privately buying there (gun show, flea market, classified ad, etc.) and bringing your booty back home (be careful!). **If you do this, *never* tell *anyone* about these illegal purchases.** Remember my rule from *Bulletproof Privacy*: Trust only when you *have* to, and then only when you *can*.

Interstate shipment of firearms

You may send *and receive* a firearm through a common carrier (e.g., FedEx, UPS, etc.) to a repair facility directly from your home without the assistance of an FFL. When sending to a non-FFL, you must declare in writing to the common carrier that you are sending a firearm.

Interstate transportation with firearms

The NRA has a good pamphlet on this. *Generally*, if your gun is legal at your destination, then you may carry it *unloaded, cased, and locked in the trunk* of your car.

Many states (Mass., N.Y., N.J., Ca., etc.) are quirky about this with handguns and semi-automatic rifles. *Beware.* You may take an unloaded, cased, locked and declared gun in your checked-through airline baggage. The airline may *not* place on your bag any identifying "steal me!" gun tag, but they *will* code the tag, usually with an "FFFFFFFFFFF."

Open carry of firearms

Only 22 states allow this. States in bold also allow the unrecorded private transfers of firearms: **Alaska, Arizona, Colorado, Delaware, Idaho, Kentucky, Louisiana, Maine, Mississippi,** Missouri, **Montana, Nebraska, Nevada,** New Hampshire, **New Mexico,** North Carolina, South Dakota, **Vermont,** Virginia, **West Virginia,** Wisconsin, **Wyoming.**

Concealed carry of firearms

Some 31 states have what's called a *"shall issue"* concealed carry weapons (CCW) permit system. As long as you're not a prohibited possessor and take a safety training course, the state *must* approve your CCW permit application.

In a dozen or so states, the local police chief or sheriff has the arbitrary power of refusal (and they use it *frequently,* most infamously in Kalifornia).

In Illinois, Kansas, Missouri, Nebraska, Ohio, Wisconsin, and D.C. there is no provision for CCWs. *Zip. Nada. Keine.*

Only *Vermont* perfectly recognizes your right to be peaceably armed *without* permit--openly or concealed. So, Sarah Brady and Josh Sugarman--why isn't Vermont a hotbed of gun violence when it *should* be by your arguments? Conversely, why are NYC and Washington, D.C. our nation's murder capitals, where they've *banned* handgun ownership? CCW states have lower crime rates. This is indisputable. Every Swiss male keeps at home his *fully-automatic,* militia-issued rifle (along with grenades, mortars, etc.), and Switzerland has the lowest crime rate of the West. Look, you clowns, opposing political views are one thing, but you don't have the *decency* to be intellectually *honest!* You are liars, creeps, and cowards.

FUTURE GUN CONTROL

We've got a tidal wave of more gun control on the way, with the goal of, first, total registration, and then total confiscation. This has *already* happened in NYC. Visit **www.gunowners.org** for the latest. (I *highly* recommend joining Gun Owners of America, the most focused, effective gun rights lobby group.)

Here's my forecast of what to expect in a logical sequence. I think we have about 1-3 years before registration, and 2-4 years after that before confiscation. Post-2005 should be fun.

Quantity limitation on dealer purchases

Currently there is a *"Twelve Is Enough"* H.R.12 bill introduced by Charles Schumer (who else?) which would limit buyers to no more than one handgun per month. Since most of the public doesn't relate to a need (or simple desire) to own multiple handguns, this bill might go through. *"Why, anybody buying more than twelve pistols in a year must have criminal purposes!"* (That's like saying anybody who buys more than 12 gallons of gas per week must be an interstate drug smuggler.)

Outlawing future *imported* semi-autos

Rifles and pistols first, then shotguns. (Just after I wrote this, Klinton signed an executive order 60 day ban.)

Outlawing *all* future imported guns, *period*

This will be easy, as the foreign manufacturers have no political clout in Congress, the domestic manufacturers will love it, and not enough of American gunowners will care.

Outlawing privately-sold handguns

This will probably be the first private sale ban, followed by semi-auto rifles.

Outlawing private sales of *all* guns

Gun shows are almost totally free of state and federal regulation despite a 1993 federal investigation that found stolen military weapons being routinely sold at them. (Yeah, right! BTP)
 -- 28 December 1997, *The Chicago Tribune*

In *Brady* Ø200,000,000 was allocated annually to the Attorney General for a NICBC system online by 30 November 1998. This will affect *all* dealer firearm transfers--not just handguns. I'll wager that all existing 4473s must be turned in for computerization. (If you're ever questioned, say that you needed the money and sold all your stuff at a gun show to private buyers.)

Once NICBC is in place, I forecast that private (non-dealer) gun sales and transfers will at last be prohibited. In the 24 states (mostly in the South and the West) which do *not* restrict private transfers, this will *kill* the gun show and classified ad sales. It's no accident; it was *meant* to do so.

After that, how can *strangers* network? How will you *trust* one another during a forbidden private sale? You *won't*, so the only people you'll be able to buy from or sell to without federal paperwork will be *reliable* friends, neighbors and relatives. Will they have *exactly* what you need in the future? *Doubtful.* **The odds are against an excess supply amongst your trusted people.** Can pressure be exerted on them to give up your name and arsenal? *Absolutely.* **Buy now, *privately and without paperwork*, while you still *can*.**

Gun-Free School Zone enforcement

Credit goes to GOA for killing HB163 which would have given BATF agents power to stop vehicles and seize otherwise legally owned firearms that were in violation of the school zone ban. I expect that a near-future Supreme Court will expand the *Terry* doctrine to allow the full search of autos (including the trunk and locked containers) *without* probable cause. This is *de facto* practice in New Jersey. Done nationally by the BATF, this may indeed prove to be the spark of insurrection.

When the BATF and your local police set up checkpoints within 1,000' of schools to search for weapons, I expect some shooting incidents. **Folks, if we allow gun-search checkpoints, then we've *lost*.** If this won't be your "line in the sand," then nothing will be. Cordoned-off blocks and house-to-house searches will be next. Man or mouse? Decide in advance.

Outlawing future *domestic-made* semi-autos

Once the foreign stuff can no longer get in, they'll deal with domestic stuff. Now it begins to get *difficult* for Congress, as they're messing with *American* jobs and companies. Congress nearly banned new domestic *"assault rifles"* in 1991 (including the Colt AR15), but didn't quite have the nerve.

Look, the congressional graffiti is on the wall already. You're supposed to shut up and pay up. Why's a good little slave like you wanting a nasty "assault rifle" anyway?

Outlawing rifle ammo as *"armor piercing"*

Velocity is the key to penetration, and therefore *all* rifle ammo is "armor piercing" in a technical sense (though it's not designed to be). Pistol calibers pale in power and range compared to any centerfire rifle caliber. Expect the feds to realize this in a couple of years.

Concentrate on *rifles*. Like the Afghans, if we're going to win this thing, it'll be through the competent use of *rifles*. (60,000 dead Soviets can't be wrong.) Pistols are what you use to gain time and distance from your assailants to grab your rifle. You shouldn't be so close as pistol range to the enemy anyway. Get a good .308 or .30-06 scoped bolt-action, a good .223 or .308 battle rifle, and *lots* of ammo for *lots* of training. Become "one" with your rifles, *quickly*.

Mandatory registration of "assault weapons"

Semi-auto mag-fed rifles will be transformed into quasi-Title II weapons. (California, Connecticut, New Jersey, and NYC have already done this.) You'll have 30-90 days to register yours, or it's contraband. In those Hitlerian states of Kalifornia and New Jersey, less than 3% have so far complied, so the "ball" is in the state governments' court. They'll need federal help.

The raids are coming. It'll be interesting. I suspect that some (maybe many, but not most) people will resist and the state governors will declare martial law and cry to the feds.

Mandatory registration of all handguns

After the 30-90 day window, they're contraband. All CCW permit holders will have their handgun tied to their Card. Can't buy ammo or parts for handguns without a Firearm Ownership Card. Ask any Massachusetts person how this works.

Mandatory registration of "sniper rifles"

This will mean any rifle with, or capable of accepting, a telescopic sight--which means *all* rifles, even down to .22s. Hunters will bitch, but since most hunters *already have* their rifles, they won't bitch much.

The day some "Manchurian Candidate" (going through *Prozac®* withdrawal, I'll bet) snipes somebody, rush out stock up on scopes, mounts and rings for Rugers, Winchesters, Remingtons, AKs, SKSs, Mini14s, AR15s, etc. You'll eventually be able to sell them for 5x what you paid for them.

No purchase of gun stuff without Card

No more filling up a basket at WalMart and paying with cash. Your Firearm Ownership ID Card will have its bar code scanned and the Federal computers will instantly upgrade your known inventory. Purchase permission can be denied onsite if the transaction is deemed *"suspicious or excessive."*

"Gun-related items" will include books, paramilitary gear, reloading equipment, holsters, mags, firing pins, etc.

Tagging gunpowder for detection and ID

A report was due on 30 September 1997 from a special panel which investigated whether tracers in gunpowder will:

❶ pose a risk to human life or safety;
❷ help law enforcement;
❸ harm the quality and performance of gunpowders;
❹ harm the environment;
❺ cost more than its worth.

In addition, the panel must project:

❶ the cost to make tagged powders;
❷ the cost to regulate the system;
❸ the costs and effects on the consumers;
❹ the effect on consumer demand for ammunition;
❺ how hard it'll be for "terrorists" to evade taggants;
❻ if taggants could be evaded by homemade powders.

The moral is: Stock up on ammo and gunpowder *today*. You can't lose with Bullseye, Unique, H335, IMR4320, IMR4895, and other versatile powders. (If you have a pet load with VihtaVuori or something else a bit exotic, be sure to get plenty of that, too.) Get a lifetime supply for you, your family, your friends, and any future family and friends. **There's no such thing as *too* much ammo.** Remember, guns can last forever, but ammo is *quickly* used up. Have at least 5,000rds per pistol, 1,000rds per scoped rifle, and 10,000rds per battle rifle.

What you don't use, others will eagerly buy or trade from you, as most people will *not* have stocked enough. *Count* on it.

Mandatory *"arsenal"* license and inspection

The BATF already requires an additional form for 5 or more handgun purchases within 7 days from the same FFL.

Anybody with more than 2 guns or 1,000rds of ammo now has an *"arsenal"* and must be visited by BATF prior to getting a Ø200 arsenal permit. Undeclared stuff will get you ten years.

Severe regulation/closure of gun ranges

The EPA has already begun this tactic. Outdoor ranges are hassled over noise regulations, and indoor ranges are closed because of alleged lead pollution. If there's no public place to shoot, then we won't be able to sight-in and practice as easily. Shooting skills, like any other skills, erode from disuse.

Mandatory registration of everything else

Yeah, sure, the trapshooters will complain, but so *what*? They kept quiet all this time because their Ø6,000 Perazzis weren't affected, and now that it begins to hit home for them, it's too late. It's 2004 and we're now like 1997 England.

Federal law banning the carrying of firearms

Senator Frank Lautenberg (D-NJ) has already proposed this in S.707, which would override state concealed-carry and open-carry laws. I warned you about precisely this in 1997 (*Bulletproof Privacy*; 14/2-3). It *will* happen someday--probably by UN resolution to give Congress its *"our hands are tied"* excuse. If you have a CCW permit, your name will be on a handy list. Read *Bulletproof Privacy* and disappear. Lock and load.

Turn 'em in folks!

Now that they know who you are, what you have and where you store it, the confiscation raids can begin. Will you "Pass" or will you "Play"? Will you be a Man or a Mouse? The English and the Australians are going through this *right now*, and they've all chosen *"Mouse"* without a squeak. Fine, those Testicle-Free losers don't deserve their guns.

So, this could be *your* story--*our* story--if we don't wake up and grow some gonads, *quickly*. Or, be defanged and get sent to the camps. Your manacles are waiting--trust me on this. *"Hey, this is America! This can't happen here!"* That's exactly why it *can* happen here; because it's too incredible for most people to even contemplate.

Don't ever think it can't happen here. It has happened here. **We have a shameful history--don't ever forget it.** *In 1932, twenty thousand World War One veterans peacefully assembled...in Washington [D.C.] to urge Congress to give them their war bonus early. The military drove them out at gunpoint. General Douglas MacArthur had full armament, including foot soldiers with rifles and bayonets, cavalry with pistols and sabers, and tanks. MacArthur led his troops into a place where twenty thousand unarmed American war veterans were camped, and he burned them out. The soldiers shot and bayonetted some of the veterans, their wives, and children. Babies died from tear gas inhalation. The result of this horror is that Hoover was defeated and Franklin Roosevelt was able to seize power and drastically expand the government's reach into your lives. Part of that meant passing the unconstitutional National Firearms Act of 1934, which was the beginning of the terrible situation we now face. What happened at Waco and the disaster we face now is nothing new. It started sixty years ago with Franklin Roosevelt, it's gotten worse ever since, and we let it happen!*

    -- John Ross, *Unintended Consequences* (1996), p. 566

Gun registration and confiscation has preceded *every* modern genocide in history. Ask the murdered Sioux Indians of the 1870s. Ask the dead Moroccan Jews of 1912. Ask the starved Ukrainians of the 1930s. Ask the dead Jews of Nazi Europe. Ask the gulaged Soviet dissidents. Ask the 65,000,000 dead post-1948 Chinese anti-Communists, and the 2,000 massacred students of 1989 Tiananmen Square. If these groups had been *armed*, would they have been shot, flattened by tanks, or herded into gas chambers?

Prompt defensive measures (this means shooting back, folks) *are the most effective means for the prevention of genocide.*

    -- V.V. Stanciu, Secretary of the International Society for
    the Prevention of Genocide (Paris, France)

Stay armed and stay *free*. England was expelled from America in 1781, from Ireland in 1920, and from Palestine in 1948; France and the U.S. from Vietnam; Portugal from Angola; the U.S.S.R. from Afghanistan--all because the counter insurgents had both the will *and* the *means* to resist insurgent troops.

    And here's the moral:

When they come for your guns, *give 'em the ammo first*.

GUN CONFISCATION ABROAD

Several countries are following the NYC model: registration, then confiscation. This works when people are wimps.

England

Following the mass murder of 16 Scottish school children and their teacher by the homosexual child molester Thomas Hamilton, Britain rode the wave of media hysteria and collected over 100,000 handguns larger than .22 caliber.

Knives, pepper spray, etc. are also strongly discouraged. Unarmed victims *can* say, *"Stop! Or, I'll say 'stop!' again."*

Australia (see www.ssaa.org.au/)

By September 1997, over 600,000 firearms were coercively purchased by the government following Australia's worst mass killing of 35 people in Tasmania by Martin Bryant.

On a humorous note, 40,000 Aussies used their government check to purchase another firearm. The buy-back program merely assisted the "exchange" of one gun for a better one.

New Zealand (see www.ssanz.org.nz/)

No confiscation yet, but their government is pushing for mandatory registration of all firearms. A mass murderer is obviously the next prerequisite... Stay tuned.

Canada (see www.nfa.ca/)

After Marc Lepine slaughtered a number of college women with a Mini14, the Canadian parliament passed Bill C-68 requiring the registration of all firearms by 1 January 2003. Warrantless home searches are now authorized. Half of all handguns are outlawed, and the other half cannot be sold but must be destroyed upon the owner's death. The province of Alberta (the "Montana" of Canada) has sued to block the plan.

Notice any *pattern* here? Armed madman with criminal record kills many people, creating outrage over gun ownership which results in new gun control laws. This formula was invented here in America. (One wonders if some of these murderers were not intentionally destabilized through *Prozac®* withdrawal, etc. Rent the movie *The Pallalax View* sometime.)

UN GUN-CONTROL

What Congress doesn't have the nerve to outlaw the UN will. **"Disarmament" doesn't mean just nuclear weapons-- it also means your own firearms.** On 22 December 1995, the UN announced a study of individually held small arms which:

> *are increasingly associated with crime, accidents and suicides, and form a major source of illicit profits for transnational criminal networks...*
>
> http://www.un.org

I expect an international "War On Guns" within 5 years. The only well-armed citizenries left are those of Switzerland and America. Wherever the UN moves in (Somalia, Rwanda, Haiti, Bosnia) it forcibly disarms the populace. We're next. *Good.* It'll wake up millions of fence-sitters, and our vigilant Citizens won't mind defending their rights against baby-blue helmeted foreign troops from Bulgaria. (If we're lucky, the UN might even send the French, *oui*?) The Smurfs will have *big* problems.

WHAT ABOUT OUR RECENT SUPREME COURT VICTORIES?

Technically, we're 4 for 4 in the last five years: ***Thompson Center*** in 1992 (BATF interpretation regarding short-barreled rifles), ***Staples*** in 1994 (knowledge required to prove illegal possession of an automatic weapon), ***Lopez*** in 1995 (overturning the *"Gun-Free School Zone Act of 1991"*), and ***Printz*** in 1997 (overturning the background check mandate for CLEOs). *Boston sez:* Hold off on the party balloons.

Point #1: A new broom sweeps clean. Four victories in five years does *not* constitute a solid, irreversible trend.

Point #2: They were all 5-4 decisions. Expect Rehnquist or O'Connor to flip soon. The Scalia/Thomas "glue" won't hold.

Point #3: Two of those cases involved *federalism* challenges, *not* 2nd Amendment challenges. The Court could have by now struck down *NFA34* and *GCA68*, but has so far denied *cert* to the potentially landmark gun cases.

Point #4: The Court is unwilling to go "too far" in restoring our 2nd Amendment rights. For example, it *could* have killed Brady's 5-day waiting period by now, but has not. Nobody, not even Scalia, has ever joined Thomas's concurrences.

Point #5: Even if these victories *are* a trend, and even if the 5-4 majority *does* hold firm, and even if the Court *were* serious about upholding our rights, there's still the presidential power of executive order (based on some nebulous "national emergency"). Show me just *one* executive order overturned by the Supreme Court in the last 60 years!

I trust I make my melancholy case. Even if I'm wrong, it's still no huge problem for the more pesky Justices to drown in 2" of bathtub water, have a fatal one-car accident, or, best yet, shoot themselves in an unprecedented, baffling moment of suicidal despair. (Ask Vince Foster how this works.)

With or without the Court's blessing, the feds are going to try to strip away more and more of our self-defense rights. They've got a timetable to keep, they're on a roll, and, most importantly, they're not afraid of us.

They won't stop until--*unless*--they become afraid of us. History has proven that in countless, unanimous examples. In *The Gulag Archipelago*, Alexander Solzhenitsyn persuasively argued that had Stalin's goons been assaulted at least with wooden chairs and kitchen knives during the initial raids, the police state would have collapsed from a lack of thugs willing to volunteer for such hazardous duty. Thugs became thugs in the first place because they're *jackals* at heart. They shoot nursing mothers in the face from 200yds and pour helicopter machine gun fire on whole families in homestead churches. *Cowards*.

We'll have *no excuse*. We have the best firearms in history, we are the most armed people on the planet, we have an ingrained tradition of Liberty, and we have the priceless benefit of historical hindsight to understand not just the *process* of gradual tyranny, but its ugly finale of roundups, camps, and executions. **We'll have *no excuse* not to resist.** A people of sheep gets a government of wolves--we *know* that from history! Let's not have it demonstrated first hand. *Gun confiscation? Screw that!*

When they come for your guns, give 'em the ammo first.

PISTOLS & REVOLVERS

Let's face it, if you *knew* in advance that you had to shoot a bad guy, you wouldn't choose a *pistol*, would you? No, you'd get a 40mm automatic cannon and let him have it from a distance. That's safe for you and deadly for him.

I exaggerate to make this point: a pistol is a weapon used to fight your way *back* to your *rifle*--which you shouldn't have left far away. Pistols are concealable weapons for sudden and terrifying lethal emergencies. A defensive round (MagSafe, Glaser, Corbon) in a powerful caliber (.40S&W or .45ACP) competently wielded will *usually* solve such a problem.

If your assailant has *any* kind of shotgun or rifle, then you're at a disadvantage, but not *necessarily* "undergunned." If you drop an angel-duster with a 12ga before he shoots you, then you *weren't* undergunned. You're only undergunned (or undertrained) if you shoot and *miss*--and *he* shoots and *hits*. Undergunned means, *first,* not hitting your target. However, hitting *without effect* is *utterly* undergunned.

As long as you understand the purpose and limitations of pistols, you won't expect too much of them and get yourself into an inappropriate tactical situation.

DEFENSIVE AUTOS

These were not designed for plinking or hunting, but to quickly drop a lethal assailant in his tracks. Such a pistol must be utterly *reliable,* and sufficiently *powerful and accurate.* **Above all they must be *reliable.***

Autos vs. Revolvers

While revolvers have their small place in a defensive battery, a good auto is the way to go. When autos weren't as reliable, then perhaps revolvers had the nod--but no longer. Autos are chambered for the excellent .40S&W and .45ACP, hold 8 to 16rds, and can be reloaded within 2 seconds after practice.

Which auto caliber?

This choice is crucial. You are delivering kinetic energy to a hostile, adrenalized, lethal assailant--and the goal is to stop his actions. Obviously, you want to give him as much KE as possible. **My rule: Carry the *largest* pistol you can *conceal*, in the *most powerful* caliber you can *handle*.**

.22LR and .25ACP (Automatic Colt Pistol)

Unless you can place shots with eyeball accuracy *without fail*, these calibers will likely merely enrage your assailant. Granted, those shot by them often die, but only *hours* later, which is no consolation to you in that dark, terrifying alley.

7.62x25 Tokarev

This is a zippy Commie round which punches through most Kevlar vests. Available in the excellent CZ-52 for Ø125.

.32ACP and .380ACP (9mm Short, 9mm *Kurz*, or 9x17)

These are popular in Europe, where all the *Gendarmie* have to do is wing a bad guy for him to give up. These are still too weak to reliably drop a truly nasty dude (unless using MagSafe or Glasers). The .380s are a good choice for smaller shooters. **Remember, *any* gun will do, if *you* will do.**

If you've just *gotta* have a .32ACP and don't mind spending Ø600+ then get the superb, tiny Seecamp auto. The Beretta Tomcat in .32ACP is a Seecamp competitor for only Ø240.

9x18 Makarov

In between the .380 (9x17) and the 9mm Luger (9x19), I consider this Commie round to be the *absolute* minimum. When loaded with MagSafe, this is a fairly capable caliber--although I'd still prefer something much more powerful.

9x19 Luger

While the 9mm was once the only reasonable alternative to the .45ACP, it's not any longer because of the .40S&W. The 9mm, if loaded with *very* hot (1300+fps) 115gr Hornady XTPs or other zorchy defensive loads (MagSafe, Glaser, CorBon), can be quite deadly, however, standard loads are not very impressive. Since most 9mm pistols also come in .40, there's no compelling reason to keep (much less *buy*) a 9mm for your primary defensive pistol. If it comes in 9mm, it'll likely also come in .40, so why (unless you've weak wrists) have it in the lesser 9mm? Yeah, more people have probably been killed with the 9mm than any other pistol caliber--so *what?* Before spears, knives, and bows were around, more people had been killed by rocks. Progress, folks. There's little need for the 9mm today.

.38 Super
Developed in the 1920s to penetrate early body armor, Elliot Ness used 1911s and *Thompsons* (cool!) in .38 Super. A dying caliber whose performance is exceeded by the .357 SIG.

.357 SIG
A shortened 10mm case necked down to 9mm, giving 125/1375--duplicating a 4"bbl .357 Magnum. Barrels for Glocks (only Ø75-90 from CTD) drop in the 22/23/27 models and use the same mags. Because its .355 bullet is feeding into a .40 chamber, the .357 SIG is known for malfunction-free operation. Best factory loads are the 125gr CorBon and Speer Gold Dot. Dies and factory ammo now exist. Stopping power *should* be excellent, however street data on this 1995 caliber is still scant.

This new caliber has a *lot* going for it. Stay tuned.

9x23 Winchester
This a 9mm "Magnum" which gives 125/1500. While very hot with a 9mm's mag capacity, not many pistols are yet made for it. A Glock in 9x23 would be great, but since it could only have a 10rd mag, stick with the .40S&W or .357 SIG.

.40 S&W
Basically a .41AE without the rebated rim or a 10mm Lite, the .40 S&W (135/1300) measures exactly between the 9mm (.355) and .45, and is a fine compromise between the 9mm's capacity and the .45's knockdown power. For example, the same sized pistol mag will hold 15/9mm, 13/.40, or 10/.45.

Introduced in 1990, most badges now use the .40 (usually in the Glock 22) so ammo is very common. Its real-world effectiveness (far superior to the 9mm and 95% as good a stopper as the .45) has been well-proven by the police.

10mm

Jeff Cooper's rule of thumb for a minimum defensive pistol caliber is a 200gr .40 at 1000fps. He was instrumental in developing the 10mm (200gr at 1200fps, which is near wimpy factory .41 Magnum specs) and its original pistol, the Bren Ten. Since the Bren was a Ø1,000 pistol and mags became as scarce as hen's teeth, the 10mm nearly died on the vine until Colt came out with the Delta Elite in 1987. Once Glock introduced their Model 20, the 10mm's survival was assured.

The 10mm is about the best stopper of any common auto caliber; better than the .40 or even the .45ACP. This does not come without a price, however, as it's a handful to control.

The 10mm also makes an excellent trail gun caliber for those insisting on an auto over a revolver.

.400 CorBon (Call CorBon at 800-626-7266)

A shortened .45 Win Mag case necked down to .40 for 135/1450 and 155/1300. Basically, 10mm velocity from a Colt 1911A1 with a simple barrel change, although frame battering from excessive slide velocities is common unless you add a stiffer recoil spring. As good (or better) a stopper as the .45ACP, with superior penetration.

.45ACP

Designed by John Browning in 1905 with a 230gr/820fps load, the .45 has been historically proven an excellent stopper. While not noted for its penetration, neither is a brick, but either will put 'em down. I like the .45 except for its reduced mag capacity (the same sized mag will hold 3 *more* rds in .40S&W).

.45 Super

This is made from .451 Detonics brass which has a much thicker case. Cut to .45ACP length, the .45 Super feeds and chambers in any .45ACP, but you will need a 35% stronger recoil spring. This hotter .45 will give you an extra 200fps, thus 10mm/.400 CorBon muzzle energy. Robar can set up your gun.

The winners are...the .40S&W, 10mm, and .45ACP

Their one-shot stop performance is 90+%, many pistols are chambered for them, and ammo can be found anywhere. The .357 SIG, .400 CorBon and .45 Super are *great* defensive rounds, but not yet very common. That will probably change.

I didn't even include the 9mm, since the .40S&W is available in 80% of all modern 9mm pistols. All you whining 9mm devotees should simply get a .40 and install a .357 SIG barrel.

So, which *is* it--.40S&W, 10mm, or .45ACP?
This choice is by no means clear cut, as all three calibers are very fine stoppers. For me, one edges out the other two, but you may disagree based on your personal needs and opinion.

If I were carrying around a *full-size* pistol in a belt holster, and caliber commonality with my other guns or with my buddies wasn't a big issue, then I'd wear a **10mm** Glock 20. I don't mind the 10mm's recoil--you've got to *take* it in order to *give* it--there's little getting around Newton's Law.

The **.45ACP** is also excellent, although mag capacity suffers, and few compact autos are available (Glock 30, Detonics, Para Ord P-10, Colt Officers ACP, AMT, and Star PD).

I think the **.40S&W** is the most *efficient* caliber as it delivers 95% of the .45's KE from a more compact round. This is usually quite ample since modern pistol technique demands two shots to the body. If two solid hits with a .40 won't do it, then it seems unlikely that using a .45 or 10mm would have made the difference. Therefore, I'd rather have the extra mag capacity of the .40 without the 10mm's recoil.

I will, nevertheless, also discuss pistols in 10mm and .45ACP, just in case you're already set on one of these calibers.

Single-action, double-action, or Glock?
Now that we've decided on one of three calibers, which kind of trigger and safety operation is the best?

Single-action (SA)--Colt 1911 style
To fire your first shot (we're assuming a chambered round) you must either thumb cock the hammer from Condition Two, or drop the safety from Condition One. In duty mode, carrying in Condition One is preferable, although proper training is essential. While better than a DA from Condition Two (because of the DA's longer first trigger pull), the Glock is better.

Good SA pistols are the Colt 1911A1 (and quality clones like the Para Ord, Argentine 1927 Sistema, Ballester-Molina), H&K USP, Browning Hi-Power, Astra A-70, Tokarev, Star M40 Firestar, SIG P210, Polish Radom (WWII), Swedish Lahti, Helwan Brigadier, Star Model B, and CZ52.

Double-action (DA)--Beretta 92, etc.

Since the trigger will both cock the hammer and drop it (thus the double action), a DA pistol may be ready carried in Condition Two and needs no thumb cocking or safety manipulation to fire your first shot.

This sounds real neat, *however*, that first trigger pull needs 10-15lbs of effort, and all successive shots are single-action pulls (since the slide cocks the hammer during its cycle). The SA pulls are only 4-6lbs. So what, you ask? Try to put two fast shots to the body from a DA sometime. You'll usually pull one of them off target because of the trigger effort difference. (The Daewoo DP51 minimizes this with its clever lightweight DA pull, but a disparity still remains. The DAO pistols like the Colt 2000 and some S&Ws were another try.)

While this can be overcome with *a lot* of practice (like *"swimming the English Channel without flippers"* according to Cooper), there's a much better way--the Glock.

Good DAs are Walthers, H&Ks, SIGs (220, 225, 226, 228, 229, 239), Beretta 92s (and Taurus clones, which are better than the Berettas), Astras (A-75, A-80, A-90, A-100), AMT Backup, Hungarian FEG FP9, Makarov, Daewoo DP51, Colt Double Eagle, and Browning BDA. S&W autos *suck*, period.

The CZ 75 and 97B (and quality clones, like the Tanfoglio TA90, EAA Witness, Beretta 92M9, Springfield P9, Taurus PT92/99 and PT52S, Jericho 941, etc.) are SA *and* DA. You can carry in either Condition 1 (cocked and locked in SA) or Condition 2 (hammer down, safety off, DA pull).

Avoid DAOs like the plague (except for the Seecamp).

Glock "Safe Action"

Gaston Glock, an Austrian engineer, made a quantum leap on several levels with his Glock 17 in 1981. Regarding the trigger system, there are no manual slide safeties. A trigger safety bar protrudes from the trigger face and is automatically pressed by the finger when pulling the trigger. Further pressure unlocks an internal safety and the final pressure cocks the striker (there's no hammer) and then releases it.

This means that the chambered Glock is carried in sort of a Condition Two and that a mere pull of the trigger will fire the pistol without any SA 1911-style safety manipulation. **The real beauty is that the first trigger pull is the *same* as the rest.** Until you've trained with a Glock you can't appreciate how superior this is to a DA, or even a SA.

Because the Glock has no manipulative SA safety, there's no safety to miss on the draw stroke or accidentally thumb up when firing--and believe me, either can happen to the best of shooters. Because the Glock's trigger pull never changes (as do the DAs), you will shoot better in adrenalized conditions.

With the Glock, you must *flawlessly obey* Rule 3 discipline. (Rule 3 should be flawless with *any* weapon, but it's *especially* important with the Glock.)

S&W blatantly copied the Glock trigger/safety system for their sucky Sigmas. Gaston Glock sued for patent infringement. After realizing that Glock was *serious*, S&W settled for Ø3,000,000 and agreed to alter their Sigmas. Heh!

Glock vs. the world

Not only is the Glock trigger/safety system the best, the Glocks are the most rugged and reliable of *any* auto pistol. (The Glock factory has a 17 with over *380,000*rds through it.) You can run over a Glock with a truck, dunk it in a swamp, drag it through the dirt, and it'll still work.

The Glock is made of just 35 parts (the Colt 1911 has 57 to nearly 80), and uses a polymer/metal insert molded hybrid frame for lighter weight and better recoil absorption (which H&K copied in their USP). The slide is CNC milled, so it's efficient to produce. The Tenifer finish is 99% saltwater corrosion-resistant and 69 HRc hard (a metal file is 62-65; an industrial diamond is 70), and just about rustproof. It field strips easier than any other pistol. It feels good and points well.

Look, the Colt 1911 *was* a brilliant design (which is why it still shines 87 years later), but, hey, progress *is* progress. In my pistol classes were students with Ø2,000 1911s constantly in the shop. (Too bad Browning didn't make his Hi-Power in .45ACP. The .40S&W version, however, is great.) A Ø450 Glock works out of the box, *period*, and I've owned or shot about *everything*. Only the SIGs and tuned Colts are slightly more accurate (though not as reliable).

Get a Glock, and be *done* with your auto pistol needs so you can move on to other matters deserving more time and money (like battle and sniper rifles). In summary, the Glock is accurate, insensitive to dirty conditions, field-strips easily, and is as reliable as a pistol gets. There may be a better pistol for *you*, but there's none better than a Glock, and there won't be for a very, *very* long time. Probably not until Gaston designs it.

Shooting the Glock

This pistol is the easiest for novices to train with, as it has none of the difficulties of the SAs and DAs. There are now drop free mags, so speed reloads are just as fast as in the 1911.

The students who've had problems with the Glock are those who didn't use a *firm* shooting grip. Since the Glock is so lightweight, it has less mass of its own to recoil against and needs your firm grip as a backstop. With proper training and practice, most small-framed shooters can master it.

If you absolutely *cannot* "resonate" with the grip size, then try the grip reduction process from Robar (602-581-2648/2962) which makes the 20/21/29/30s feel like a P-35 Hi-Power. Go to another pistol if you must, but *do* give the Glock a fair try. (I'd nonetheless train with 1911s and DAs for familiarity's sake.)

Which Glock for *you*?

The Glock numerology is purely sequential in order of design. (The pistol was Gaston Glock's 17th patent, hence the beginning number.) Models in bold are the best choices.

17	9mm full size (17+1)
17L	9mm full size (17+1) long slide
18	9mm full size full auto selective fire for cops
19	9mm compact (15+1)
20	10mm full size (15+1)
21	.45ACP full size (13+1)
22	.40S&W full size (15+1)--size of the 17
23	.40S&W compact (13+1)--size of the 19
24	.40S&W target long slide (15+1)--*very accurate*
25	.380ACP compact (not available here), 19/23 size
26	9mm micro (10+1)
27	.40S&W micro (9+1)--size of the 26
28	.380 on 26/27 frame sold in Central/S. America
29	10mm compact (10+1)--size of the 19 and 23
30	.45ACP compact (10+1)--just like the 29
31	.357 SIG full size ("15"+1)--22 size and mags
32	.357 SIG compact ("13"+1)--23 size and mags
33	.357 SIG micro (9+1)--27 size and mags

So, we've decided on .40S&W, 10mm, or .45ACP. This gives us *six* choices (not counting the 24 or 29 models).

Why not the Glock 29?

In 10mm we finally have the compact 29, which holds 10+1. It's the same size as the 23, but with a bit fatter grip. This is an awesome conceal piece, though it has one big problem: the shorter barrel reduces velocities to .40S&W levels--so what's the *point* of it being in 10mm? None. Carry a 27 or 23 in .40S&W or a 30 in .45ACP. Sorry, Gaston.

Why not the new Glock 31/32/33s in .357 SIG?

While I've every confidence in the .357 SIG's effectiveness, let's wait for the street data to be sure. Ammo is still uncommon, although that will change. Finally, these are too new to find on the used market. Just get a 23 or 27 and install a .357 SIG barrel (Ø75 from CTD). The .357 SIG uses .40S&W mags.

The .357 SIG loses 70fps from the 33's 3½"bbl vs. the 32's 4"bbl, however, simply install the 32's 4"bbl in a 27, which is what I'm doing since I have both a 27 and a 23. (The 31's 4½"bbl only gains 40fps at best and isn't worth the length.) Every .40S&W Glock owner should have a .357 SIG drop-in barrel.

compact (27 or 23/.40S&W), (30/.45ACP)

Concealability is the goal here. (If you can *reliably* conceal a *full*-size pistol, then by all means carry that, as they hold more rounds, are more accurate and easier to control.)

The **.40S&W** micro 27 is amazingly tiny yet holds 9+1--a superb *deep* cover pistol which can use the 13-15rd mags of the 23 and 22. I highly recommend the Ø9 Pearce grip extension (from CTD) which improves feel. (I don't recommend a +2 floorplate in the 27 because the mag spring is too short.) For the novice, the 27 is a more challenging to train with than the 23.

If you can conceal a mid-size gun, the 23 is hard to beat. It holds at least 13+1, and can use the 15rd mag of the 22 and/or the +2 floorplate. Though not tiny, it conceals fine.

The new **.45ACP** Glock 30, which is the same size as the 23, is a real winner. It conceals well enough, yet holds 10+1 (or 13+1 if using the 21 mag). You won't likely find any used ones for sale for a long time, so that means a papered sale. If adding the .40 is out of the question, and you're sticking with the .45, then the Glock 30 is your compact pistol. They work *perfectly* right out of the box, whereas the 1911s are much more finicky.

Carry the 13rd mags in your mag pouch, because if the 11 in your 30 didn't do it, then you're in some kind of *bad* trouble.

For *deep* concealment, the 27 is just unbeatable.

For larger conceal guns it's a choice between the Glock 23 or the Glock 30. The 23 holds 3 more rounds, is a bit thinner and has a little narrower grip which feels better to me. Therefore, between a 30 and 23, I'd choose a 23. (If a 30 drops in my lap, I'll take it, but since I've already got its big brother 21 I won't go out of my way for a new 30.)

full size duty (22 or 23/.40S&W) (20/10mm) (21 or 30/.45)

The "duty" pistol is one worn daily in a belt holster, therefore, the smaller size of the concealables isn't needed. The Glock 23 and 30 are more concealable duty sized pistols, and they do hold 10-13+1, which is probably sufficient. Any of them would be a fine choice if you could afford only *one* defensive pistol for alternative belt and concealed carry.

The 20 and 21, though fat (send it to Robar for grip slimming), are great. They carry 13-15+1 (or 15-17+1 with the +2 floorplate) without being much larger than a 1911. Sixteen rounds of .45 or eighteen rounds of 10mm should please *any* hostile crowd. If you *never* envision having to conceal your belt pistol, then a 20 or 21 is for you.

For *me*, however, I'd probably prefer a more compact 23 or 30 since mag capacity is sufficient (and you can use the longer mags anyway), and they're more concealable. You never know when you'll have to hide your pistol in a hurry.

So, what's *my* choice of Glocks?

If I could afford only one, it would be the micro 27. Two, I'd add the 23. Three, I'd add the 30. Four, I'd add the 20. Five, I'd add a 19 (or 26), just to have a 9mm. Six, I'd add the 21. Seven, the 24. I've no use for the 22 over the 23, or the 17 over the 19.

Customizing your Glock

Glock Works (800-710-5202; www.glockworks.com) has all the custom gear you could want, and then some. Glocks don't need much, so don't go crazy. Here are my thoughts:

Ported or compensated barrels

They ruin your night vision, and are unnecessary with good training, a strong shooting grip and sufficient practice.

Extended mag and slide releases

Generally unadvised--stock controls usually work fine.

Lasers

Don't you dare. Forget about the Buck Rogers junk. Lasers don't stay aligned, are hard to see in daylight, and the battery will crap out in the cold or when you need it the most. *Simpler is better.* Learn to use your front sight.

Sights

Adjustable rear sights are *not* suitable for a combat pistol. Instead, I recommend a glow-in-the-dark Trijicon Ashley Express (www.ashleyoutdoors.com, or from CTD, 817-625-7557). The ghost-ring rear from Tactical 2 (818-962-8712) is also good.

Magazines

The newer factory Glock mags (with the squared "U" at the rear of the lips) will drop free when empty (compared to the rounded "U" mags). The steel body U.S.A. mags will also drop free, but are hard on the plastic mag catch. The aftermarket polymer high-capacity mags are somewhat junky.

The post-ban factory 10rd mags (20/21/23; 9 in the 27) are very reasonable (Ø18 from CTD) and excellent for practice.

Save your Ø75 high-capacity mags for actual duty carry. If you've got a 27 or a 23, you might as well get the *15*rd 22 mags for spares. If you *have* to reload, then by definition you're in a firefight, so wouldn't you rather that second mag have *15*rds instead of a mere 9 or 13? Logical, eh?

The +2 floorplates are clever, but sometimes come off the mag body when firing, so experiment thoroughly *before* relying on them for duty. Glue them in place with Loctite Surface Insensitive Formula.

Belt holsters and mag pouches

With Glocks, Kydex® gear is the way to go, *period.* It's a tough thermo-molded polymer which is impervious to salt, sweat, water, oil, gun cleaners and most chemicals and solvents. Leather and Cordura just can't compare.

The indisputable originator of Kydex® gun/knife gear is SEAL A.T.A.K. knifemaker Kevin McClung of **Mad Dog Tactical, Inc.** in Prescott Valley, Arizona (520-772-3021/3022fax; www.northlink.com/~maddog). Other firms rip off his ideas, but nobody designs and makes stuff better than Mad Dog.

Made in America by Americans with American materials, all Mad Dog products come with a no-sniveling Lifetime Guarantee--not that you're likely to ever need it.

I like the Taylor ThunderBolt™ (co-designed by shooting instructor Chuck Taylor) and the Tactical Low Ride™. Get mag pouches for your Glock and AR15, a Sure-Fire Flashlight holder, and a Leatherman (or Gerber multi-tool) pouch.

Concealment gear for your Glock

Two good books on concealed carry are *Hide In Plain Sight* by Bloodworth and Raley (Paladin Press) and *CCW: Carrying Concealed Weapons* (ISBN 0-941540-24-3) by Ahern.

For *best* deep concealment, Thunderwear (Ø54.45ppd.; 800-375-4433) has no equal. You'll need loose fitting slacks. I also like the Pager Pal (from CTD, 817-625-7557) and the faux cell-phone case (Phone-E-Pak; 800-209-7904).

For jogging, etc. the ActionPac™ for Ø54ppd is the ticket (800-472-2388; www.action-direct.com).

With an untucked shirt, vest, or jacket, a behind-the-back Inside Pants Mad Dog holster works very well. It's nearest your center of gravity, easy to hide, yet quick to draw. Quicker still is in the front of your body under an untucked shirt (don't ND...).

Fanny packs worn in front work well, but are by now very well known. So, if you're illegally concealing without a permit, understand in advance that the cops might spot the pack and ask to see your CCW permit. Nevertheless, these packs *do* have their place. I like the Bagmaster products (800-950-8181). Model HLFP-M has a discreet 1¼" belt (the 1¾-2" belts on other packs are too obvious) and will hold the Glock 23 and 30.

I *don't* care for shoulder holsters. They're off-balanced and print through your jacket too obviously.

Ankle holsters work only for small pistols and create a slight limp, but are fine for a backup .32LR Beretta or AMT.

Bargain autos

If reliable, any gun is better than *no* gun at all. Remember the first rule of gun fights: Have A Gun.

If you're on a *real* budget, then the Ø165 Makarov 9x18 pocket pistol (derived from the Walther PP) is a great bargain. The 9x18 is more powerful than the .380, though not quite up to the 9x19 Luger. The quality is very good, with the best being East German, then Bulgarian, then Russian. MagSafe makes hot defensive ammo for the 9x18, and a 1,000rd case of training ammo goes for about Ø150.

The Tokarev 9mm (or 7.62x25) is only Ø130, but is a fairly clumsy pistol which will not conceal like the Makarov.

From J&G, the CZ-52 is a very fine pistol for Ø125 and its 7.62x25 is a real zinger. (They're also in 9mm for Ø150.) The Ø100 CZ-70 is in .32ACP. In fact, *any* CZ pistol will be a well-made bargain.

There are a lot of surplus 9mm Browning Hi-Powers coming in for about Ø300. Fine pistols, and mags and parts abound.

The Argentine "Modelo 1927/Sistema Colt" .45 1911 for Ø240 is a *very* solid auto (made of Swedish steel), with full parts interchangeability. The Ø175 Ballester-Molina is also well made, although only the barrel, bushing, link, pin, mag, recoil spring and guide, and mag will work in the American Colt.

The KBI and FEG Hi-Power/Walther clones from Hungary are well made and very good values. The GKK45 (a .45ACP DA Hi-Power clone) from Birmingham Pistol (800-951-4867) is a red-hot bargain at only Ø186. Unfortunately, it is nearly impossible to get spare parts, mags, and accessories for these pistols.

WWII pistols

I have a weakness for these. If you're going to collect something, then at least these autos are serviceable as well as nice to look at. I like the Luger, Sauer 38H, Walther P-38 and PPK (or PP), and Swedish Lahti. I recommend only matching numbered guns in 90+% condition without an import stamp (it's usually on the barrel). Such will go for Ø300-600. Find an original holster, mags, etc. for each and you'll have a fun collection of historical shooting irons. While the Luger is too ammo temperamental, the P-38 and the Lahti are *very* reliable combat pistols. SOG (800-944-4867) has good prices on both. The *Finnish* Lahti is a *true* collector's piece, going for at least Ø1,000. (The Lahti was designed for sub-zero temperatures, and it *works*.)

Autos to *avoid*

The Ruger P series run poorly, feel just *awful* and have stupid controls. Can't stand 'em. Besides, Bill Ruger was making them with 10rd mags *before Congress even required it*.

Did I mention that S&W autos suck? I like their *revolvers*. (The opposite is usually true for Colts--except for the Python and Diamondback, Colt aren't not known for their revolvers.)

Do *not* buy pistols by Davis, Lorcin, Jennings, Kel-Tec, High Point, or Bersa. The *gangsta* TEC-9s are worthless crap.

Basically, use good judgment. **Quality is almost always *discernible*.** If you've never heard of a "Yugo Arms" and it looks crappy and feels crappy--then it probably *is* crappy. A decent quality auto will always cost at least Ø125. Pistols less than Ø125 are priced that way for a reason. Autos demanding and getting over Ø300 are usually pretty good.

REVOLVERS

While I enjoy revolvers, I'm not *gaah-gaah* about them. To me, they have two general purposes: a decent defensive pistol for those who cannot (or will not) spend the time needed to master an auto; and trail weapons against big cats, bears, etc.

Calibers

In my opinion there's only several to consider.

.38 Special

Introduced in 1902, it's sort of the .30-30 of revolver rounds. While not a great stopper, the P+ load is just under a hot 9mm. A good caliber for ladies and backup guns. Derringers in .38 Special are great hideout guns.

.357 Magnum

Its case is 0.125" longer than a .38 Special, with three times the energy. Its 125gr/1600fps load is historically *the best* one shot stopper, at 98%. You'll need at least a 4" barrel to wring out this round (6"+ is better).

.41 Magnum

Between the .357 and .44 Magnums, it gives 914ft/lbs from 210/1400. It's powerful, accurate, tolerable and *uncommon*. While a fine round, it's a "neither-fish-nor-fowl" 16 gauge. Carry the .44 instead, just like the 12ga over the 16ga.

.44 Special

The .44 Special at 200/900 (360ft/lbs) approaches the .45ACP in stopping power, and *far* outshines the .38 Special. A very good caliber in a snub-nose, as a long barrel isn't needed for velocity. Also, it can be fired from .44 Magnums.

.44-40
An Old West round from 1873, offering 200/1150 for 587ft/lbs. Uncommon in modern revolvers, but fun cowboy stuff. Handloading it is a real bitch, and factory ammo is pricey.

.44 Magnum
A fantastic caliber--powerful, versatile, and easy to load. The classic revolver load of 240/1450 (for 1121ft/lbs) is pretty stompy. 265/1400 (1154ft/lbs) or 300/1250 (1041ft/lbs) will take black bear and elk within 75yds, and deer out to 100.

.45ACP
Colt and S&W make revolvers in this, using ½ and full moon clips. Fun and gentle shooters with good power.

.45 Colt
The .45-70 of revolver cartridges. Between the .44 Special and .41 Magnum in energy (250/950 for 500ft/lbs), this century-old cowboy round is fun for the hobbyist, but better and more common calibers exist.

.454 Casull
Makes the .44 Magnum look positively anemic. Sort of like a .45-70 Lite, throwing a 250gr at 1800fps for 1800ft/lbs. Gee. (This would make a fantastic carbine caliber.) The .454 Casull revolvers can also use the .45 Colt ammo, just as the .357 Mag can fire the .38 Special. Unless you're in grizzly country, this monster round is too *beaucoup* for most souls. A great penis enhancement caliber, however.

snub nose (.38Sp.; .357 Mag.; .44 Sp.)
(S&W 60 and 640; Ruger SP101, Charter Arms, Taurus, Rossi)

This is a great gun for the nightstand, as it can be kept loaded forever without stressing any springs. They're sometimes only 5-shot instead of six, but that's the price of small size. Go stainless whenever possible. Use MagSafe or Glasers.

In **.38 Special**, I'd go for a 5-shot S&W 60 or 640. I prefer the hammer to be shrouded, if not fully concealed. Or, choose a 6-shot, as in the Colt Cobra. Taurus has greatly improved their quality (and, to a lesser extent, so has Rossi). I'd avoid the cheaper revolvers. (Guns, tires, and tools are *not* the things to sacrifice quality to price.) As the standard .38 Special round is pretty anemic, load it with MagSafe, Glaser Silver, or CorBon. Practice your two-shots-to-the-body in DA, and speed loading with strips and HKS speedloaders.

For the stainless **.357 Magnum**, in order of preference are the Ruger SP101, the S&W 640-1, and the Taurus 605. The 2½ Python 6-shot stainless is also a beauty, though big ØØØ.

Barrel length should be as long as you can conceal. Compact .357s are a real handful, so attach some good grips by Pachmayr or Hogue. Practice with full-house loads. Muzzle-blast from 2" snubbies is literally stupefying, therefore a poor choice for low light conditions. You might consider frangible Glaser Silvers in your .357 for the nightstand.

Best choices in **.44 Special** are the 3" S&W 29-3, Taurus M431 or M445CH, Rossi M720, or older Charter Arms Bulldog.

Forsake the newer Charco Bulldog Pug and its abysmal quality for an older Charter Arms Bulldog. Don't put a trillion rounds through it, as they loosen up quickly.

Revolver -- Magnum (.357 or .44)
(Colt Python; S&W 19 or 66, 29, 629; Ruger)

Those in bear or big cat country should carry at least a .44 Magnum (or even a .454 Casull), as the .357 is *not* a reliable stopper for the big and mean stuff. In fact, the .44 is preferable to the .357 in about every situation, though I included the .357 for those who can't handle the .44. You won't need such a revolver unless you're often in the field. Load your first chamber with snake shot and the other 5 with game loads.

The best DAs are the S&W 29/629 and Ruger Redhawk. (Though the S&W is no weakling, the Ruger is stronger.) Ruger makes great SAs, the Blackhawk and Super Blackhawk. I've got a 629 and Super Blackhawk, and love 'em both. I do not recommend the Colt .44 Anaconda Magnum.

Hunting with a good .44 Magnum is extremely gratifying. I'd choose a 629 or Redhawk with 6-7½" bbl. and a trigger job. Some swear by scoped models, but get proficient with iron sights, first. Use 265gr or 300gr bullets.

Bargain revolvers

There's an import glut of very decent WWII S&W Model 10 .38 Specials for Ø100 (two for Ø90) from SOG. These are nice collectible pieces and excellent values. For future *wampum* when private sales have been outlawed, a Model 10 and box of ammo will be *very* desirable. You might consider picking up a dozen or two, individually shrink wrapping them with 50rds, and burying them for that upcoming rainy decade.

The police trade-in .357 Magnum S&W 65s and 66s are very nice for Ø180-250. The 66 is more solid than the 65.

Revolvers to *avoid*

Same rules as autos apply to revolvers: If it feels like junk, then it probably *is.* All of the Spanish cheapies are abysmal. You can rarely go wrong with a Ø100-250 S&W which appears to be in decent condition.

The only Colt revolvers I like are the Pythons (.357 Mag) and Diamondbacks (in .22LR and .38 Special). The modern King Cobra and Anaconda are pretty sloppy.

.22LR PISTOLS

While these aren't what you'd choose for defense, .22LR pistols are good for initial training, plinking, and pest control. Also, they're just plain *fun.* One of my students, a high-school junior, enjoyed my Ruger Mk.II *so* much, that she *kissed* it good-bye! (Talk about a gun making a lasting impression.) I can train a novice for a .40 or .45 *much* more quickly by starting with a .22LR for an hour to shed fear and gain confidence.

.22LR ammo

Avoid **the Mexican and Russian stuff--it's *bad.*** Use any copper-coated ammo and avoid the leadfingers. Stingers, Yellowjackets and Vipers are the hot loads for pests. At least one .22LR pistol is a necessary gun in most batteries.

Auto -- full size .22LR

The Ruger Mk.II stainless is the way to go. Extremely accurate (particularly with a 5½" bull barrel) and good pointers. You'll pay Ø175 for a used one. The Mk.II has a slide stop and can also use Mk.I mags, whereas the Mk.I can use only its own 9rd mags. The older Mk.Is are fine, though I prefer the Mk.II.

Other good .22 autos are the Colt Woodsman and High-Standard). I also like the scaled-down Luger and P-38 copies.

Get a Ø15 surplus Swedish Lahti 9mm leather holster from Sarco or The Gun Parts Corp. The Ruger and mags fit perfectly. Mad Dog Tactical also makes their excellent Kydex® Gun Glove holster for the Ruger.

Auto -- compact .22LR

Once you've got your Ruger, then you might like a micro .22LR. They're not vital, but they do have their place. They are good for snakes/pests at close range, or *deep* conceal backups.

Spend Ø160 for the Beretta 21A or Taurus PT-22; the cheaper Jennings, etc. are a false savings (they misfeed often). I've tried two of the Iver Johnson Walther PP clones, but both were jammers, to my sad surprise. The stainless Walther TPH is Ø350, but a real Mercedes. The American version malfs often, so stick with the German model, expensive though it is.

Practice making *headshots*--forget the body, as the .22LR will *not* stop your bad guy there. If you can *reliably* place with eye-socket accuracy, then this pistol might someday save your life. Keep it spotlessly clean and lightly oiled--all .22s are sensitive to powder buildup.

What about the .25ACP? *Nah.* Ammo is at least 15¢/rd compared to 2¢/rd for .22LR, with no appreciably greater stopping power from its whopping 80ft/lbs. Stick with the .22LR.

HIDEOUT HANDGUNS

These are smaller than even the Glock 27 micro. We're talking *last-ditch* handgun, carried in the bra, groin, etc. This is what you'd use to fight your way back to a "real" pistol!

These serve well: Seecamp .32ACP (Ø600+!), NAA .32 Guardian (a Seecamp clone; www.naaminis.com), Beretta .32ACP Tomcat (Ø240), or Derringer (I'd choose the stainless M-1 in .40, a common caliber that doesn't need a lot of barrel to perform well; 800-642-7817; www.amderringer.com). Practice your discreet, flawless drawing and shooting *extensively*, as this is your "last chance" firearm. You simply *cannot* fail with it.

❖ 5

SHOTGUNS

Shotguns are especially good for defense in urban environments, and certain kinds of hunting (birds and heavy brush game with slugs). Since these situations are not very common for me, I'm not into shotguns all that much.

Pump vs. Auto?

The better autos (Remington 1100 and 1187; Brownings; H&K; Benelli) are no doubt fine shotguns, but a pump is more reliable and easier to clear malfunctions. With training and practice, a good shooter can hit just *almost* as quickly with a pump (e.g., Kurt Russell in *The Thing*, even though he managed, without reloading, *11* shots from a 4+1 Ithaca). I think that a good pump with a total of three barrels will handle just about anybody's shotgun needs. Finally, pump shotguns were not affected by the "Crime Bill," but autos were.

An 18" barrel auto, however, *is* a good *car* shotgun as the driver can fire it one-handed. (The High-Standard Model 10B bullpup comes to mind here...) Alternate slugs and 00 buck.

Remington 870 (3" Magnum w/20" Remchoke)

Use #4 buck for attackers, and 00/000 buck or slugs for barricades. Other rounds include DragonsBreath, flechettes, smoke, CS gas, etc. (All Purpose Ammo, 800-870-2666).

For urban dwellers, such is *the* first line of defense. Condo bee-hivers should use only birdshot (#2 is best) to avoid wiping out your neighbors just beyond drywall.

While the Ithaca and Mossberg pumps are fine, the Remington 870 is really the best choice. The Winchester 1300 Defender is also a very fine pump, and even less prone to malf than the 870, although barrel changing is not as convenient.

Find a 3" Magnum if you can--it'll fire all sorts of specialty rounds which aren't often in 2¾". A 20" barrel with Remchoke and ghost-ring sights, +3 mag tube extension, Choate pistol-grip full-length stock, forestock with Sure-Fire flashlight, sling, and 6-round Sidesaddle make for an awesome weapon. The two other barrels are a long vent-rib for hunting and a rifled slug barrel with iron sights (rumored to soon be outlawed by the BATF as a *"destructive device"*).

I highly recommend a *good* defensive shotgun course (e.g., Louis Awerbuck's Yavapai Firearms Academy in Prescott Valley, Arizona) to maximize your effectiveness.

RIFLE / SHOTGUN COMBINATIONS

In his *Survival Guns* Mel Tappan praised the versatility of the Savage Model 24 over/under combo guns. I have some and like them very much. Made in .22LR/20ga, .22WMR/20ga, .223/20ga, and (at one time) .30-30/12ga, they make excellent backpacking guns to handle most any game within 50yds. The shotgun barrel can throw a rifled slug for bigger game, although this is often not accurate enough past 50yds.

Their biggest drawbacks are poor sights and *abysmal* triggers--both of which can be addressed. I'd send it out for a rust-resistant finish (Parkerizing, Teflon, etc.), install an ammo butt cuff, sling, and good sights. Threading the barrel for a Remchoke is also very worthwhile.

For the shotgun barrel you can even get some rifle caliber insert barrels (in .223, .30-30, .44 Magnum). O-ringed sealed inside your barrel, these aren't known for their accuracy, but will work out to 75yds in a pinch.

Smaller shotgun gauge inserts are also available. I pack many .410 shells and a few 20ga shells to save weight. With practice, a .410 will drop *nearly* as many birds as a 20ga.

Within their limitations, the Savage 24s will accomplish much for one long gun. It's a good gun for a young boy to hone his skills with. It's also a good gun to break down and pack in the truck or camper. Used, they go for Ø125-225. The ones with the .22 Mag or .223 barrel are quite versatile, since they're much more powerful than the .22LR, but you can still shoot .22LR with inexpensive brass chamber inserts.

❖ **6**

BOLT-ACTION RIFLES

What a rifle delivers is highly-accurate power at long range. Versus battle rifles, bolt-actions are usually chambered in more powerful calibers and are also much more accurate, therefore they far eclipse battle rifles when shooting at hard and far targets. Basically, your battle rifle is for threats up to 400yds, while your scoped bolt gun handles stuff past 400yds. If you'll never shoot past 400, then you might not even need a bolt-action, but I'd always have one, regardless.

ALL-AROUND CALIBERS

Basically, we want to be able to kill elk out to 250yds, mule deer out to 400yds,, and bad guys out to 700. The caliber must be accurate, tolerable if not comfortable, easy to reload, and *common*. While it's not a varmit or bear caliber, it'll do either in a pinch from a good man. In short, this rifle/caliber will do 90% of anything a bolt-action is expected to do. (I omit the overbore Magnum calibers.) For *specialized* needs, you'll need *specialized* rifles. Underlined calibers are the semifinalists.

.223   .22-250   .220 Swift
Throwing a 55gr pill at 3300-3700fps, these are varmit calibers *only*. I wouldn't dare hunt whitetails with any .22 caliber, even though it's probably done.

.243   6mm Rem.   .250 Savage   .257 Roberts
Throwing a 100gr at 3000fps, these are excellent varmit and whitetail deer calibers, though a bit light for mulies, and decidedly unsportsmanlike to use on elk. The .243 (6-08) is the

most widely available and renowned for its accuracy, but it and its ballistic brothers are *much* too light for general purposes.

.260 Rem.   6.5x55 Swede   7x57   7-08

Now we're getting somewhere. Throwing a 140gr at 2700-2900fps, these are great for mule deer (and elk under 175yds). The ballistically excellent 6.5 and 7mm bullets are *very* efficient. Good for intermediate sniper use, too.

The 6.5x55 Swede and 7x57 Mauser

These are excellent 1890s European military calibers, giving good power with little recoil. However, they are long-action cases, and there are much better calibers (e.g., the .30-06) for such actions. While I wouldn't buy a *modern* rifle in these two, I have an absolute crush on the Swedish military rifles in 6.5x55. In 7x57 I'd also probably be rather tempted by an FN-49 or a M98 made by Loewe or DWM for South American in the 1920s.

The .260 and 7-08

These two are merely the .308 case necked down to 6.5 and me, and are two of my favorite short-dated calibers. They ballistically duplicate the 6.5x55 and 7x57 in short cases. One of these is what we *should* have gone to in the 1950s, as their ballistics are *much* better than the stubby .308. Bullets top out at 160gr for the 6.5mm and 175 for the 7mm.

6.5RM   .284   .270   .280

These four give nearly identical performance--150/2900. The 6.5RM and .284 are short-action calibers, while the .270 and .280 are long-action rounds derived from the .30-06 case. Maximum bullet weight for the 6.5mm and .270 is 160gr; for the .284 and .280 (both 7mm) is 175gr. These four are excellent for any 400yd deer, and great for elk and black bear within 250yds.

What about the 6.5mmRM?

A neat short-action round, but I'm just not into belted Magnums, especially when the beltless .284 does a better job.

The .284 Winchester

Technically, I like the .284 a lot. It gives excellent .280 ballistics from a *short* (and stronger) action. For a light and handy pack rifle in open deer country, a .284 can't be beat.

Finding a *rifle* in .284, however, is a problem. Only a few manufacturers ever made rifles in .284, and *nobody* does today.

If desperate, you could get one in 7-08, chamber ream it for .284 and widen the feed rails. This is a bit of work for an extra 200fps over the 7-08, but, hey, occasionally these projects have an irresistible (though somewhat illogical) appeal.

.270 and .280

Although you can find .280 rifles and ammo easily enough, only the .270 could be considered *widely* available. While the .280 with its wider/heavier bullet selection is a better *ballistic* choice, the .270 of 1925 simply has 32 years on the .280. For all-around use on anything up to mule deer, the .270 is great. Personally, I'd rather have a .280, .30-06, or 7mmRM over the .270 as I like at *least* 175gr bullets for elk or black bear.

.30-30   .30-40 Krag   .300 Savage

Throwing a 150gr from 2250-2650fps, these three offer usable performance, though it's not enough.

.30-30 Winchester

From 1894, a real veteran. Although ballistically anemic, having a used Ø175 Marlin lever-action for the trunk isn't a bad idea. Within 150yds, the .30-30 will drop any deer. If you don't expect too much from it, the .30-30 is still pretty effective.

.30-40 Krag

Between the .30-30 and .308 in power, the rimmed .30-40 was obsolete when designed in 1892 (because of the 7x57 Mauser). The only reason to have a .30-40 is for that velvety Old World Krag action, but if you've just *got* to have a Krag, then get instead a Norwegian model in the lovely 6.5x55 Swede.

.300 Savage

Introduced by Savage in 1921 in their excellent Model 99 lever, the idea was to give near .30-06 ballistics in a short-action. Basically it's .30-40 power from a short case. Given the .308's overwhelming superiority in the same action, there's no reason to *choose* a .300 Savage--but if you already have and cherish Grandpa's 99, then simply chamber ream it to .308.

.303 British   .308   .30-06   8x57

Throwing a 180gr at 2550-2800fps, these four are military in origin and well-proven on the battlefield.

.303 British

Too bad the English didn't make it rimless in the 1890s when the 7x57 Mauser showed us how. Not a *bad* round, but the rimmed case is a loading hassle. For somebody on an *extreme* budget, a surplus Lee-Enfield No.4 Mk.I for Ø80 can't be beat. It's 90% the power of a .308, and will take elk or black bear within 200yds. Sierra just came out with a long overdue 174gr HPBT MatchKing bullet. Still, save up for a .308 or .30-06.

.308

The best post-WWII cartridge, giving 95% the power of a .30-06 in a short case. Supremely accurate, easy to reload, and its cheap brass make the .308 hard to beat.

.30-06

Inspired by the 7x57, this 1906 .30 caliber was a home run. It is *the* most popular centerfire cartridge in the world, and justifiably so. The .30-06 will do just about *anything*.

8x57 Mauser

The 7x57 necked up to 8mm, this is a very good cartridge, but the .323 bullet and shortish case combine to rob it of truly long range potential. No reason to have a 8x57 unless you just like WWII German Mausers, FN-49s, or Hakims. (You could chamber ream it to 8-06 to use the plentiful .30-06 brass.)

.260, .270, 7-08, .284, .280, .308, or .30-06?

All of these are excellent general purpose cartridges. Of the seven, two shine slightly brighter than the others.

.260 Remington (6.5-08)

Great, but uncommon. Fine for deer and bad guys, but a *bit* light for elk and black bear as bullets top out at 160gr.

.270 Winchester (.277-06)

An excellent plains caliber. *Very* flat shooting and very common, but bullets top out at 160gr.

7-08 Remington

More common than the .260, and bullets available up to 175gr. In some ways, I like the flatter shooting 7-08 over the .308. As good as it is, it's still lacking 200fps on the .280, and it's not *quite* common enough.

.284 Winchester
While the .284 is superb and my *theoretical* ideal (giving long-action .280 ballistics from a short-action), it's just *not* common at all (brass is as expensive as the .45-70!).

.280 Remington
The .280 is much more common than the .284 and has a better bullet selection than the .270, but it still shares one 7mm problem: bullets top out at 175gr, which isn't *quite* enough for brush hunting elk or bears. The Nosler Partition is a great 175gr bullet, but a 200gr .30 is better. (Too bad the .30-284 doesn't exist.) Also, the .280 isn't as common as .308 or .30-06.

And the finalists: The .308 and .30-06
While I love the BC and SD of 7mm bullets and believe that a 190gr bullet is feasible, reality is a stubborn thing. I hate to dismiss the above excellent 7mms, but *realistically* it's between the .308 and .30-06 due to their unsurpassed availability, wide use, versatility, and heavier bullet weights up to 220gr.

.308 or .30-06?
For bad guy work out to 700yds either of these do well. Both are excellent rounds with very similar in performance. Bullet weights range from 110 to 220gr, so these two .30 calibers have bullets to handle about anything. Which is better?

.30-06 pros and cons vs. the .308
Jeff Cooper is fond of saying: *"If you can't do it with 180 at 2,700, then you probably can't do it."* He's talking about a .30-06 load of 180gr/2700fps. It's ballistically superior to the .308, with an average edge on velocity of 150fps. While not huge, it *does* give the .30-06 an indisputable 100yd advantage. It also throws the higher BC 190-220gr bullets with adequate velocity, such being a bit too heavy for the .308. It's probably a tad more common in very remote *Deliverance*-class areas.

There is no current U.S. military ball in .30-06. It is heavier and more expensive than .308 with very little velocity advantage. Finally, the only battle rifles chambered for it were the M1 Garand and FN-49.

.308 pros and cons vs. the .30-06
It's an *extremely* efficient case, giving 95% the velocity of a .30-06 in a ½" shorter round. By most accounts, it is also a *tad*

more accurate. It requires only a short-action, saving you ½lb in your bolt gun. Since you will *rarely* have a 600+yd shot during a routine patrol, the .308 is an excellent round for most threats. Brass is more plentiful. Best of all, modern battle rifles are chambered for .308 (7.62x51), so one caliber can serve for both bolt and battle rifle. The .308 is a great round for intermediate distances and *can* be stretched out in *really* good hands. A wealth of sniper dope exists on the .308.

The .308 won't *quite* reach out there like the .30-06 with 190-220 grainers. The .308 is fine with 168-180gr out to 600yds, but is pretty much out of gas by 800. (Yes, I *know* kills have been made at 900-1000yds with the .308, but that was by "excellent" shooters, who *would* have chosen at *least* a .30-06 had they known such a distant shot was likely.) The .308 just doesn't have the case volume to deliver much past 600yds where wind resistance becomes increasingly more crucial.

Caliber commonality of .308 between bolt and battle rifles

Regarding caliber commonality of the scavengeable 7.62x51 NATO--I say "fine," *to a point.* Pull up a chair.

Using military .308 M80 ball is O.K. for your FR8s, 740s , and battle rifles, but it *isn't* accurate enough for your scoped .308s past 400yds. (Most M80 groups only 2-4". Foreign stuff is worse, often up to 6"!). If your "very good" riflemen are using .308, they'll have to carry their own matchgrade ammo to be deadly past 400yds anyway. **My point is this:** for accurate .308 bolt-gun work, M80 might as well be in *another* caliber, so its commonality loses much of its *prima facie* advantage.

As M80 is unsuitable for "very good" riflemen who must train/equip with matchgrade ammo--why not simply field them with the more potent .30-06 or .300WM? If you're good enough to wring out a .30-06, why not *carry* one since you'll have to pack matchgrade ammo *anyway?* Why sacrifice that 100yds of extra .30-06 range and "very good" riflemen skill for the puny advantage of .308 commonality for NATO ammo? (Besides, in an utter pinch, the .30-06 rifleman can *temporarily* fire .308 with a Ø10 chamber adapter. This is obviously less accurate because of the bullet's required ½" jump to the lands, but nonetheless deadly out to 400yds.)

For these reasons, I can't see why the .308 *must* be the caliber of your "very good" bolt-action riflemen. If, however, your riflemen are only "good" then the .30-06 would be rather wasted, and the .308 would be the more logical choice.

So, what's the answer--.308 or .30-06?

It depends on the situation. For example, if I *positively didn't need* the extra 100yds of the .30-06, *or* the firepower of the battle rifle, *and* my field activities insisted on a lighter rifle, then I'd feel quite comfortable with a .308 bolt gun.

If I envisioned some longer shots, then I'd field with at least a .30-06, which is clearly superior to the .308. (I *might* even have a 7mmRM or .300WM over the .30-06.)

Battle rifle vs. bolt-action rifle

If I thought that short range action against assailants was more likely than 400+yd shots, then I'd carry a .223 battle rifle.

If both concerns were *equally* likely, then I'd field with a *very* accurate .308 battle rifle. While I could stalk within sniper range of my FAL, I could *not*, conversely, transform my bolt-action to 20rd/semi-auto firepower. **If multiple bad guys are at** *all* **likely, then carry a** *battle* **rifle.**

Since I enjoy rifles and can afford them, I have bolt-actions in .308 *and* .30-06, and battle rifles in .223 *and* .308.

Those with limited budgets (or limited interest) would be adequately armed with a *very* accurate .308 battle rifle (skipping the AR15 and .308 bolt gun), *or* a .223 AR15 and .30-06 bolt gun (skipping the .308 for the .30-06's extra range).

Other good bolt-gun calibers

Regarding other fine similar calibers, such as .250 Savage, .264WM, 7mmSTW, etc., their main drawback is relative scarcity of ammo versus the .308 and .30-06. Sure, they're around *now*, but in 2013 it may like trying to find a box .256 Newton today. This goes triple for the wildcats, which are often the tastiest calibers. I know the .358STA is awesome, and the .22 Cheetah is a neat prairie dog round, but let's stay *realistic*. We've got to be able to *feed* these things far into the future.

You might have to live off the ammo you've acquired within the next few years *for the rest of your life.* Even if they don't cut off ammo production (or tax it out of existence), they'll be putting detectable chemical taggants in the gunpowder.

Many of our elderly Patriots have a lifetime of field experience (hunting and warfare) and have settled on their rifle. If he's *really* good with it, so *what* if it's in 7x57? If a 400+yd man had a *choice* 400+yd rifle (whatever the caliber) and was *really* dialed in with it, I wouldn't budge him out of it for a .308. He's probably already developed his pet load for it and can group 1" or better. A proven combination of man/rifle/caliber is a "magical" thing and should *not* be broken up. **Remember, *hitting* is the thing.** If he and his rifle are so well-bonded, you're nearly there already. His rifle is already well-sorted out and wouldn't need anything. (If ain't broke, don't "fix" it! The only modifications *might* be a rust-resistant finish, a composite stock, and a *really* fine scope.) What he needs is *plenty* of ammo and quality sniper gear. Have him stock up on at least 1,000rds of his pet load, make sure he has a complete spare parts kit, and concentrate on training him for counter-sniper work.

RIFLES

It's hard to really goof with *any* modern commercial rifle. In order of personal preference, I like Sako, Ruger M77II, Winchester 70, and Remington 700. I have at least one of each, so I know them well. The M77, 70, and 700 will comprise about 60% of all used bolt-actions at the gun shows.

While I've never owned a Savage 110, I've heard that they're *quite* accurate. Extremely expensive and "pretty" rifles would be the fine Colt-Sauer, Kleinguenther, and Weatherby.

Sako

These Finnish rifles are of extremely high quality and have an integral scope mount receiver base (as does Ruger). Choose the older L-579 (later called AVI) actions for .308, or the L-61 (AVII) Finnbear for .30-06, over the modern actions (which are more cheaply made--a sad sign of the times).

Other manufactures used Sako actions: Model 52 J.C. Higgins (.222), the Colt Coltsman (.243 and .308), Browning (.22-250), and H&R Model 317 (.223). Howa of Japan copied the L-61 in their .30-06 Model FSD-43.

If you plan on building a *choice* rifle, then you can't beat an older Sako action. My custom .308 is a real jewel.

Ruger M77II

This is a near copy of the pre-64 Winchester (which is a commercial version of the M98 Mauser). Besides the Mauser claw extractor, the M77II has many nice features. I like the slab-sided action which looks more modern and beds better than round actions. I like the Winchester 70-style three position safety (the older M77s have a Fire/Safe tang safety) which allows the safe operation of the bolt to load/unload. The trigger is adjustable down to 2lbs.

What I *really* like is the integral base on the receiver, so no screw-on mounts are needed. Plus, steel rings come with each rifle, so you save a total of Ø30-60. The Sako-style mounting system is extremely rugged and keeps its zero well.

I'd get the stainless version, and replace the cheesy, fluted, non QD-stud stock with a McMillan, etc.

Every Ruger I've had has been not only very accurate, but a *bargain.* Rugers are Ø50 cheaper than the 70 or 700 because their receivers are made from investment casting instead of machined parts. Once an issue years ago with some, the technique has by now proven its quality. The Rugers only downside is that their barrels shoot out a tad early, by 15,000rds. (So what? Replace then it with a premium aftermarket barrel.)

I found a used M77 with 4x scope (which I replaced with a Tasco 3-9x) for only Ø300. So, for Ø350 I've got a quality .30-06 truck rifle that shoots ¾MOA. Now, *that's* a bargain!

Winchester 70

While the pre-64s (<700,000 serial #s) command a Ø550-800 price, they are not *quite* as accurate as the modern 70s. I don't care for the cheapy version made from 1964-1968 (700,000 to 866,000 serial #s). The post-68 model (>G866,000) is what you'll see most of these days, and it's a very good rifle for the money. A stainless model is now available. I think that the 70 is a little more rugged and handsome than the 700, and I prefer its safety and extractor.

The new "70 Classic" is a revived pre-64 action. It's a great rifle; very accurate with its hammer-forged barrel, and available in stainless. A bit pricey, but *well* worth it. A good choice for your .300WM sniper rifle. Get it with the BOSS.

Remington 700BDL

While I favor the Ruger and Winchester over the Remington, such is more a matter of personal taste as there's nothing *really* wrong with the 700. It is the Army and USMC choice for their .308 sniper rifles, as well as for most SWAT teams.

Winchester lost their lead in Vietnam when they stupidly replaced the pre-64 Model 70 with the 1964-68 model, and the military snipers changed to the Remington 700. Today, the 700 over 70 stems more from post-Nam inertia than any difference in quality or performance (of which there's very little).

The BDL has a mag floorplate (the ADL has a blind mag). The Model 7 is a carbine in .223, .243 .260, 7-08, and .308 and is a very handy little field rifle. The older 721s and 722s are pre-700 actions, and very good values for the money.

Browning A-Bolt II with BOSS

This a quality rifle from Japan with a short bolt throw. I had one in .308 and liked it O.K., *"But Chuck, there just wasn't no love connection!"* It's funky and uncommon enough to give the owner difficulty in finding bases, stocks, triggers, etc. I'd go with a Sako, Ruger, Winchester, or Remington.

The BOSS is muzzle break tunable for each barrel's "sweet spot" of least vibration, which adds *significantly* to accuracy. The BOSS can be added to any rifle for Ø185. It *works*.

In summary

A good .308/.30-06 is probably the most rifle an average Patriot can accurately shoot and *afford* (usually about Ø500 with decent scope). In "good" hands at prone, it hits reliably (95%) out to 300yds. In "very good" hands, out to 500. Rarely will longer shots be expected, and rarely will greater than "very good" skill be available. A good .308/.30-06 will handle *most* rifle situations for *most* skilled Patriots, so it should be the general bolt-action arm of Liberty.

If Ø is no object, then get a Win. 70 Classic or an older Sako (AVI, AVII). If you're on a budget, then get a Ruger M77II. If you somehow don't like the Ruger, then get a Winchester 70 or Remington 700BDL. Other decent bolt-actions are the Remington 721, 722 and 788, and the Savage 110.

Get a stainless if possible, as the steel and corrosion resistance is superior. The shiny finish will stand out in the field, so you'll need to camo it with Bow-Flage paint.

If on a *really* tight budget, try a lever-action Savage 99E or Remington 740 auto at around Ø250. At 2½-3MOA they won't be tack-drivers the way bolt-actions can be, but accurate enough out to 400yds. Most 99Es and 740s I've seen were well-used and *not* fabulous shooters, so choose well--or save up the extra Ø100 for a Winchester 70 or Ruger M77II.

Setting up your rifle

As with most things in life, you generally get what you pay for. For a non-Magnum/<700yd rifle, there are three levels of price/performance. Pareto's Law, or the 80/20 rule, is amply demonstrated here: **Level 1** rifles will give you 80% of Level 3 performance for 20% of the cost. **Level 2** gives 95% for 35-50% of the cost. **Level 3** gives 100% for 100%. Performance is just a matter of money--how much accuracy can you *afford?*

The question is probably more correctly posed inversely: how much accuracy can you afford *not to have?* If terrain and threat are limited to 400yds, then a Ø450 Level 1 rifle will suffice, but if you're living in flat country and expect bad boys with bolt guns, then you'd better get a Ø3,000 Level 3 rifle.

GENERAL PURPOSE RIFLES OUT TO 400yds

Affordable, decent performance--Level 1

While these clearly are *not* sniper-grade rifles, they give fine performance (<1½-2MOA) for *much* less money. They are remarkable weapons for Ø350-500 and will do 80% of anything ever asked of a bolt-action rifle. Several of these can be had for one Ø2,500-4,000 sniper rifle, so many "good" riflemen can be well-armed for no more than Ø500 apiece.

A good Tasco or Simmons 3-9x scope costs Ø200 less than Ø300 Leupold. These are decent scopes for the money, and your rifle will be capable out to 400yds.

For example, assuming a .308 throwing a 168gr Sierra MatchKing at 2700fps, if you zero your rifle at 275yds, you will be within 5" above or below line of sight out to 325yds. This is known as MPBR (maximum point blank range), meaning that you should be able to hit within a 10" circle out to 325 with a center hold. Exact holdovers for 300, 400, and 500yd shots are 2.3", 16.4", and 39.7" respectively. As it becomes nearly impossible to accurately holdover more than 36" (½ a man's height), such scopes limit your rifle to about 400yds.

For game, use the 180gr Sierra GameKing (a soft nosed MatchKing, no re-zeroing!), Nosler Partition, or Barnes X (if your rifle will shoot them accurately). Carry cartridge adapters from MCA (760-770-2005) in .30 Carbine and .32 ACP (this capable of fairly quiet 50yd headshots), along with a broken shell extractor, firing pins, extractors, and ejectors.

The Jeff Cooper Scout rifle

His concept is a rifle capable of taking 200k (440lbs) targets out to 400m, in a package no more than 1m in length (39.36") or 3.5k (7.7lbs). Usually in .308, this rifle is known for its Burris 2¾x scope, barrel mounted *in front* of the action.

The advantage of this arrangement is that you keep *both* eyes open, track with your *left* eye, and once you're about on target you then focus through your right eye for the shot. Since the magnification is low, there's no significant image disparity between the eyes. It's *extremely* quick, and *the* best bolt-action rifle sighting system for moving targets. Years ago I visited Gunsite and watched students in an API 270 class *routinely* bust thrown clay pigeons with their .308s. Way impressive.

The Scout rifle is lightweight, utterly handy, and well serves as a day-in/day-out general purpose rifle. Since the action is not covered by a receiver-mounted scope, the Scout is quick to reload (especially in a military bolt-action with stripper clips). I've seem some which even took M1A 20rd mags (Robar Technology in Phoenix adapts M77IIs and 70s for these).

If you don't want a 500+yd range .308 bolt gun (saving that work for a .30-06, 7mmRM, or .300WM), then a Scout .308 might be just the ticket. Steyr Mannlicher just unveiled their production Scout, a project shepherded by Jeff Cooper himself. It looks and shoots great. Price is a *very* Austrian Ø2,595.

Other rifles suitable for the Scout treatment are the Marlin lever-actions (with their good power and quick operation), the Lee-Enfield (with its short bolt throw and detachable 10rd mag), and the Remington Model 7 (it's already light and handy, and the Burris Scout scope mount uses the rear sight screw holes). Springfield Armory recently introduced their Scout M1A--neat! I've made two inexpensive test Scouts, and was very impressed with their performance.

For unsurpassed funkiness, I think I'll get a stainless Remington Model 7, give it a BOSS 24"bbl in 6.5-284, and Scout it. My load will be the Sierra 155gr MatchKing at 2900fps. MPBR will be *360*yds (300yd zero!), with a 10.5" holdover at 400yds (1773ft/lbs) and 27.7" at 500 (1555ft/lbs). This is *very* flat shooting with a *lot* of energy at long distance. Compared to a .308's 168/2700, my 6.5-284 has 400 more ft/lbs and 12" less drop at 500. That's amazing. At 7¼lbs, it will make a *great* backpacking rifle with .270 ballistics from a short-action. **This is** *tres chic.* (Other fine calibers: .260, 7-08, .284, and .308.)

OUT TO 700yds
Spending Ø1,200-1,500 for a Level 2 rifle

Your "very good" shooters deserve a bit more rifle. With this rifle, not only will they be effectively fielded, but they'll have a weapon to hone their skill--possibly emerging as "excellent" riflemen deserving 1000yd Magnums. This .308/.30-06 *must* shoot at *least* ¾MOA to be effective out to 700yds.

Pay for a *very* good Ø350+ scope (with BDC, if possible): a Redfield, Leupold VariXIII, or Burris . (If it doesn't have Mil-Dots, then send it to Premier Reticle (540-722-0601) for Ø100.)

I recommend a *good* composite stock--professionally pillar-bedded and floated; a bead-blasted matte blue finish, Harris bi-pod, 3lb trigger, titanium firing pin, etc. **Don't skimp on this weapon. Pay for** *quality* **and get it** *right.*

Total cost will run Ø1,200 minimum, because of the glass. I know it's tempting to attach a cheaper scope--*don't*--such suffices only for your "good" shooters. For *affordable* clarity and ruggedness, you can't beat a Leupold or Burris, and your "very good" riflemen deserve such. Lesser scopes tend to lose their zero or fog at the worst moments. Take my word on this! Excellent vs. average accuracy adds 200+yds to your effective range.

If it won't group tightly, try a Douglas or Shaw stainless barrel (recommend 1-10" twist for .30-06, and 1-12" for .308). This should turn it into at *least* a 1MOA rifle. This rifle will do 95% of whatever asked of a bolt gun.

Handload to your rifle's taste. A good .30-06 load is the 168gr Sierra HPBT MatchKing atop 58gr of IMR4350 (the .308 likes 42.5gr of IMR4895) and CCI Mag primer, which gives an honest 2875fps. For ultra-long range or windy conditions, try the 190 or 200gr Sierra HPBT.

Dropping Ø2,000+ and doing it right--Level 3

From CFI (817-595-2485) is the superb .308 Steyr SSG PIIK with 20" barrel and 10x Hensoldt (military Zeiss) ZF500 scope (¼min. clicks, 500m BDC *and* Mil-Dot) for Ø1,995--which is a whopping bargain. GSI (800-821-3021) might still have the PII 26"bbl, 800m package. Robar (602-581-2648) makes a *very* nice Ruger M77II based .308 rifle with M1A mags (cool!).

For value and proven performance in a turn-key package, I recommend the Precision Marksman Rifle from L.O.D. For only Ø3,395, this Sako action comes with a Krieger barrel, custom stock, stainless-steel pillar bedding, epoxy and Teflon coating, *and* an Ø1,100 Leupold Mark 4 M1-10x scope (the undisputed best for serious distance work in a .308). Designed by one of the country's sniping and night vision experts, this rifle will make 600yd *headshots* and 1000yd torso hits.

> *L.O.D. designed this rifle to bridge the [price] gap between Accuracy International's AWP and the rest of the field. Developed to be as ergonomically correct as possible, the L.O.D. rifle significantly diminishes the physical stresses on the shooter, which increases his ability to put the round precisely on target. At half the cost of other premium systems, this rifle is, without a doubt, the best value on the market for the serious shooter.*
> -- Billy B. Martin, President, L.O.D. (713-668-1428)

Once you have an L.O.D. rifle, get down to Billy's in Houston for the best sniper training available to civilians. Practice thoroughly with your rifle past 400yds and become *awesome.*

700-1000yds--Level 4

Any decent .308 or .30-06 Level 1 rifle will, out of the box, will hit pretty well out to 500yds. Accuracy out to 700yds, however, requires steeper expenditures in time and money for your Level 2 and 3 rifles. **If your ranges are past 700yds and you are an absolute dead shot** ("excellent"), then go to one of the *common* Magnum calibers (7mmRM or .300WM). For 1000yd work, you'll need a Ø3,000+ **Level 4** rifle. Scopes, barrels (replaced every 2-4,000rds), etc. are more expensive.

Handloading for this kind of extreme range is *highly* meticulous, demanding: precisely neck-turned brass (water weighted), deburred and uniformed flashholes, perfectly seated Federal Bench Rest primers, absolutely consistent powder weights, precise bullet seating depths, and dozens of hours of experimentation. You see, every rifle is an enigma and you must send many different loads down the barrel to discover *the tastiest* combination of bullet, bullet depth, brass, powder and primer. *To get less than* ¾*MOA* (which means hitting vs. missing past 700yds) requires an awesome Level 4 rifle with lovingly-made handloads; plus just one other thing:

The man behind the rifle

The rifle and ammunition are 2nd and 3rd to the ability of the *shooter.* A top man with average equipment will beat an average man with top equipment--*count on it.* Don't be lured into the common trap of spending all your money on weapons and gear. A Ø3,500 Level 4 rifle will not hit at 1000yds if *you* can't deliver at 500. You must *deserve* such a quality weapon by first learning to consistently outshoot Levels 1, 2, and 3 rifles. Walk before running.

Only when *your* accuracy equals a Level 3 rifle, *and* your tactical situation *demands* 1000yd capability, should you go with an expensive Level 4 rifle. Be prepared, however, to spend Ø2,500+ for the rifle, Ø1,200 for the scope/rings/mount, and another Ø1,000+ for ammo and supplies. You'll need countersniper gear such as laser range finder (the Bushnell Yardage Pro 800 is affordable at Ø450), spotting scope, notebook, ghillie suit, etc. And finally, there's the training.

Pay for quality training, while such is still legal, and *practice.* Past 700yds, wind is the crucial variable. Practice and log your shots. Work out the kinks, acquire your data, endurance, and patience *beforehand.* You won't have the opportunity to play "catchup" when the Balloon Flies. Reading, thinking, and gun polishing alone won't do it. You've got to get out there, sweat, get dirty, and suffer the bugs. **The more you sweat in training, the less you'll bleed in battle.** There is no time for games. Get serious, or give your stuff to the *serious* man who has the mettle but not the gear.

Choosing between the 7mm Rem. Mag and .300 Win. Mag

A 7mmRM throwing a sleek 175gr Sierra SBT (.533 BC; .310 SD) at 2900 makes for an ideal countersniper round at distances 200yds past the effective range of the .308/.30-06. The Secret Service snipers use 7mmRM. The 7mmRM needs less bullet, powder, and recoil to do *nearly* the same job, with almost twice the barrel life of the .300WM.

For harder targets and/or windier conditions, the .300WM throwing a 200gr Sierra HPBT (.565 BC; .301 SD) at 2900 is far superior to the .308/.30-06. Bullets identical, the .300WM throws *300*fps faster than the .30-06, with a 200yd down range velocity equal to .30-06 at the *muzzle*. It edges out the 7mmRM with 150 more ft/lbs at 1000. The U.S. military uses the .300WM, so it's well-sorted out ballistically with lots of field dope. *Police Sniper* by Craig Roberts discusses a *900 yd* .300WM headshot. Wow. It's an awesome caliber. If a .300WM won't solve your problem, then you're in *real* trouble.

Since the .300WM can send 200-220gr bullets (vs. 175gr for the 7mmRM) and has 15% more case capacity, the .300WM is the Level 4 caliber choice. (The 7mmRM does, however, make an excellent Level *3* caliber.)

The .300 Weatherby, Dakota, and Imperial mags (not to mention the wildcat mags) are *very* hot, but you'd have to stock up on a lifetime's supply of brass and forsake all the .300WM data. Such isn't worth it for an extra 200fps. Besides, if the .300WM is too sissy for your needs, then a mere 200fps increase won't melt your butter, anyway. You'll need a Level *5* rifle.

1000-1500yds--Level 5

If the .300WM won't do it, then the seriousness of your situation is growing geometrically. You'll need one of these three: .30-378 Weatherby (250/3200), .338 Lapua (8.6x70; 250/2950), or .375-50BMG (barrels from Pacnor). The .300 and .330 Dakota Mags are also good Level 5 calibers.

The long-range .308 and .338 calibers

Weatherby offers their excellent rifle in the now factory .30-378. In .338 Lapua, the Accuracy International SM for Ø3,825, and the Dakota Arms T-76 for Ø4,250.

My personal favorite is the .338 Lapua. While .30-378 Weatherby has a slight ballistic edge with their sleeker bullets, they are *way* overbore and burn out barrels quickly. (For this reason, I didn't even mention the .300 Phoenix.) The .338 Lapua will do the same work without you needing to carry a quiver full of spare barrels.

1500+yds--Level 6, the .50BMG

The Level 5 calibers are good out to about 1500yds, so after that you'll need a .50BMG. This kind of distance work requires *big* bucks and *lots* of practice. My motto is, *"If you can't do it with 700 at 2,900, then you probably can't do it."* A .50BMG has a mere *13,075*ft/lbs of ME. This is more for busting up equipment than for sniper work. Get in touch (under an alias and mail drop) with the Fifty Caliber Shooters Association at 11469 Olive St., Suite 50, St. Louis, Missouri 63141. Here are some manufacturers:

Harris M-96 semi-auto. Ø6,800. (602-230-1414)
More accurate (1MOA) than the Barrett.
Barrett M82A1 semi-auto. Ø6,750. (615-696-2938)
Used by our military in the Persian Gulf. 2MOA.
AMAC 5100 bolt-action. Ø2,995. (208-756-6810)
Very accurate (¾MOA/1000yds) and an excellent value.
Used to great effect by the Afghans against the Russians.
Redick Model 650 bolt-action. (501-636-3188)
One of the most rugged and accurate (½MOA).
Barrett M95 bolt-action bullpup. Ø4,650. (602-230-1414)
5rd box mag, 22½lbs, 29"bbl, 45" overall
Maadi-Griffin bolt-action bullpup. (602-854-3434)
Well-regarded, ¾MOA/1000yds accurate rifles.
L.A.R. Grizzly bolt-action bullpup. Ø2,570. (801-280-3505)
State Arms Gun Corp. (608-849-5800).
Giant copy of the Rem. 700. O.K. accuracy (1½-2MOA).
McMillan M88 bolt-action.
An oversized Rem. 700. *Extremely* accurate.
Robar RC50 bolt-action. Ø3,750. (602-581-2648)
Rem. 700-style action, but better barrels than the M88.
Rib Mountain Arms M92 bolt-action (605-957-4249)
Very accurate and high quality custom rifle.
RMC Mfg. bolt-action (605-348-3736)
For Ø2,259-3,150.

Scope for the .50BMG

The scope for a .50BMG is Leupold's Mark 4 M1-16X (adjustable to 65MOAs up/down, which is capable of 100 to 1500yd shooting). Older scopes send to Premier Reticle for Mil-Dots.

.50BMG Ammo

Regular U.S. military ball is only 3MOA stuff, which means up to 30" at 1000yds. O.K. for equipment, but not accurate enough for bad guys past 500yds.

The M2 AP (black tip) is more accurate (2MOA) than ball. Major Plaster fired his AMAC with M2 at a 55gal drum 1250yds away and hit 70%.

The AP exploding Raufoss (green/silver tip, RDX core) is more accurate still, though apparently illegal for us to own-- darn it. When you can find Raufoss, it'll run you Ø15-25/rd (it costs the Government Ø9/rd). Fun stuff, I hear. Don't drop 'em!

River Valley Ordinance (314-926-3076) sells pulled G.I. bullets for about 60¢/rd: M1 Incendiary, M2 AP, M8 API, M17 Tracer, and M20 API-T.

Many excellent benchrest bullets exist (most are mono-lithic steel, brass, or bronze), such as the Thunderbird Cartridge Co. match, the Hornady 750gr HPBT (BC .86), the Dabco Bieber Bore Rider (BC .91), and the Barnes double ogive 700gr bronze with a 1.015BC (higher than an F-16!). Benchrest shooters routinely place 5 shots in a salad plate at 1000yds. (The current record is 3¼"!) Any of these bullets from an excellent rifle will print 85% in a 8'x10' panel 3000yds away. That means that parked enemy equipment can be perforated at *1¾ miles*.

CLOSING COMMENTS

In short, to each according to his *ability*. Most of your people, **"decent" riflemen** (*Bronze* quality and 80% of your men), get carbines in .223 (or Commie 7.62), .30-30s, and .303s for effective ranges of 250yds. Your **"good"** (*Silver*-16%) get a Ø500 Level 1 .308 and can reach out to 400yds. They can handle 80% of distant threats. Your **"very good"** (*Gold*-3%) get Level 2 and 3 rifles which can reliably kill 700yd threats, 95% of your distant problems. Perhaps one in ten "very good" riflemen can be honed into **"excellent"** (*Platinum*) and kill out to 1000yds, and he gets a Level 4 rifle, lots of gear, and a spotter.

What about *past* 1000yds? This demands an **"artist."** (We're talking near Carlos Hathcock here, who was truly *gifted*.) If you're uncannily blessed with an "artist" then you *must* provide him with a superb fire team and .338 Lapua which can reach out to 1500yds. If the .338 Lapua is too pansy, then a .50BMG is your answer. Either way, you'll be untouchable.

❖ 7

OTHER RIFLES

.22LRs

These are *essential* for training, pest control, and small game hunting. You shouldn't be without a .22 rifle any more than a chef would be without a paring knife.

.22LR semi-auto takedown

The advantage of a takedown is that it stores away easily in your backpack, trunk, boat, etc.

Charter Arms AR7

Some of these are O.K.--but test fire them first, as they often malf. I've collected a few over the years, but had to sort out a couple of real lemons. The buttstock doubles as the waterproof, floating carrying case--neat. The iron sights are poor; accuracy is only fair. They are not dovetailed for scope mounts. I'd pass on the AR7, generally--unless you find a *really* good one, and even then, delegate it to secondary/stash status. It's a shame they weren't better made and with decent sights.

Browning

This is a little jewel of a gallery rifle with its buttstock mag tube. They're collector items, however, Norinco makes a decent copy (and even *these* are hard to find).

Marlin Papoose M70P

This is lot of rifle for 4lbs and Ø140. The Papoose disassembles into a package as short as your forearm and packs in its own little floating case. Attach a compact 4x scope and you'll have great little woods rifle. Headshot countersniping is possible out to 100yds with practice. Get some 15rd mags.

Spend another Ø50 for the stainless M70PSS, and camo it with removable Bow-Flage paint.

If you can afford only *one* .22LR rifle, make it a Papoose. It's 90% as accurate as the Ruger 10/22, yet more versatile.

.22LR semi-auto full-size

While these aren't as handy as the takedowns, the full-size rifles hold more rounds and are a bit more accurate.

Ruger 10/22

This is the finest .22 auto, and fairly compact in a folding stock, though 1½lbs heavier than the Papoose. Can be found used for Ø120-150. It is quite accurate and mag capacity runs from 10 to 50rds. Parts and accessories abound. A real staple in one's battery. You gotta have one.

Marlin 60 tube mag

The Marlin 60 is just like the Papoose but with a 14-18rd tubular mag and fixed barrel. It single feeds .22 Shorts and Longs as well as Long Rifle; versatility which may be vital someday. It typically runs Ø60-90; a real bargain for often half the cost of a 10/22. Stock up on several and outfit younger kids, the elderly, and random guests. A barrage of .22LR from your random party guests will keep the marauders' heads down at minimum, if not inflict some real injury.

Other .22LR rifles

Many other .22 semi-auto rifles exist (Sears, Savage, etc.) and many can be had for under Ø75. While these are often O.K., there's no reason to stray from the cheap and plentiful Marlin 60. Stick with a proven winner.

The Winchester and Rossi pumps are nice (tube mag and manual action means that you can use Shorts, Longs, and LR), but a bit uncommon.

Bolt-action .22s are ironically more expensive than the semi-auto Marlin 60, but are good for children to develop single shot accuracy and reliable bolt-action experience so useful with your centerfire bolt-actions.

I prefer, however, lever-action .22s over bolt-actions. They usually have a capacious mag tube (vs. a small detachable mag), will accept/feed the Shorts and Longs, and they are more fun to operate. The Marlin 39 and the Browning BL-22 are superb rifles, and superior to the Winchester. These are hard to find at gun shows, so keep your eyes open.

Customizing your .22LR

As I'm an accomplished shot, and a good .22LR has headshot potential out to 100yds, I prefer to scope my more accurate .22LRs. A scope detracts little from the rifle's handiness, increases effective range by 50yds, and can quickly be removed if necessary. A small Ø35 4X is sufficient (Tasco, Simmons, Bushnell, Norinco, etc.). Don't forget a sling.

Closing thoughts on .22LR rifles

Every **vehicle and** *every* **domicile should contain a .22 rifle and 1,000rds of ammo--for survival's sake, at least.** Never be without a gun, even if it's a modest Ø60 .22LR. Such could easily feed you or save your life. (A woman alone at home, barricaded in the corner behind her bed, quietly waiting for the intruder to come to her, could easily repel an attack.) For less than Ø100 and a couple of hours practice, *anyone* could become proficient enough to prevail in such a defensive scenario. Those not willing to invest *so little* time and money are simply not serious about preserving their lives in these perilous times. **If you look like food,** *you'll be eaten.*

Take at least basic steps for your own self-defense. Folks, stop whining for more police, or else we'll *get* a Police State.

SPEED & ACCURACY OF ACTIONS

From fastest to slowest, they are: auto, slide/pump, lever, bolt and single. It's no coincidence that this order also corresponds to least best to best accuracy. The looser the action type, the quicker and less accurate it is. You'll have to decide the right balance between speed and accuracy, and actions will differ 2-3X more in *speed* than accuracy.

An auto is more accurate than a single-shot is quick. Levers offer a good compromise, though a well-practiced bolt can be almost as fast but with better accuracy. It's advisable to become proficient in operating *all* the different actions. **What you're untrained for is exactly what you'll be forced to someday use.** Call it "Boston's Law."

SPORTING AUTOS

I'm not a big fan of these rifles. Granted, they cycle more quickly than bolt-actions, but somewhat at the expense of accuracy and reliability. The H&K 770 in .308 is nice, but eccentric. Some of the Browning BARs are very accurate. I've taken a few deer with a Remington 7400 .243 and liked it, but I think I'll just stick with a bolt-action. If you've already got an *accurate* auto that you like, keep it, but train with a bolt gun.

SPORTING PUMPS

The Remington 760 comes to mind. A friend of mine has one in .30-06 and can shoot a 2½" 300yd group, so they can be quite accurate. *Personally*, I just don't care for them, but if *you* resonate with the slide-action rifles, then fine.

LEVER-ACTIONS

These are very handy, hold at least 7rds, good for leftys, their ammo is available anywhere, and they travel well. Typically Ø150-200, they're a great bargain and make fine car/truck rifles.

Winchester 94 or Marlin?

While there's nothing actually *wrong* with the 94 (and the Rossi copies), I prefer the Marlin as it's more rugged and side ejects (which allows a top-mounted scope, if desired, though unnecessary in its 100-250yd calibers). To me, the 94 *seems* fragile, and I *really* don't like its loading gate and follower. Also, the Marlin has a decided edge on quality.

Marlin (.30-30, .35 Rem., .44 Magnum, .45-70)

The **.30-30** can be found *anywhere* in the Americas. Choose the 170gr bullets over the 150gr. It'll take deer up to 200yds and elk within 100yds. The .30-30 will do if *you* will do. The Model 30AS is the no frills version of the Model 336. Used, they go for Ø150 to Ø195, depending on model and condition. I'd stock up on bargain Model 30ASs for trading *wampum*.

The **.35 Remington** is a necked-up .30-30 and a better brush caliber, though not quite as common.

In .44 **Magnum**, this is a fun poodle-shooter out to 200. For deer, the .44 is limited in power and accuracy to only 100yds (4MOA with only 1,000ft/lbs). Used, the Model 1894 is hard to find and folks want at least Ø250 (even though new wholesale is about Ø285). I found a used Marlin Limited (16¼"bbl) at a gun show and I absolutely love it. I added a Weaver peep rear sight and a custom-made leather butt cuff holding 10rds. It is *sweet*. When I pull the rear stock off, it packs into any suitcase or bag.

For elk and bear country, Marlin offers the 1895SS in the stompy **.45-70**. (A *great* Scout rifle platform.) When handloaded to 40,000cup (near its *real* potential--*far* beyond Springfield Trapdoor specs), the .45-70 can take all but the *big* bears. Use 300gr/2050fps for deer, the 350/1900 for elk, and 405/1750 for black bear. (You can load up to 50,000cup in the Browning 78 or Ruger No. 1 to approach within 300fps of .458WM velocities, though such isn't necessary but for griz.)

The **.444 Marlin** (a .44 Magnum *Magnum*) is also a fine round, but since its 1-38" twist doesn't stabilize 300gr bullets well, 150yd elk is really about the most its 265gr load will handle. In truth, the .444 really *can't* compare with the .45-70.

A final note on the Marlins: **Don't dryfire them off safety.** Their firing pin has no return spring and dryfiring will eventually break the pin. Have a couple of spares.

Other lever-actions

Browning BLR

This lever-action in .22-250, .243, 7-08, .308, .270, .30-06 and 7mmRM with detachable mag (so it can use spitzers) is a lovely rifle, though you'll pay at least Ø475 for a nice one. (Pick a Belgian over a Japanese.) A good 6x scope does well here.

Savage 99

This has a very strong action, can use spitzers in its rotary mag, and is generally well regarded--however, I didn't have much luck with the three .308s I've tried. Mine just weren't accurate enough. The tightest group I got was 2¼", and I won't keep a .308 which can't give me at least 1¾".

Besides, I prefer the exposed hammer of the BLR and Marlin. I hike with a chambered round, hammer down, safety off. For a shot, I thumb back the hammer while I unsling, and this is a very fast technique--less than 3 seconds for a standing

100yd shot. The Savage won't allow that, and a hammer-down Marlin feels a bit more safe to me than a cocked/locked Savage.

Winchester 88
No longer made, the 88 was about the strongest of all the lever-actions and very accurate, but the trigger pull was lousy. For a great brush gun, get an 88 in .358 (.35-08).

Ruger M96/44
It holds only 4+1 (.44 Magnum), but has a very quick lever throw. The Marlin is a much more handsome rifle, has an exposed hammer, plus it holds 3-5 more rds.

BOLT-ACTION MILITARY
These rifles have strong advantages: they are powerful, rugged, battle-proven, caliber common, and modern bargains. While I wouldn't field with one over a modern battle rifle (which has better controls and semi-auto firepower) or a sniper rifle (which is 3-8x more accurate), these old workhorses are very capable out to 400yds and will handle combat conditions.

Lee-Enfield No.4 Mk. I or II .303 British
From 1888 to 1950, the .303 well served Great Britain. The .303 is 90% as powerful as the .308 (60,000 dead Soviets in Afghanistan can't be "wrong"), and is adequate for any North American game. Finding ammo is no problem. Its short bolt is *twice* as fast to throw than the M98 Mauser's.

The real modern advantage of the Lee-Enfield is good .30 caliber power in a 10rd detachable box mag for Ø100. I don't readily add calibers to my battery, but the Ø100 Lee is so rugged and affordable. **Stick with the No. 4 Mk. Is and Mk. IIs**. The older No. 1, 2, and 3s are more relics than serviceable shooters. Cut the barrel down to 18" and remove as much wood as possible to create a 8lb carbine. Have several; they're great as vehicle rifles (if confiscated or stolen, you're out a whopping Ø100). When folks catch on to these Ø100 rugged, powerful rifles with their 10rd box mags, they'll at last be cleaned out.

Mine are surprisingly accurate: I can consistently hit man-size boulders up to 500yds off hand. Speer 150gr spitzers max load to 2755fps with 46.2gr of R-15--pretty hot (but your cases won't last long given the spongy Lee bolt).

Krag-Jorgensen (.30-40 or 6.5x55)

This funky 1890s rifle is known for very smooth action and hinged box magazine. Since the Mauser M98 actions are more modern, the Krag is really just a fun game or collector's rifle. Original condition Krags are worth Ø500+. Most Krags, however, have been sporterized by now. The .30-40 is adequate for deer and 200yd elk. Or, the action can be rebarreled in .444 Marlin (1-16" twist) for a great brush rifle. The Norwegian Krag in 6.5x55 is a fine deer rifle.

Mauser 98

Developed in 1898 as an improvement on the Model 1896, the Mauser boys created one of the best (if not *the* best) turn bolts ever. It is very simple, with only 10 parts. (Only the P17 and the Arisaka, with 7 and 6 parts respectively, are simpler-- and they're M98-based, anyway!)

Except for its longish lock time, there is really nothing of the M98 to complain about. Strong and smooth, it is today copied by FN, Winchester and Ruger, and many others.

Made for every European and South American country, there are literally millions of these excellent war rifles around. While most M98s are in 7x57 or 8x57, the boltface is the same as the .308/.30-06, with new barrels widely available. Any made by DWM, Loewe, Mauser, FN, or CZ between 1920-1943 is fine.

Argentine 1908 and 1909

These were made by DWM and Loewe in the 1920s, and the quality is superb. The caliber is the nice 7.65x54 Argentine, which has the same boltface as our .308/.30-06. The 1909 has a blind mag, while the more desirable 1909 has a mag floorplate.

Mexican Mauser 1910

No, they weren't *Hecho in Mexico*, but *for* Mexico by Germany. These are small ring M98s and perfect actions to add the barrel of your choice. J&G sells them for Ø180.

Spanish FR8 M98

If an additional caliber is totally out of the question, then the Spanish Mauser FR8 in .308 is a real bargain at Ø150. They're solid 98 Mauser actions with 18" barrels. Though most are a little rough, some are quite nice with *excellent* bores. Remove the bayonet attachment and stone the sear, as the trigger is quite poor. If you've more time than Ø, the FR8 tarts up nicely. Consider a Tasco or Simmons 4x or 6x scope (a 3-9x is wasted on these rifles). Back in 1994 the gun shows had *scads* of them, but they've been snapped up. Don't despair, however; you'll find one if you're diligent enough.

Do *not* buy the junky *M96* Spanish or Chilean .308. The one I tried wouldn't even hit the paper at 100yds. The M96 action doesn't have the third locking lug of the M98 and is really only a 45,000cup action (the .308 runs to 52,000cup). Distinguish the M96 by its cock-on-closing bolt throw.

Steyr M98 .308

SOG has these Mausers in original .308 for only Ø130, which is great deal (and better made than the Spanish FR8). They'll go quickly (as did the FR8s) and you'll never see them thereafter at gun shows. Folks, the good, rugged stuff is being salted away, so get going.

Belgian FN 1950s Mauser

I had a very nice 1952 in original .30-06 which I found for only Ø225. Since the rifle was quite accurate at 1½MOA with iron sights, I added a Timney trigger and a forward-mounted Burris 2¾x scope (to test Jeff Cooper's Scout rifle concept). This created a very sweet package (fed by stripper clips, since the scope wasn't covering up the action). With scope it shot ¾MOA and was extremely quick, well-balanced, and handy.

I sold it to a young friend (who cherishes it), so at least it has a loving home. If you run across one of these Belgian '06s, snap it up! The quality is excellent, and it will be very accurate, especially for a military bolt-action.

Springfield 03A3 .30-06

After the German Mausers made their impressive showing in Cuba, we dumped the Krag and basically copied the M98 Mauser. Some improvements were: magazine cutoff to allow single loading on top of a full mag; graspable cocking piece to manually recock and refire a hard primer.

The 03 actions numbering higher than 800,000 (Springfield) and 285,507 (Rock Island) received the double heat treatment and are stronger than the "low numbered" actions. All 03A3 actions were double heat treated.

The Springfield was a very good military bolt-action, and they sporterize nicely with many available accessories. Mine shoots ¾MOA. While I wouldn't alter one that was in *very* good original condition, anything less is ripe. You'll pay Ø150-300 for a non-collector grade.

P17 Enfield

This is a U.S. WWI Mauser-style .30-06 altered from the P14 .303 British. It was exceptionally well made and finished. These are very good rifles, although the leaf spring extractors are weak (Christy's Gun Works has a replacement *coil* spring).

I once had a gun show table, and some creaky Old Duffer shuffled up to ask me what I'd give for his P17 he had in the truck. I told him at least Ø125 if in nice shape, so he went to fetch it. Meanwhile, a friend of mine stopped by, and, knowing that he was hot to find an original P17, I told him that one was due by soon. Old Duffer came back with his rifle, and it *wasn't* in nice shape. It was in *perfect* shape. The wood was beautiful and the bore was mint. It even had the original leather sling. I thought my friend Steve was going to pass out from shock. Old Duffer wanted Ø150 (which was a great deal) and I nearly bought it for myself, but I couldn't do that to Steve (who was about to burst). So, I let him buy it. His eyes glow whenever he talks about that P17 and its 1½" groups.

Swedish Mausers (6.5x55)

Only available in quantity since about 1994, these are the most accurate and finest quality of *all* military bolt-actions. If a rifle didn't shoot within 1½MOA, it was rejected. They are chambered for the excellent 6.5x55 Swede (140/2750).

In 1995 these were being *given* away for only Ø60. You should pick a WWI M1896 or WWII M1938 Carbine from Sarco for Ø130, and *fast*. **The last lots to come in have arrived are going quickly.** Compared to 11,500,000 German K98ks, the Swedes made only 804,000 Mausers. As Doug Bowser in *Neutrality through Marksmanship* (an excellent book from Sarco) put it, *"Although...not rare, we will be wondering where they all went in about 5 to 10 years."* Just so. I have an unissued, *perfect* 1914 M1896 that I bought for *Ø140* at a gun show. What a treasure. All I need is an M1938 Carbine, and M1941B sniper with the German Ajack 4x scope (Sarco has these for Ø1,200--*groan*).

SURPLUS SEMI-AUTO RIFLES

Here's a summary of the *commonly* available military semi-autos in the surplus market. Many are foreign rifles shut off from further import, so act quickly.

M1 Garand (.30-06   USA, 1936-59)

Our WWII workhorse. The 454V8 of battle rifles. You'll pay Ø500+ for a nice one. Parts abound. Watch your thumb.

Tokarev M1940 SVT (7.62x54R   USSR, 1939-45)

The "M1 Garand of Russia." *Very* nicely made and good shooters, they wholesale for about Ø300. Hurry.

M1 Carbine (.30 Carbine   USA, 1942-)

Many folks love these carbines, puny caliber notwithstanding. Prices vary widely depending on condition and make.

AG42B Ljungman (6.5x55   Sweden, 1942-62)

Beautiful, funky, and 1½MOA accurate--my favorite. It uses a gas tube (no piston) and Tokarev SVT40/FAL-style bolt (though with no exposed handle to eliminate its receiver clearance and dirt entry). With its excellent trigger pull and quick adjustable 100-700m rear sight, the Ljungman is fine shooter and probably the most accurate of any service-grade semi-auto. Ljungmans today go for Ø350-400. I found one at a pawn shop for only Ø300 (they didn't even know what it was!).

Springfield Sporters (412-254-2626) has most Ljungman parts (including Ø40 barrels, Ø8 blank firing devices, and Ø7 night sights w/leather case!). Sarco sells the original maintenance kit for only Ø25 and original leather sling for Ø5.

In 1959 the Swedish government converted 10 AG42Bs to 7.62x51. Seven of these FM59s are in European collections, and the other three are (were?) for sale by Sarco for Ø8,650. Wow.

The Danish copied the Ljungman in 1949. Commercially offered in 7x57, .308, .30-06 and 8x57, the Madsen is, sadly, nearly never seen here. A .30-06 Madsen would be *tres chic*.

Hakim and Rashid (8x57 and 7.62x39   Egypt, 1960s)

With Swedish engineering help, the Egyptians adapted the Ljungman to 8x57. The Hakim has a 7-position gas regulator (clockwise to close--the 7 o'clock generally works best; use a ¼" nut driver with a small notch cut in it for the tool). Fashion a case bumper around the operating handle from rubber auto hose and electrical tape. This fine rifle can be had for <Ø300 and is a better bargain than the 8x57 FN-49.

After the Egyptians saw the Soviet SKS, they adapted the Hakim to create the Rashid in 7.62x39. With a 10rd mag and folding bayonet, only 6,500 were ever made. It's the only Ljungman model with a bolt handle, and has a Hakim-style gas regulator. The Rashid is more accurate than the SKS, but the springs wear out rather quickly. Several years ago, these rare rifles could be had for only Ø150. Hunter's Lodge (800-533-8540) is at press time wholesaling the very last lots at Ø440. Hurry. Sarco sells the original web sling for only Ø7.50.

G43 (8x57   Nazi Germany, 1943-45)
Made in large quantities, this Tokarev-style gas-operated rifle has a 10rd detachable mag and weighs 9.5lb. The G43 is a very unique and interesting rifle for about Ø650-1,200.

Simonov SKS (7.62x39   USSR, 1946-)
These are beautifully milled and make the ChiCom versions look like crap. For Ø150-200 at any gun show.

FN-49 (7x57, .308, .30-06, 8x57   Belgium, 1950-58)
The father of the FAL. A pre-WWII design and too expensively-made for most countries, only eight countries adopted it. The Belgian .30-06 is the choicest model (though at Ø500+). (Convert a Ø300 Egyptian model from 8x57 to .30-06 with a Ø100 bbl.) My next favorite is the South American rifle in 7x57.

In 1996 a few hundred of the rare 2,200 Argentine Naval FN-49s in *.308* w/detachable mag were imported for Ø400. Good luck finding one today.

MAS-49/56 (7.5x54   France, 1951-65)
Not a bad rifle, but the French just *had* to avoid the 7.62x51 NATO caliber. An interesting collectible. Burns Bros. and Classic Arms (800-383-8011) wholesales them new/unissued for Ø230. Stock up on *lots* of ammo for this bird.

vz-52 (7.62x45, 7.62x39   Czechoslovakia, 1952-59)
A fantastically over-engineered rifle and great Ø85 curio. Most are pretty crude. Federal Arms (612-780-8780) sells 7.62x39 chamber conversion kits for Ø35.

Dragunov (7.62x54R   USSR 1963-)
The Commies' sniper rifle. *Way* overpriced at Ø1,800+ and it gives only 1½MOA. The scope is only fair. I'd pass.

RIFLES IN PISTOL CALIBERS

Except for the Marlin 1894 .44 Magnum, I don't care for these (the 9mm/.45ACP Marlin Camp carbines, or the new Ruger 9mm/.40 carbines). Yeah, they're fun to shoot *because they don't recoil*. **Little recoil means little muzzle energy.** You've got to *take* it in order to *give* it. Besides, if you're going to pack a rifle and its weight, then you might as well have it in a *rifle* caliber, even if it's only in .223. While a .44 Magnum comes alive from a 16-20"bbl, the 9mm, 40S&W, and .45ACP do not. Also, I'd rather have a 12ga over a 9mm rifle.

MUZZLELOADERS

There are two ways to go: replicas of antique rifles or modern designs in composite stocks, stainless steel, etc. I've never gotten into muzzleloading, which seems to me more of a hobby than a practical shooting discipline. Comparatively, they're slow, inaccurate and cumbersome. While I'm not trying to utterly discourage you from trying them, you should at least have completed your primary gun acquisitions beforehand.

One interesting advantage to muzzleloaders is that they are not considered *"firearms"* under *GCA68* and are thus largely unregulated. You can even buy them through the mail!

AIR RIFLES

These are great for pest control and indoor practice. The Chinese models are very powerful and reasonably accurate for only Ø35-60. The German Feinwerkbau are the BMW of air rifles--beautiful and accurate for hundreds of Ø. I found a nice English Webley and Scott at a flea market for only Ø75. Whatever you buy, get thousands of pellets (target and hunting).

BATTLE RIFLES

These rifles were not designed for plinking, although they are great fun for such. They were not designed for target shooting, although they can be accurate to 1MOA. They were not designed for deer hunting, although some can suffice.

Rugged and self-loading, these rifles were designed for incapacitating and killing men in great numbers and at great distances. Owning battle rifles is no cause for shame. Sometimes, by their lethally aggressive behavior, men deserve to be shot. When they appear singlely and suddenly at close range, a pistol will usually solve your problem. When they appear at greater distances and/or in greater numbers, only a battle rifle will do. Remember, guns are only tools. Lethal emergencies vary, and so will the tools necessary to deal with them.

One very possible lethal for country folk is an attack by a pick-up truck full of marauders. A quality battle rifle, along with the will and training to use it, is the best tool to solve your problem. City dwellers during severe civil unrest could take to their rooftops with battle rifles to protect their neighborhoods from the hordes of arsonists and looters. (e.g., the L.A. riots.)

Another likely lethal emergency is the armed assault on peaceable (though politically incorrect) American gunowners by government thugs dressed in Nazi SS black. They probably will be carrying one of three long guns: an H&K MP5 9mm subgun, an M16A2, or a Remington 700 sniper rifle in .308. It is essential that your entire family be equipped and trained with battle rifles to counter this likelihood. (The dress rehearsals were Ruby Ridge and Waco.) As Jeff Cooper put it in *Art Of The Rifle*, *"Pick up a rifle and you instantly change from a subject to a citizen."* Just so.

The politicians know full well that you won't like what they've got planned for you. They know that they've squeezed us into corner and we're as mad as hell about it. They also know that we'll eventually say *"Enough!"* and fight back--and this terrifies them. Whenever they see a picture of an AK47 or AR15, they envision it wielded at themselves. These are "evil" guns to our "leaders" for the simple reason that they expect to face the muzzle of one some day enroute to the noose.

If they *really* knew anything about guns, they'd have tried to confiscate all the scoped hunting rifles. They're getting around to this, however--e.g., the proposed ban on *"cop killer ammunition"* able to pierce bulletproof vests. (Which means, practically speaking, *any* rifle cartridge with a muzzle velocity over 2000fps. Say bye-bye to your .30-30, your .30-06, etc. Heck, even a *.22LR* will penetrate most vests.)

If you *truly* cherish your residual liberties, then you must have a battle rifle. I'll cover the six general designs of self-loading, semi-auto military-style rifles:

AK (including the SKS variants)
Garand (M1, M1 Carbine, M14/M1A, and the Rugers)
FAL
H&K
AR15 (and South Korean Daewoo)
bullpups (AUG, FAMAS, L85A1, Bushmaster M17)

WHAT ABOUT FULL-AUTOS?

As Clint Smith of Thunder Ranch puts it, *"They only turn money into noise."* I rather agree. Tactically, "spray and pray" full-auto stuff is wasteful of ammo and your rounds/KIA ratio goes way up. In WWI the ratio was 10,000, in WWII 25,000, Korea 50,000, and in Vietnam it was over *100,000* rounds/KIA. Folks, firepower is *hits* per minute--*not* rounds per minute. Snipers in all of these wars averaged *1.5*rds per confirmed kill.

This aside, lawful Title II *NFA34* weapons are Ø2,000+, not to mention the Ø200 BATF tax stamp, the fingerprinting, the 4-6 month wait, etc. Finally, Title II owners can expect their 200,000 lawful weapons to be confiscated within 10 years. Do you *really* think that the feds will continue to allow Americans to own M16s, .30-06 BARs, .50BMG M2s, and 20mm Solothurns? No matter that *not one* of these registered weapons has *ever* been used in a crime since the *NFA* began in 1934. "They" cannot allow us to retain this kind of weaponry.

While finding (or converting) unregistered full-auto stuff is apparently easy enough, the risk probably too steep. You'll have to store it away from home. Finding a remote place to practice without being turned in is a real hassle. Getting caught with it is a felony, and you'll lose your 2nd Amendment rights (what little are still left). All in all, it's more trouble than it's worth.

If our situation ever turns into a full-blown guerilla war, then you'll have your chance to fire all the M16s you'd ever want. But until then, don't mess with them.

PROPER BATTLE RIFLE HANDLING

A superior battle rifle must meet the following criteria:

❶   Deliver high energy projectiles.
❷   Deliver them accurately.
❸   Function flawlessly in combat conditions.
❹   Handle well.
❺   Reload quickly.
❻   Field-strip easily.

Let's cover elements ❹ and ❺, which are often overlooked.

Ergonomics and handling

A battle rifle is simply a specialized hand tool. It is held and operated by human hands, and a good ergonomic design fully takes that into account. Some rifles have better controls than others. As I'll soon explain, the AR15 has the best, and the AK47 has the worst.

A battle rifle's controls are the bolt handle and stop/release, the safety, the mag release, the trigger, and the sights. How they are laid out and how they work is crucial. Remember, if you have to resort to firing a battle rifle at somebody, then things must be pretty serious. You need every edge possible. You need a rifle that works *with* you, not against you.

Your hands

Your strong hand (90% of shooters are right-handed) holds the rifle and pulls the trigger. *Ideally,* it should also thumb the safety and index finger the mag release.

Your weak hand steadies the rifle at the forestock and reloads. *Ideally,* it should operate the bolt handle and release.

A good design allows your hands to work in concert with each other. The right hand holds and fires the rifle, while the left hand loads, reloads, unloads, and clears malfunctions.

Reloading

Since battle rifles are reloaded often, the next three controls are very important. When you're reloading under fire, speed is everything. The difference between, for example, an AR15 (2 seconds) and an AK (4-6 seconds) is crucial. In a firefight a *lot* can happen in those extra 2-4 seconds an AK needs.

Bolt handle (left-hand control)

This control is probably the most operated of all. It is used to chamber, to clear malfs, and to unload. It must be accessible and hand friendly under exertion.

As a left-hand control, the bolt handle should be on the left. Unfortunately, only the AR15 (left-side operated rear drawbar), FAL, and H&K are so set up. The AKs and the Garand systems require the left hand work from *underneath* the rifle--an awkward concept. (The Galil at least has a top manipulated bolt handle, which is the best of the AK variants.)

Mag release button (right-hand control)

While your left hand is moving a new mag to the rifle, the right hand should be pushing the mag release, which should gravity drop the empty mag. Only the AR15 and the Daewoo are set up correctly. (Some *very* recent .223 FAL and H&K variants also have this release for the NATO-standard M16 mags.)

All other battle rifles require the *left* hand to operate the release. This is a faulty design as the left hand is *already* busy holding a new mag. (*Never* dump the old mag before gripping a new one.) Therefore, specialized techniques are necessary for successful "double-duty" of the left hand.

Leisurely tactical loads behind cover during a lull in the fight present no problem for any battle rifle, however, when a speed load is demanded, the AR15 and Daewoo are best.

Bolt lock/release button (left-hand control)

The bolt should lock back after the last round. After some practice, you'll feel the sensory difference and automatically know to change mags and release the bolt. (Neither the AK nor the H&K have automatic hold-opens. The AR15 does, and the bolt release button is properly placed on the left side.) Once the new mag is inserted, the left hand then trips the bolt release to charge the chamber, and smoothly moves up to the forestock.

The FAL has a proper left-hand bolt stop/release, though not a right-side mag release. The AR15 is still much better.

The H&K bolt can lock back in an MP40-style notch and is slapped forward by the left hand enroute to the forestock.

The SKS bolt locks back, but has no release button.

The AK is the worst offender. Since it has no bolt lock, you won't know you've run dry until pull #31 goes *"click!"* Now, you've got a terrifying 4-6 seconds of empty gun panic while the AK's crappy ergonomics become obvious. The left hand must (after changing mags) go underneath the rifle to rack the bolt, then return to the forestock. How 1947. Atrocious.

Safety (right-hand control)

Only the AR15, H&K, FAL, and Galil have *thumb*-operated safeties. The AK (except for Galils) and Garand systems require the trigger finger.

Again, the AK is atrocious. The right hand cannot simultaneously retain a shooting grip and operate the safety.

Overview

While this discussion has probably awakened you to the necessity of well-designed controls, you can't fully appreciate this until you train with different rifles and *personally* learn their differences. While the AK is cheap and utterly reliable, its controls are *abysmal*. While the AR15 is expensive, complex and a touch finicky, its controls are just about perfect.

If you want a bargain rifle to blast away with on weekends, then the Chinese MAK-90 is your toy. But, if you're *serious* about your battle rifle, then you'll choose an AR15, FAL or H&K. Superior controls are vital to staying alive. If I've convinced you of this point, then get to Thunder Ranch *ASAP* for Rifle 1 class. Until you've been to gun school, you can't appreciate what you don't know. Go now, while you *can*.

The AK47

History of development

Before WWII, the Germans had learned in the 1936 Spanish invasion that 90% of a soldier's shots were at targets within 300 meters, so why should he have to lug around a long-barreled rifle and its heavy 8x57mm ammo? Since the 9mm MP40 subgun was anemic past 150 meters, an intermediate round was designed--the 8x33mm, or 8mm Kurz (Short). Controllable in full-auto, yet effective out to 300 meters, the 8mm Kurz filled a crucial niche.

This cartridge was fired by a totally new class of weapon, the gas-operated MP44 (later called the StG44, as Hitler personally named it the *Sturmgewehr*, or "assault rifle"). The Wehrmacht and Waffen SS loved it. Although introduced far too late in the Russian campaign to make any real difference, Soviet tanker sergeant Mikhail Kalashnikov saw the genius of the MP44 and ran with it. His version was called the AK47.

Instead of using expensive, heavy, machined parts, the AK was constructed of cheap and light stamped steel. While not at all accurate (4" groups at 100yds are typical), it is *absolutely* reliable and can be field-stripped by a monkey. It uses a gas piston instead of an easily-fouled tube (e.g., the AR15).

Its cartridge, the 7.62x39, was also an improvement over the German 8mm Kurz. Heavily tapered for easy extraction, it gives the 30 round magazines their distinctive "banana" shape. Physically, the AK is probably the most recognizable of any gun in history--a characteristic amply assisted by the sheer number of AKs in existence; some *50 million*.

AK variants
Nearly all AKs were/are made by Communist countries (USSR, Czechoslovakia, Hungary, East Germany, Bulgaria, Yugoslavia, and China) and in the "Commie 7.62" caliber. Egypt makes the Maadi. China and Romania also produce it in our .223, although mags are a bit harder to find.

The Commie AK
The Hungarian AKs are probably the finest in quality, followed by the East German, Bulgarian, and Romanian. The Chinese clones (MAK-90, NHM-91, etc.) are a fairly shoddy, but they *do* work well--a testimony to the sound AK design.

The Finnish Valmet
This is a high-quality AK with cast aluminum receiver. They're beautifully made and accurate. The Valmet is the most pleasant shooter of all .308s. Downside: Valmets are Ø1,000-1,600, the AK control ergonomics suck, and mags are nearly *im-*

possible to find, even at the Ø150 they usually command. Galil mags *usually* work, though they're "only" Ø125. While you *can* alter M1A mags with spot-welded tabs, such is rather tedious.

Unless you're very wealthy and can afford *at least* a couple dozen of them, dropping a Ø150 mag in a firefight might cause you a crucial second of hesitation. For exactly this reason a friend traded his .308 Valmet for an Argentine FAL.

The Israeli Galil

Never shy about co-opting a good design for themselves, the Israelis produce their own high-quality version of the AK in both .223 and .308. The bolt handle protrudes to the top rather than to the right, so you can rack the bolt with the left hand from above (rather than from underneath). The best AK bolt.

The Galil has a milled receiver (Valmet is cast aluminum), a right thumb-operated safety (unlike any other AK variant except for the South African R4s). The folding stock is great, and a retractable bipod is standard. For the desert, the Galil is King.

My comments on the Valmet can be used nearly verbatim for the excellent Galil. AK-based ergonomics aside, the Galil is an outstanding rifle. It is also *extremely* expensive. Used ones start at Ø2,000+. Factory .308 mags are Ø125 and aftermarket mags begin at Ø50 (call Forrest, Inc. at 619-561-5800).

If you've just *gotta* have a .308 AK and can't afford a Valmet or Galil, then try the Yugoslavian version for only Ø600. The quality is good, and 20rd mags are only Ø29 from CDNN.

The SKS

Basically a pre-AK without the dust cover and detachable mag, it's a great spare rifle to keep in the barn or your trunk. For Ø100-150, the Chinese Type 56 is quite a bargain. If pre-11/90, install the 20rd fixed mag and a flash suppressor (not muzzle brake, which isn't needed). I prefer the 16"bbl version.

The advantage of the *fixed* mag version is that it escapes the *"assault rifle"* classification and is thus less risky to trunk in your car. Buy your ammo in stripper clips, as it's the quickest way to load the SKS. Carry the 120 or 200rd ammo pouches.

The Chinese also make a detachable mag version which uses the plentiful Ø8 AK 30rd mags (though *not* the 75rd drums without grinding down a bit of the magazine well). This is my favorite SKS, and I actually like it better than the AK.

For those on a *real* budget, the SKS isn't a bad deal. The 7.62x39 caliber is even a decent whitetail deer caliber out to 150yds and adequate 4x scopes and mounts are about Ø70.

The Russian 1950s Type 54 version is *very* nice, though you'll pay Ø175-200 for one. BATF classified it as a *"curio or relic"* so it can keep its bayonet without legal problems.

Ergonomics of the AK

Since Communists are anti-human at heart, it manifests in their weapons' ergonomic design, which is just awful.

AK bolt handle

Although the German MP44 correctly placed the bolt handle on the left side, this feature, sadly, was not appreciated by Kalashnikov. Proper technique with the AK is to rack the bolt with the left thumb from *underneath* the rifle. While awkward and requiring practice, it's the best that can be done with such a poor design. (Left-handed shooters, however, will find the right side handle an unexpected bonus!) The bolt handle is far too thin, and your left thumb will get cut on the knife-edged safety unless you radius its edges and/or practice.

The Galil protrudes to the top. The SKS bolt handle is fat and round, with nothing nearby to slice your thumb.

AK bolt lock/release

It has none. Since the bolt does not stay open after the last round, you must rack the bolt to charge from a new mag.

AK safety

It's abysmally located. Not only can it not be operated without the right hand releasing its shooting grip, it's inexcusably noisy (just what a soldier wants on a night patrol). You can spotweld a second horizontal tab at the rear which is now reached by your trigger finger. (Call 619-931-5304 for an improved safety for Ø19.95ppd.) This alteration merely makes tolerable an atrocious design.

The SKS safety, however, is in the trigger guard and can be operated with the right finger. It's quiet, too.

AK magazine release button

Also abysmal. It cannot be correctly reached by the right index finger, but needs the left thumb.

AK magazine locking/unlocking
Really bad. The mag's front corner is first inserted to (hopefully) catch the receiver notch, and then the mag is rocked back to the release lever catch. While very securely holding the mag in place, all this takes considerable practice and the mag will not drop free by itself (as in the AR15). In a speed load, you can hit the release button with the new mag.

AK sights
Crude but rugged. The front sight is hooded and adjustable for windage/elevation zero, and the rear tangent sight is fairly on for distance elevation (dehorn the leaf corners).

AK handling
Fair. The AKs feel a little clumsy and the Commie stocks are usually a bit too short. In brief, not terrible, but not great.

AK reliability
The best. AKs work, *period*. During double-feed malfunction drills in rifle class, one guy had a MAK-90 and it was difficult to jam up *on purpose*.

AK accuracy
Poor to fair. A 100yd group tighter than 4" is gravy, especially in a Chinese gun. (I happen to have a Norinco SKS paratrooper which groups 2½" with iron sights. My scoped SKS groups 3".) Assuming a 4MOA gun, this means a 12" group at 300yds and 16" at 400yds--clearly a limited rifle (not to mention that the 7.62x39 is out of gas by 400, anyway). By comparison, AR15s will typically group 2MOA, which I think is a reasonable standard for a 400yd carbine.

AK field-stripping
Sublimely easy. The dust cover pops right off, exposing the bolt carrier and spring for simple removal. Gas piston slides right out. Bolt strips easily due to its less-is-more design. Not that this is often necessary, as AKs run without regular cleaning (although I'm *not* recommending laziness).

Final comments on the AK
By all means, you should spend a lot of time behind an AK because you are likely to encounter one in the field someday (either in Billy Bob's MAK-90, or in some UN Bulgarian's AK.) However, I don't believe that an AK should be your *primary* bat-

tle rifle because of its inferior ergonomics and caliber. (A .223 or .308 Galil is the only AK exception.) While an AK will "make do" just fine and ammo can probably be forever scrounged up (or reloaded), I prefer the ergonomics and parts/caliber availability of the AR15. To me, ergonomics settles the matter hands down. The AK works *against* the shooter, and while you *can* "swim the English Channel without flippers"--why should you *have* to?

If the Commie AK or SKS *is* to be your battle rifle, I'd prefer the SKS Sporter over the AK since it's Ø50 cheaper, uses AK mags, scopes more easily, and has superior controls and a better sporter stock. It's about as reliable as the AK, too.

If you're set on an AK, however, at least get it in .223 so you'll be able to feed it with domestic ammo.

THE GARAND FAMILY

M1 Garand

John Garand, the brilliant gun designer at Springfield Armory, gave our WWII troops his superb M1 in .30-06. Robust and extremely reliable, the M1 gave our boys a real edge over the German's slow bolt-action Mauser. The Garand was a fairly accurate and very powerful rifle. Since we made 6,034,000 of them, they're easy to find. Its real design flaws were its weight, lack of a detachable mag, and poor ergonomics.

While I don't recommend that you *choose* a Garand, I wouldn't pass it up if one landed in your lap, either. It's heavy, slower to load, and only fairly accurate (unless tuned), but a real reliable 454V8 of a battle rifle. You can still get one for Ø310 from the Civilian Marksmanship program (419-635-2141).

M1 Carbine

Designed for support troops, this was a light and handy little rifle using a Garand bolt but with a detachable mag. Sadly, its unique caliber (the .30 Carbine) is inexcusably weak. They *should* have created a rimless .40 (say, 10x45, at 200gr/2200fps for 2150/ft/lbs) and designed the Carbine around *that*. A detachable mag, auto-rimmed 10x45 Carbine would have *really* been the thing out to 250yds.

While there was a firm which used to convert the .30 Carbine to .44 Auto Mag and .45 Win Mag (cool!), the little bolt just couldn't handle the power and many of them simply blew up. *Cuidado.* I'd rather pay Ø375 for a used Ruger .44 Carbine.

While these little M1 Carbines *are* fun to shoot, the SKS is just as much fun and a better field weapon. If an M1 Carbine is the only military-style rifle you have and you can't afford anything else, *sell it* and get at least a Ø175 detachable mag SKS or a Ø250 Chinese MAK-90. Don't limit yourself with that puny 50yd.30 Carbine caliber. Dump your Carbine on some sucker.

M14

Basically an M1 Garand in .308 with detachable mag, the M14 was an excellent weapon, though a handful in full-auto, which is why our military switched to the .223 in Nam.

Semi-auto M14 variants

Springfield Armory makes the very good M1A. Used ones go for Ø800-1,000. If you've chosen the M1A, then pay a bit extra for the more accurate National Match version. Avoid the short barrel "tanker" models--the muzzle is too close to the gas port, so they're not as accurate. Mags are plentiful at Ø15-20 each and spare parts are no problem. This is a fine field rifle which scopes well and can double as a sniper rifle out to 600yds.

The Italian BM59 is an M1 tanker converted to .308 with a 20rd mag. Accuracy sucks, and muzzle blast is *brutal*.

The Chinese (Norinco and Polytech) made a clone of the M1A. While they use M14 mags, not all M14/M1A parts interchange, and the bolt and receiver need to be heat-treated to approach M1A temper and longevity. This aside, these clones are reliable and fairly accurate, and thus a very good value for those who can't afford an M1A but don't want (or can't find) an FAL. No longer imported, you might get lucky at a gun show or flea market for around Ø525. (I'd still much rather have an FAL.)

The Ruger Mini14 (.223) and Mini30 (7.62x39)

I've owned several of these over the years and *tried* to like them, but I just can't. None of mine were ever very accurate so I reasoned that I could shoot the same crappy 3-4" groups with a MAK-90 for Ø150 less money.

At one time, the Mini14 was *the* only affordable alternative to Colt's AR15 (when AKs and SKSs weren't yet allowed in), and had more market leverage. Today, AR15s are less expensive than they were, and bargain Commie rifles abound.

In .223 I'd much rather have an AR15. In 7.62x39 I'd much rather have an AK. Therefore, regardless of caliber, the Mini just doesn't blow my skirt up. Some people really like their Minis, and I won't try too hard to talk you out of yours. They make a good wife rifle for those husbands with an M1A, since the rifles have the identical operating/ergonomic system.

Ergonomics of the M14 rifles

M14 bolt handle
Right side and operated with an underneath left hand. At least the handle is smooth and wide, unlike the AKs.

M14 bolt lock/release
It not only has one, but it's even on the left side. Good.

M14 safety
Unique in that it's inside the trigger guard and thus easily operated, although it's a bit too noisy. Better than the AK, but not nearly as good as the AR15 or the FAL.

M14 magazine release button
Center mounted AK-style. Too bad.

M14 magazine locking/unlocking
AK-style, though a little easier to catch the front corner.

M14 sights
Excellent. The fixed front is wing-protected, while the rear is a fully-adjustable peep.
The Ruger front has no wings, and the rear is fragile.

M14 handling
Good enough, though not great, and it's a bit heavy. Only the A2 version has a pistol grip. The FAL is better balanced.

M14 reliability
Excellent. The Garand bolt is simple and strong.

M14 accuracy
Good to very good, meaning 1½-2½". Unless it's a National Match M1A, the average FAL is usually more accurate.

M14 field-stripping
Easy. The trigger guard hinges down to release the trigger group, and then the barreled receiver comes out of the stock.

Final comments on the M14 rifles and clones
I've had many Springfield M1As and Chinese clones, but sold them all once I fired my first FAL. Still, I *do* like these rifles and wouldn't feel at any *overwhelming* disadvantage if I

had to field with one. They're solid, reliable, and fairly accurate. They scope well and easily. Parts and Ø15-20 mags abound. For the .308, I just like the FAL better, as I'll soon explain.

FAL

The FAL is hands down my favorite .308 battle rifle. Used at one time by *93* countries, most of the free world concurred. (When did *93 countries* ever agree on *anything*?) It's been utterly battle tested and has many very nice control features copied from the WWII German MP44.

Ergonomics of the FAL

FAL bolt handle

Correctly placed on the left side and forward of the bolt for easier operation. The best!

FAL bolt lock/release

Also correctly placed on the left, and just where the left thumb will be after loading a mag. Although a bit cramped behind the mag release button and requiring a downward pull (instead of an inward push as on the AR15), it's still very good.

Because of the bolt handle's rearward travel ending just above the bolt release button, the bolt can be retracted *and* locked back with only the left hand, something that even the AR15 cannot boast. Superb.

FAL safety

On the, you guessed it, left side and well designed for the right thumb. The AR15 has a tad shorter travel and is a little quieter, but the FAL is a close second.

FAL magazine release button

AK-style. At least it's not centered underneath (as in the AK and M14), but off to the left.

FAL magazine locking/unlocking

Similar to the AK with its nose-in-rock-back movement, although unquestionably the best of that variant thanks to the helpful right side receiver bridge and forgiving forward notch.

FAL sights

O.K., but could be *much* better. The front is a winged, threaded post. The rear is a fully-adjustable peep with elevation clicks out to 600yds--and, to me, it's a bit flimsy with too much mechanical play. The M1A's is *far* superior.

FAL handling

Very good with its pistol grip and fine balance. A bit muzzle-heavy, but I'd cut the barrel down to 16½", anyway. Only the Valmet and AR10 handle better, but not by much.

FAL reliability

Very good, especially those with sand-cut bolts. It's even got a hand adjustable gas regulator valve with *12* positions. Proper adjustment for normal semi-auto fire is to gradually close off the valve until the bolt begins to short cycle, then open it back up a couple of notches. This ensures that only just enough gas gets to the piston, which reduces fouling. Blocking off the gas flow entirely will turn the FAL into a manually-operated single shot for either grenade launching or suppressed fire without bolt clatter. Neat.

FAL accuracy

Very good at 1¼-2" and slightly better than the M1A because of the more precise bolt lock-up. While dust cover scope bases exist, the cover has far too much play and is too long to reasonably serve as a solid base, so I wouldn't bother trying to scope it. DSA claims that their Ø95 base (#620-A) keeps its zero.

FAL field-stripping

Upper receiver hinges up like the AR15 to easily remove the bolt and clean the bore. Lower strips out easily. Though not often a required procedure (unless you're swapping buttstocks), the buttstock concentric springs are a *real* pain to cram back in, so beware. Use a ¼" aluminum tent peg (the one with eyelet).

Final comments on the FAL

Ergonomics are excelled only by the AR15. The gas regulator valve is outstanding. Reliability and balance are great. Parts are no problem, whether for inch pattern (U.K., Canadian, Australian, N.Z.) or metric pattern (Belgian, Israeli, Brazilian, Argentine, etc.). Mags are plentiful at Ø7-15 (metric pattern mags work in inch guns, but not vice versa). For those wanting a *real* battle rifle in a *real* caliber, the FAL is tops.

Treat yourself to a pre-ban Argentine or Belgian (Ø1,400-1,900), preferably with the folding stock (about Ø2,200). Yeah, it's a lot of dough, but if you're *serious* about fighting with a battle rifle then just how important is that *jet ski*, anyway?

DSA (847-223-4770) domestically manufactures their modern CNC SA-58 *with pistol grip stock* for Ø1,395. Great quality. (Replace the short safety with a longer L1A1 safety.) The 16¼"bbl carbines lose 250fps with increased muzzle blast, so stick with the 21"bbl models. (I do not recommend the FALs from Hesse Arms. Their quality isn't up to DSA.) Temporarily "sporterize" the stock to add a vortex flash suppresor. (On a post-9/94 semi-auto, you can have one, but not both.)

Springfield Armory imports the new Brazilian FAL, which they call the SAR-4800. These are very well-made and accurate rifles (often 1MOA), but they have that stupid sporter stock. Get an American DSA with a pistol grip for the same Ø.

You could *theoretically* buy a surplus parts kit (has everything but upper receiver) such as the Ø175 FN FAL Steyr STG 58 (the best) or the Ø110 Israeli FAL and assemble it on a new metric upper. Entréprise Arms (www.entreprise.com) and others sell new-made inch receivers (an FFL purchase). *Warning:* assembling pre-ban parts on a post-ban upper is a felony--and, gee, I wouldn't want you to break the law... Obey Congress and defend yourself with kitchen knives and BB guns while congratulating yourself for being a good slave--I mean, "citizen."

On a budget? How about a *Ø400* FAL?

The new import hybrid (Canadian inch lower on Brazilian metric upper) was a *whopping* deal at Ø400 (Bandet, or SOG). Although I don't care for its folding bolt handle, plus it has that crappy "sporter" stock and no flash suppressor--but for Ø400 it was an *incredible* bargain. I say "was" as they've gone up in Ø.

You can order the original stock, pistol grip and flash suppressor for only Ø45, but *don't* get caught with these parts on a post-ban sporter. Since this Sporter doesn't have a forbidden pistol grip, you *can* have the barrel threaded for a vortex flash suppressor (see p. 3/7-8). Once "the gloves come off" simply put the original pistol grip and buttstock back on. If you *fully* revert a post-ban rifle, don't *ever* take it to a gun show or the range. Keep it hidden for that imminent rainy decade. (Or, install an improved Sporter stock from DSA for Ø75. Part #090-DI).

Stock up on as many of these and their mags as you can afford. I've had good success finding them at gun shows, so far. I even traded even a Polytech M14 for one--*heh!* Americans have yet to appreciate the FAL and think that the M14 is better. For Ø1,400 you can have an FAL, 10 mags, and 5,000rds of Portugese ball ammo. Now *that's* affordable firepower!

News flash: Klinton just signed an executive order banning for 60 days the importation of foreign semi-autos. Prices on these import FALs will increase significantly. Buy now!

The H&K

In .223 (Model 93) and .308 (Model 91), the H&Ks are typically German: high-quality, expensive, complicated and heavy. They are very robust rifles, accurate and reliable (a modernized MP44 using an MG42-style delayed roller-block action--no gas tube or piston).

Ergonomics of the H&K

H&K bolt handle
Well placed on the left side of the forestock. It folds down and remains stationary during firing.

H&K bolt lock/release
It can manually lock in an MP40-style forestock notch, and is bumped forward to release. Not ideal, but not terrible.

H&K safety
Correctly placed on left side and above the pistol grip.

H&K magazine release button
Most are AK-style, while some in .223 are AR15 push button style (though placed too far forward from a shooting grip).

H&K magazine locking/unlocking
Depends on the release button, AK or AR.

H&K sights
Front is a shrouded post. Rear is a rotating drum peep out to 400m (which should have been out to 600m) which seems quick and rugged, though not all owners like it.

H&K handling
The 93 is too heavy for a .223, but the 91 is about average weight for a .308 (though 8oz heavier than an FAL). Balance is O.K., though slightly muzzle-heavy. An FAL is better.

H&K reliability
Excellent. *Slightly* better than the FAL and equal to the M1A. Whad'ya expect from the Germans?

H&K accuracy
Excellent. Equal to a National Match M1A and *slightly* better than an FAL.

H&K field-stripping
Very easy, using the MP44-style hinged upper.

Final comments on the H&K
Mags are plentiful, though rather expensive at Ø20-50. Parts and accessories abound. It's the Mercedes Benz of battle rifles, and a little funky. The feeling of quality is very strong and reassuring. It's employed by some 60 armies, nearly as many as the FAL. It *does* destroy brass, however.

Give one a try if you can *afford* it. Inter Ordnance imports their SLG-95 for only Ø899 (704-821-8337). Springfield Armory imports the Ø1,200 SAR-8 Brazilian version, or you can spring Ø2,000+ for an original German model.

The AR15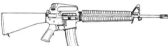

Finally, an assault rifle with well-designed controls! I only wish that it were in my *Sturmgewehr* 6.5x48 (I'll explain later). The first version got off to a rather poor start in Vietnam, primarily because of normal teething problems, insufficient cleaning by the troops, and an unforgiveable gunpowder change which caked up tremendously.

The modern A2 version can be called a triumph of engineering over design and works very well. I didn't use to like ARs at all, but have grown convinced of their utility. Regardless of whether or not you choose an AR for your .223 battle rifle, train with one as you may face them in the field.

The A1 (pre-1985)
This has the triangular forestock, simple rear sight, and a 1-12" twist (suitable only for 55gr ammo, like M193 ball).

The A2 (1985 on)
This version has the rounded forestock and improved rear sight. It will have at least a 1-9" twist for 62gr ammo.

Ergonomics of the AR15

AR15 bolt handle
On the left side, though sadly at the *rear* of the receiver so that the left hand has to move way off the forestock. No big deal, however, I wish it were placed *forward* (as in the FAL).

AR15 bolt lock/release
Perfectly placed on the left side where the left thumb naturally reaches for it after replacing a mag.

AR15 safety
Perfectly placed on the left side where the right thumb has natural access. Range of travel is a nice and short 90°. Best of all, it's *quiet*.

AR15 magazine release button
Perfectly placed under a straightened trigger finger.

AR15 magazine locking/unlocking
Mag drops free as in an auto pistol. So obvious, but nobody did it in a rifle before Eugene Stoner. Mag inserts straight up without any nose-in-rock-back gymnastics and locks with pressure. Superb design--the standard against which all others should be measured. In Michael Mann's *HEAT* you'll see how fast a mag change can be, even by an *actor* (Val Kilmer).

AR15 sights
Excellent--some of the best. The wing-protected front post is adjustable for elevation zero with a bullet tip. The A2 rear sight (with small and large peep) is adjustable for windage and bullet drop out to 800yds (though the .223 is spent by 500).

AR15 handling
Superb. Lightweight, with pistol grip, and well balanced, especially with the thin 16" barrel.

AR15 reliability
Very good. ARs with their gas tube (instead of piston) and many springs, pins, and ball bearings demand thorough cleaning and oiling, but they run great if you take care of them.

AR15 accuracy
Excellent. With a Ø2 Accuwedge, they'll usually group under 2½" with ease. Only the Daewoo is more accurate. I can hit torso-sized steel at 500yds with mine.

AR15 field-stripping

Upper receiver hinges up (like the H&K and FAL) and bolt carrier slides right out. Bolt is complicated, but strips easily enough. This rifle *will* collect powder sludge more easily than the AK, so you'll have to clean it more regularly. Keep that bolt, carrier and buffer well oiled.

Final comments on the AR15

Since Olympic Arms just *had* to make an AR15 pistol in 7.62x39 they single-handedly got the BATF to rule against imported steel-core ammo since the law forbade using such in a pistol. Only one factory pistol using a rifle caliber made it also a pistol caliber, so 90% of the cheap Chinese ammo was cut off. **Moral: *Don't* buy your AR15 from Olympic Arms.**

While genuine Colts are nice, Bushmaster rifles are just as nice but not as expensive. I like Bushmaster's "Dissipator" model with the 16" barrel and full-length stock which uses the full sight radius of the excellent A2 sights. PWAs are O.K., too. Professional Ordnance offers a 4¾lb carbon fiber AR15.

I'd avoid the Colt **barrels** with their too fast 1-7" twist. A twist of 1-9" is the best compromise for *any* military ball weight, either 55gr M193 ball or the 62gr foreign SS109/U.S. M855. The pre-1985 A1s with a 1-12" twist will *not* sufficiently stabilize the 62gr, and are only suitable for 55gr.

A **flash suppressor** is a *must* on any battle rifle, as 70% of defensive shooting is done in conditions of low, altered, or failing light. Muzzle flash *without* a suppressor can be up to 2' and is quite blinding. Use the "vortex" suppressor--it's *the* best, eliminating 99% of the flash. While I haven't heard of many busts on modified post-ban guns, beware.

Pistol grip. I've tried most of them: the original A1, the A2, Pachmayr, Stock Option, etc. The A2 has that annoying ridge; the Pachmayr (although really comfy) is Ø40, heavy, and moves your hand off the controls somewhat. My solution is the old A1 grip with a piece of bicycle tubing. It's OEM, thin, cheap at Ø5, lightweight and comfy--can't beat it!

Misc. Get the plastic box G.I. earplug container with its swivel lid, and paracord it *short* to the barrel under the front sight. In the buttstock, pack in a small bottle of BreakFree or surplus LSA, spare parts (bolt, firing pin, extractor, springs, ball bearings, etc.), and cleaning kit.

Sling. *Every* rifle (and shotgun) *must* have a sling, and it's more for carrying than for shooting steadiness. Remember, a pistol is what you use to fight your way *back* to your rifle, which you probably left behind because it didn't have a sling.

> *The sling is to a rifle is what the holster to a pistol. If you have a sling, chances are you will keep the rifle with you.* If there is no sling present, you will set the rifle down. When you are at the absolutely farthest point away from the rifle that you can possibly get, you'll need it.
>   -- Clint Smith, director of Thunder Ranch

For your battle rifle, the simpler the better. G.I. 1¼" OD webbing works fine. At the forestock end there should be no excess sling, as this end and its keeper are not to be adjusted. Adjustment of sling length is to be done solely at the buttstock loop. Holding your rifle muzzle down, adjust sling for about 8-10" of parallel-to-ground buttstock slack. This will be good for both carrying and arm looping. Through both keepers, loop the sling to the outside *away* from the rifle, and then leave enough length to loop *back over and through* the keeper in reverse. This secures the sling from pulling through a keeper. (Remember *Diehard* McLane's MP5 sling doing that in the elevator shaft?)

Sights. I highly recommend a Tritium front sight post, which makes night shooting much easier.

Clint Smith of Thunder Ranch raves about the optical C-More sight (from Dillon for Ø345). The Ø1,000 Elcan 3.4X scope from Canada is also superb (G.S.I., 205-655-8299).

J&G sells Chinese copies of Colt's 4x20 AR15 scope with BDC for only Ø40 (including see-through mount). The quality is very impressive for the money, and I can easily hit steel plate out to 500yds with mine. The mount will *not* keep its zero upon reattachment, and the scope won't hold up forever, but for Ø40, *who cares?* If nothing else, this bargain scope is at least a handy monocular if it ever loses its zero.

30rd **mags** are plentiful at Ø5-15. Get about 50 of them from Sierra Supply, along with G.I. mag pouches. Get a few of the 20rd mags for easier prone firing.

The Sally Speedloader (Ø19.95; 888-773-5637) fits on your belt like an open mag well w/catch to stripper clip load mags.

I haven't had too much luck with the Chinese 120rd drum. The 100rd C-Mag works great, but pre-bans are a mere Ø625 (800-867-7999) and the the Ø225 post-bans are sold only to cops and feds, darn it.

Install a Ø60 Redimag from Dillon which holds a second loaded mag right next to the gun's mag. Also, cut some 2½" bicycle tube into ½" bands and use four of them to hold a third mag on top of the forestock. (Load to only 28rds--it's more reliable and saves the springs.) Now, your AR15 has 84 rounds as its grab-n-go package. If you can't solve your problem with *84* rounds of .223, then it *might* be your "turn" to exit the planet.

Many of these tips can also be used on other rifles, although the AR15 is unique in its customability. You can have different uppers for the same lower and swap out in 1 minute.

The AR10

This is an AR15 in .308--heh! Many (60%) AR15 parts interchange. M14 20rd mags are adapted for Ø20 each. Best of all, the AR10 has the same excellent controls as the AR15, therefore far less additional training is required. The AR10 will shoot at *least* 1MOA, and sometimes ½-¾MOA (which is sniper grade accuracy out to 700yds). Sadly, they're all post-ban and retail for Ø1,375-1,995 (www.armalite.com). I'd choose the flattop AR-10(T) National Match with 24" barrel, and top it alternately with an Elcan scope and NVD.

The Stoner SR-25 is more expensive and more accurate, but is *far* too finely tuned and fragile for battle rifle duty. The AR10 shoots just as well for half the price.

DAEWOO

This is a very good rifle from South Korea. It's basically an AR15 with an AK-style gas piston. It uses AR15 mags, and has similar controls. It is very accurate and reliable.

Ergonomics of the Daewoo
Daewoo bolt handle

Without excuse, it's on the *right* side. Boo. Hiss. The handle itself is smooth and rounded, at least.

Daewoo bolt lock/release

Perfectly placed as the AR15, however, bolt retract and lock back is a two-handed operation.

Daewoo safety
Correctly placed, but stupidly designed with a long lever requiring 180° travel instead of the AR15's 90°. Very awkward, as the right hand must leave its shooting grip (I'd just use my left thumb). No excuse for this.

Daewoo magazine release button
Perfectly done as the AR15.

Daewoo magazine locking/unlocking
Perfectly done as the AR15.

Daewoo sights
Very good. The front is completely shrouded (as the H&K), and the rear peep is fully adjustable.

Daewoo handling
Good, though not great. It's at least 1lb heavier than necessary and the sporter stock feels awful (it's also 1" too short).

Daewoo reliability
Excellent. The AK-style gas piston is much less fussy than the AR pistonless tube.

Daewoo accuracy
Excellent. A friend of mine groups 1-1½" with his, and I understand this is fairly common Daewoo performance.

Daewoo field-stripping
AR15 simplicity.

Final comments on the Daewoo
They *almost* made the ultimate .223 battle rifle using the best of the AR and the AK systems (and with a 4-position gas regulator, no less!), but they *blew* it with the bolt handle and safety. (The Singapore SR88A is like the Daewoo, but with better controls. Don't get excited, however--they aren't imported.)

Still, a *very* good rifle (a close second to the AR15) and an *excellent* value at Ø475 if you can't afford another Ø250 for an AR. It uses AR15 mags. I like the Daewoo very much. The South Koreans take their weaponry *very* seriously, and it shows. I'd still save up for an AR15, but *don't* pass up a Daewoo if one comes your way and you need a .223.

BULLPUPS

A bullpup is a rifle in which the action is located *behind* the trigger/pistol grip, with the receiver itself acting as the butt-stock. While this is a clever and efficient configuration on its face, the mag release is still on the receiver and now *also* behind the pistol grip, thus inoperable from a shooting grip. While this mechanism could *theoretically* be operated from pistol grip controls through connecting rods and/or cables, such would be extremely complicated. It's never been done, nor is it likely to be.

French FA-MAS .223

Nicknamed "the Trumpet" by the *poilus*. While by most accounts a reliable enough rifle (especially considering that it was designed by the *French*), it is unavailable to us. Boo, hoo.

British Enfield L85A1

This was proven in Desert Storm to be a very unreliable rifle. (When will the Brits learn that they're *not* gun designers?)

AKU-94 bullpup stock for the AK47, MAK-90, etc.

Just introduced by K-VAR (818-243-0151) for Ø229. I've handled one and they feel pretty good. Fine quality.

Bushmaster M17S

This is a surprisingly well-done rifle for Ø700 retail. It's 30" long with a 21½"bbl (1-9" twist). A bit heavy at 8.2lbs, but it has a built-in Weaver rail. Bolt handle is on top (good), AR15-type bolt stop/release is retained, along with mag release (and left side ambi button, too). The safety is a push-through above the pistol grip. While the bolt and carrier are proprietary, it uses AR15 mags. Overall quality is excellent, although the non-adjustable sights are far too short and good for only 25yds.

I picked up a used one for only Ø400, and added a vortex flash suppressor and a Simmons 1½-5x scope. It shoots 1½-2" at 100yds, even with its mushy trigger pull (typical of bullpups). It likes Thermold mags. A C-More sight might be just the ticket for the M17S. It'll need a chest-carry tactical sling.

Since I bought it for only Ø400, I might keep it for a trunk rifle, even though my best shooting buddy chided me pretty hard on all this. He said I have *"gun disease"* and urged me to seek immediate treatment before magazines begin to sprout from my face, and my, *ahem*, turns into a bolt.

Steyr AUG

The AUG is *the* best of the bullpups, hands down. At least its safety is pistol grip mounted and the bolt handle is properly on the left side. (Can also be ambi set up to eject to the left.) The mag release is behind the mag and can be actuated by pressing the fresh mag against it. The 1.4x optical sight with its 5MOA "doughnut of death" is quite good. The trigger pull, however, is very heavy (feels like 10lbs). AUGs cost a mere Ø2,200+ and original mags are no longer imported. It's a SWAT team favorite, cuz it looks high-tech *bad*. I've spent some time behind the AUG, and I do like it, even though it's too expensive for me personally. (For Ø2,500 I could buy *any* .308 FAL, AR-10, or H&K91 I wanted.) The AUG is neat, but no assault rifle quantum leap as some would assert.

If you've just *gotta* have one, go ahead, I guess---although I can't see how they're better than a 16" barreled AR15. Malasian ball is *very* accurate in AUGs.

DEALING WITH POST-BAN BLUES

Basically, 18 USC §922(r) applied the *"sporting purposes"* cosmetic crap to imported semi-autos made after 30 November 1990. The "Crime Bill" did the same to domestic semi-autos made after 13 September 1994. Here's an exclusive Boston guide through the rats' warren of "assault rifle" laws.

If the rifle was made in the U.S.A.,

was it made *before* 13 September 1994?

If Yes, then it is pre-Crime Bill and can have *all* the stuff.

If No, then it cannot have more than one 18 USC §921(30)(B) feature (folding/telescoping/pistol grip stock, bayonet mount, flash suppressor or its threaded barrel, or grenade launcher).

If the rifle was imported,

was it made *before* 30 November 1990?

If Yes, then it is pre-import ban and can have *all* the stuff.

If No, was it made *before* 13 September 1994?

If Yes, then it's pre-Crime Bill and *can* have multiple features *if* the 27 CFR §178.39(c) imported parts count is <10.

If No, then it *can't* have more than one 18 USC §921(30)(B) feature even if the §178.39(c) parts count is 10 or less.

In my view, a flash suppressor and pistol grip are *essential* to a battle rifle. **On post-9/94 rifles you can have one *or* the other, but not *both*.** U.S.A. semi-autos (e.g., AR15 and DSA FAL) can have pistol grip stocks. AR15 owners can simply store replacement pre-ban threaded barrels (or entire uppers).

Foreign rifles can have pistols grip stocks if the 27 CFR §178.39(c) imported parts count is 10 or less (see page 3/6). So, thread your "sporter" stocked AK, FAL, or Daewoo barrel for an *American* vortex flash suppressor *today*. Buy, but do not install the original stock. Later, "when the balloon flies" you can install that scary pistol grip which will let you reach the safety. (Or, you might simply whittle the sporter stock to OEM shape.)

If you're too nervous about flash-suppressing a post-ban rifle, then try Hornady's low flash TAP Urban .223 ammo.

THOUGHTS ABOUT CALIBERS

Let's compare the three common battle rifle calibers. I don't have figures for U.S. military ball past 500, so I used ones for Federal Match (69gr/.223 and 168gr/.308) from Major Plaster's *The Ultimate Sniper*. The .308FM shoots almost as flat as NATO M118 Match, while the 55 and 62gr .223 ball shoots flatter than the 69gr FM, though with not as good energy retention. Nonetheless, this chart is very illuminating.

Ballistic Comparison: .223 vs. 7.62x39 vs. .308   (in yards)

velocity	Muzzle	100	200	300	400	600	800	1,000
.223	3000	2720	2460	2210	1980	1560	1240	1060
7.62x39	2340	2080	1836	1606	1388	1051		
.308	2600	2420	2240	2070	1910	1610	1360	1170

energy	Muzzle	100	200	300	400	600	800	1,000
.223	1380	1134	925	750	600	375	235	170
7.62x39	1485	1172	913	699	522	299		
.308	2520	2180	1870	1600	1355	970	690	510

trajectory"		100	200	300	400	600	800	1,000
.223		zero	-3.2	-12.2	-28.3	-89	-207	-405
7.62x39		zero	-7.6	-29.2	-72.0	-145		
.308		zero	-4.5	-15.9	-35.5	-105	-228	-421

.223 or not .223? How about the Commie 7.62x39?

While the 7.62x39 has a *bit* more energy than the .223 out to 181yds, the .223 with its higher BC catches up, penetrates better, shoots flatter, and is easier to find. Granted, the above 69gr BT Fed Match will *not* (because of its lower MV) shoot quite as flat as the 55 and 62gr ball, but this rough comparison is still helpful. The .223, regardless of loading, is very flat shooting, though has meager energy to deliver past 500.

Ballistically, the 7.62x39 with its low velocity and stubby 123gr bullet quickly runs out of gas past 400yds. The overall round is inefficient, trading length for fatness, thus increasing magazine height for no good reason. If you're going to have a case head width of 11.35mm, then you might as well increase the length to 45mm for more capacity, which would have nicely made a sort of ".308 Lite." Yes, the 7.62x39 meets its design parameters, but these were quite flawed (as were the .223's).

So, regarding which of the two lighter carbine rounds, I *highly* recommend the .223 over the 7.62x39. You should train with cheaper 55gr (e.g., the accurate Malasian or Venezuelan ball) and save your 62gr SS109/M855 for that rainy decade.

We're still going with 7.62x39, since rifles are a bargain

The only way I'd choose 7.62x39 over .223 is if I had a *lot* of people to equip on a *very* tight budget.

My favorite rifle in this is the 16"bbl SKS Sporter which uses AK mags (except for the drums, and even these will work with a bit of mag well whittling). They run about Ø170; Ø50 less than the semi-auto AK47 clones (MAK-90 and NHM-91). For Ø70 you can get a Chinese 4x scope/rings/see-through mount, which will increase the effective range out to 400yds. 30rd mags are still only Ø8, and you should have at least 12 per rifle, carried in the 4 mag pouches. Be sure to invest in the complete spare parts kit for Ø35. Having an extra barrel, set of sights, and trigger assembly is also a good idea.

If a Ø170 AK-mag SKS is too expensive, then get the plain Ø100 version with fixed 10rd mag. Attach a new 20 fixed mag (the 30rd is too tall) and feed it with stripper clip ammo. Spend another Ø75 for the high quality Russian SKS, if you can.

Regarding ammo, the 10¢/rd days are long gone, but good-quality Russian ammo (NC/Berdan) can still be had by the case for about 15¢/rd--and I'd *hurry*. Boxer primed 7.62x39 exists in good quantity now, but considering the cheap Russian stuff--why reload? (This goes for .223, too.) You'll need 5,000rds for training and practice, and another 5,000rds for the field. Who *wants* to reload 10,000rds per rifle, anyway? You're spending a lot of time without saving any real money. Simply stock up while you can. Surplus can *always* be sold later. **There's no such thing as *too* much ammo.**

Stock up on tons of ammo and spare parts kits, and spend *lots* of time and ammo in training. At most, 80% could field with the SKS--the other 20% are your better riflemen using scoped bolt-actions (in .308, .30-06, etc.) to keep your attackers past 300yds while being picked off. Success in battle means hitting without getting hit. Hit and *move*. We're not going to win this thing by slogging it out at the company (or even platoon) level since we'll just get airstruck.

.223 vs. 7.62x51 NATO (.308)

I used to pooh-pooh the .223 in favor of the .308, and I still do to an extent, however, I'm now more accepting of the .223 than I was. Out to 300-400yds the .223 is *fairly* capable--assuming that you won't be shooting in the wind or through cover.

While an FAL is only 2½lbs heavier than an AR15, .308 ammo and mags take up *2½ times* more weight and *3 times* more space than the .223. For example, an AR15 three-mag/90rd pouch will hold just two .308 20rd mags. An Eagle tactical vest will hold *12* AR15 30rd mags, versus only 6/20rd .308 mags. **A .308 bullet *alone* is heavier than an entire *round* of .223.** For a long patrol, humping an FAL, 10 loaded 20rd mags, and 200 extra rounds in strippers is *work*. The same number of rounds in a AR15's system would weigh *20lbs* less, and 20lbs either way on a long patrol means a *lot*. **Question: Is it *worth* it?**

Probably. There's just something extra comforting about having a .308 vs. a .223. The .308 is effective out to 600yds and, in *very* capable hands and rifle, out to 900. Many have survived torso (and even head) hits with the .223, but the .308 seems to put 'em down for good. The .308 ball will go through ¼" of boiler plate steel at 300yds (vs. 100yds for .223), the door of a '68 Dodge at 400yds easily (vs. 300yds *barely* for .223), and a full 4" of concrete at 100yds (vs. 1.4" for the .223).

As you see, round weight *does* correlate to performance. Yeah, the .308 system *is* heavy, but TANSTAAFL. While .223 weighs much less, you'll probably have to give your targets a few rounds more to drop 'em than you would with a .308.

If I were somehow limited to only one of the two, then I'd choose the .308. You'll pay more in Ø and sweat, but it's truly an *awesome* caliber. Besides, your enemy will have at best a mere 7.62x39 or .223. Never forget that...

If you can't decide, then own *both* and choose when you need to. I'd routinely carry my AR15 on long patrols, but if a heavy scene were anticipated then I'd swap for my .308. Granted, if I *knew* that I would *not* also have swap access to a .308, then I'd probably field with an AR10, FAL, or H&K 91. Or, use the .223 indoors and the .308 outdoors.

Another option is to carry an AR15 and backpack a lightweight, scoped bolt .308 with 40-60 Match grade rounds.

WHICH .223?

Hands down, the AR15A2 is best. The Daewoo is second. The .223 SAR FAL-copy is third. The H&K93 is fourth (too expensive and too heavy). The Mini14 and Chinese AK haven't got well-designed controls, and aren't accurate enough.

WHICH .308?
FAL, H&K91, GALIL, or AR10?

Pros and cons of the FAL
Pre-ban rifles available?
Yes, so it can legally have a flash-suppressor and pistol grip stock. Used versions run from Ø1,400-2,000.

The Century Arms import is only Ø400, though post-ban. If you want to equip a lot of people with a .308 battle rifle, and don't mind illegally converting them, then this is the way to go.

How much are mags and parts?
Only Ø7-15 each, and they're very plentiful.

Final remarks on the FAL
Second best controls (to the AR10), second to the AR10 for best accuracy, and tied for 2nd with the H&K for reliability (the Galil is 1st). But this is almost hair-splitting. The FAL may run barely second in some categories, but not 2nd overall, if you know what I mean.

Pros and cons of the H&K91
Pre-ban rifles available?
Yes, so it can legally have a flash-suppressor and pistol grip stock. They begin at about Ø2,000.

How much are mags and parts?
Ø20-50 each depending on where made, but they're plentiful. Parts and accessories are also abundant, though costly.

Final remarks on the H&K91
Third best controls (to the AR10 and FAL), third for accuracy, and most reliable (with the FAL an almost tie). The cheapest post-ban H&K clone is the SLG-95 for Ø899.

Pros and cons of the Galil
Well-made, accurate, and reliable, this AK variant still suffers somewhat from AK ergonomics. Finally, the Ø125 mags make the Galil quite impractical for all but the very wealthy. Oh, and try to get *parts*... I'll have to pass on the Galil.

Pros and cons of the AR10
Post-ban rifles run from Ø1,400-2,000. The modern AR10 is so new that you will not likely find a privately sold one--*ever*.

Pre-ban rifles available?
Only the first versions, which are collectors' guns.

How much are 20rd mags and parts?
Ø65 each from Armalite, or they will adapt your pre-ban M1A mags for Ø20.

Final remarks on the AR10
The AR10 has the best controls and is the most accurate .308 battle rifle, but the H&K91 and FAL are slightly more reliable. They begin at Ø1,375 retail.

What's wrong with an M1A?
Enough. Plenty. It's 1940s technology with poor controls, and is way too heavy and clumsy. Keep yours if you absolutely love it, but other .308s are much better, so there's no reason to *choose* an M1A over an FAL or H&K91.

So, which .308 is it? FAL, H&K, or AR10?
For a legal *pre-ban* rifle, which one?

If money were no object, or if I *might* be in the desert, then a Galil. The controls aren't as FAL-friendly, and the mags are expensive--but the Galil *works*.

If the H&K91 had an AR15 bolt hold-open device and mag release button, plus a left-sided FAL bolt handle, then I'd jump on it regardless of cost or where I was fielding.

If I could *choose* my conditions *and* I was on a *moderate* budget, I'd go for a Belgian or Argentine FAL, especially because the controls are so good and mags are such a bargain. It's not *quite* as reliable as the Galil or H&K91, but more accurate.

Affordable mags/parts, and superior controls make the FAL my .308 favorite over the H&K91 and Galil. The modern AR10 was a close second, but they're hard to find on the used market, and pre-ban versions don't exist.

For converting a *post-ban* rifle (you bad boy!), which one?

If on a budget, then get a Century Arms FAL. The original buttstock, pistol grip and flash-suppressor are only Ø45.

If *not* on a budget, then get an AR10 as it's only Ø300 more than a DSA FAL or an SAR-8 H&K91 clone and more accurate. Be careful with flash-suppressing a modern AR10 as it'll be unique (unlike pre-ban H&K91s and FALs, which *do* exist).

TRIVIA TIME!

Let's see if you've been paying attention. Applicable rifles are (in alphabetic order): AK, AR, FAL, H&K, M1A, and SKS. Some answers must be extrapolated. Answers on page 17/8.

❶ Which rifle may the bolt be retracted/locked back *one-handed*?
❷ Which rifles *do not* use a gas piston?
❸ From best to least best, list the six rifles as to reliability.
❹ From best to least best, list the six rifles as to ergonomics.
❺ From best to least best, list the six rifles as to parts availability.
❻ From best to least best, list the six rifles as to affordability.

❖ **9**

IDEAL RIFLES
& RIFLE CALIBERS

For a *Sturmgewehr*, the .223 is greatly lacking, and the .308 is rather much, so I've designed a fine intermediary round between the two which provides 85% of the .308's performance at 75% of the weight and space. This caliber is sorely needed.

My *ideal* carbine caliber--the .264 Boston

In the 1950s, the British were experimenting with their .280 Enfield (7x43mm, for 140gr/2415fps from a 24½"bbl), which I think is nearly ideal--controllable in full-auto, yet effective out to 400yds. They clearly were on to something.

My ideal carbine round would throw a 140-142gr 6.5mm Sierra MatchKing at a minimum of 2500fps, preferably 2600.

It would have an intermediate case head diameter of 10.80mm (between the .223 case's 9.60mm and the .308's 12.01mm). This midsize case is just *begging* to be invented, as was the 10mm case. Happily, the 10mm Auto has a head diameter of *exactly* 10.80mm and thus could easily be manufactured to the desired length of 48mm (exactly between the 45 and 51mm lengths of the .223 and .308) with a 25° shoulder and 7mm neck. It would be very slightly tapered, dropping about 0.6mm from base to shoulder. SAAMI max of 52,000cup. Max COL would be about 2.675", or 67.94mm.

With an estimated 36gr of 748 powder, it would send a 6.5mm 140gr HPBT MatchKing (.535 BC; .287 SD) to 2600fps. I think that 2600 is very feasible given the case's likely efficiency.

Based on 2600, I calculated:

Velocity/KE:		V/KE % of M	E% of .223/.308	"drop
Muzzle	2600/2101	------	(152/83)	
100yds	2434/1841	(94/88)	(162/84)	------
200yds	2274/1608	(87/77)	(174/86)	-4.4
300yds	2120/1398	(82/67)	(186/87)	-15.4
400yds	1973/1210	(76/58)	(202/89)	-34.2
500yds	1830/1041	(70/50)	(219/91)	-61.9
600yds	1695/893	(65/43)	(238/92)	-102.0
1000yds	1249/485	(48/23)	(285/95)	-408.0

Energy of the .264 Boston

Compared to the .223/69, the .264 Boston gives *1.74x* the energy at 200yds, *2x* more at 400 and *2.38x* at 600yds.

Compared to the .308/168, the .264 Boston has 86% as much energy at 200yds, 89% as much at 400, 92% at 600, and *95%* at 1000yds. Remember, this is with *21%* less powder, *17%* less bullet, and *25%* less size than the Fed .308M.

This is a *dandy* round. At 400yds it has *more* energy than a .44 Magnum does *point blank*. At 1000yds it's got as much KE as a .40 or .45 do point blank. (I employ the handgun KE comparisons to illustrate the .264 Boston's energy at long range.) Delivering 1041ft/lbs at 500yds with only 36gr of powder is *extremely* efficient.

A hunting rule of thumb is that deer need at least 1000ft/lbs of KE for a reliable and sporting kill. That figure correlates well to the human animal, which the .264 Boston delivers out to 500, and the .308 out to 600. So, we have an ideal *Sturmgewehr* caliber: if the .223 is not enough, and the .308 is too heavy to pack, then the .264 Boston should be just *perfect*.

Trajectory of the .264 Boston

It's very flat shooting, too. At an MV of 2600, I calculate a trajectory just slightly *flatter* (+2.7" at 500yds) than the Fed .308 168gr Match. (At 2650 it would be identical to the NATO 173gr M118 Match. To reach an MV of 2650 *might* require the case length increased to 49mm, but this would still be acceptable.) The relevance of this is that many sniper scopes have BDC cams for the Fed .308M and M118, so a new cam for the .264 Boston wouldn't be needed.

With some experimentation, perhaps the 155gr Sierra MatchKing (*.570* BC; .318 SD) could be loaded to 2500fps. Energy would equal the Fed .308M at 625yds, and even *exceed* it by 27ft/lbs at 1000.

Instead of creating a ".30-06 Lite" with the 7.62x51 in the 1950s, my new round is what the 7.62x51 *should* have been (and what the British *almost* had with their .280 Enfield). It should also replace the .223 as the police sniper caliber (as the excellent .243 is now doing in many departments).

The .264 Boston rifle

The rifle would be an FAL-style short gas piston upper (18"bbl), left handed FAL bolt handle with an AR lower. Also, a 2¾x BDC scope with offset iron sights in case the scope failed.

I would demand that it shoot within 1½MOA with regular ball (which would be of M118 quality). I would also insist on 23rd mags intelligently loaded to 20rds (to save the springs) with 10rd stripper clips. These mags would be 1¾" *shorter* than the 30rd AR15 mags. Mags would have the SIG SG551-style stud and slot to attach themselves together side-by-side.

In short, you would have the accuracy and ballistics of the 6.5x55 Swedish Mauser in a modern autoloader. It would be the finest *Sturmgewehr* rifle/caliber combination, *period.*

Will some manufacturer ever create the .264 Boston?

It's probably too much to hope for. Since I designed the .264 Boston as a *battle* rifle cartridge, some nation's military would have to "see the light" and get excited enough to sell off all their 5.56mm ordinance. Not likely. There *might* have been a chance before the 5.56 NATO *really* caught on, but not now. (When I start my own country, I'll insist on a fair evaluation of the .264 Boston.)

As the private sector generally develops rifle calibers only for single-shots, and many other cartridges with similar performances already exist (6mmPPC, .243, .250-3000, 6.5x55, .260, 7-08) the .264 Boston is probably not compelling enough of a potential *bolt* gun caliber for civilian development.

So, why all this *hooha* on a never-to-exist cartridge?

Two reasons: It was fun to design, and to illustrate the gaping hole in the assault rifle caliber spectrum. I think that the .264 Boston is *"just right"* (to quote Goldilocks). The 6.5mm 140gr bullet is just begging for this intermediate width case-- the ".40S&W" of rifle calibers.

METRIC THOUGHTS

The Europeans got it right the *first* time over a hundred years ago with the German 7x57 (in 1892) and the Swede 6.5x55 (1894). Too bad that we didn't "go metric" instead of the .30-40 Krag (a mere ".30-30 Magnum"). Even Teddy Roosevelt's Rough Riders charging up San Juan Hill in 1898 couldn't ignore the accurate firepower of the excellent 7x57 German Mausers.

Just eight years later we had our own superb high-velocity spitzer, the .30-06 (7.62x64). It *should* have been, however, in 7mm. Winchester basically confirmed this in 1925 with their .270 (not *quite* a 7mm/.284 cal.), and Remington *finally* got it right in 1957 with their .280 (a 7x64mm).

The versatile .308 case (with 5 caliber loadings)

It's been very successfully necked down to 6mm (.243 Win.), 6.5mm (6.5-08, or .260), and 7mm (7-08), while being necked up to the .358 Win.--and it delivers all of them well.

I think the 140-155gr 6.5mm is the best long-range caliber for this case. For a short-action, the .260 is amazingly capable, even taking elk and moose with the 160gr round nose.

The versatile .30-06 case (with *12* caliber loadings)

It's been very successfully necked down to .22, 6mm (6-06), .257 (.25-06), .264 (6.5-06), .277 (.270 Win.), and 7mm (.280 Rem.), while being necked up to .323 (8-06), .338-06, and .35, .375, .416 Whelen. I know of no other case with *twelve* different caliber loadings.

I think the 160-175gr 7mm (.280 Rem.) is the best long-range caliber for this case. (There needs to be a 190gr bullet.) Short of grizzlies, the .280 can truly do it *all*. What a cartridge!

Why my fascination with 6.5mm bullets?

I very much like the 6.5mm (.264 cal.) for its efficiency (especially in the 140 and 155gr): high BC and moderate weight. It's sleek enough to fly well, light enough to fly fast from a small case, yet heavy enough to have good energy and penetration 300-400yds down range. I've begun a lifelong love affair with the 6.5x55 Swede, and a buddy has a *sweet* 6.5-08 which is a real ½MOA tack-driver with little recoil.

Our 7.62x51 NATO round would have been *far* better in a 140gr 6.5 or 168gr 7mm with a *.535* BC rather than the stubby 147gr .308 and its barn-door BC of .380. (Whereas the .308 is "only" excellent, the 7-08 is fantastic, and the 6.5-08 is *perfect*--which Remington finally realized with their .260.) A .308 bullet must weigh at least 190gr to achieve the high .535 BC and .286 SD of a 140gr 6.5mm or 168gr 7mm. Until a Magnum-sized case can throw a 190+gr, the .308's lower BCs simply cannot compare with the 6.5 and 7mms.

My point is this: if you wanted a 140-155gr bullet sent from a mere 51mm long case, you would *not* choose the .308 caliber (if starting from a clean design slate). The .308 is best for 180-220gr, and the .338 for 225-275gr. This generally keeps BCs above .420 and SDs above .230, and to fall below these values begins to indicate needless caliber inefficiency.

Why my fascination with 7mm bullets?

The .284 is a great caliber, especially for 160-175gr bullets, and the '06 case does very well in 7mm. The .280 Rem. gives 150/2900, 168/2800, and 175/2700 for good 700yd work.

The 7mm Mags can do even more: the 7mmRM out to 800yds with 175/2900; the 7mm Weatherby out to 900 with 175/3000; and the 7mmSTW out to 1000 with its 175/3100. If you need a 7mm Mag, the best compromise between power and efficiency is probably the 7mmRM, which outshines the .280 by 200fps (however, you'll lose one round of magazine capacity), yet is neither as brutal nor as heavy as the Weatherby or STW.

Metric summary

The .223 case *should* have been the 47mm long .222 Rem Mag necked up to 6mm to throw the 100gr Sierra MatchKing at 2800 (an autoloading 6x47), the .308 case in 6.5mm, the .30-06 case in 7mm, saving the .308 caliber for larger cases--not that I'd begrudge anyone of 80 years of wildcatting fun.

The *theoretically* six ideal rifle calibers

Had "they" asked *me*, the needs of the American riflemen could have been well met with only these six cartridges:

❶   .22LR stainless AMT
❷   .264 Boston (6.5x48) *Sturmgewehr*
❸   .284 Winchester
❹   .300 Dakota Mag (from the .404 Jeffery case)
❺   .338 Lapua (shortened/necked down .416 Rigby)
❻   .50BMG bolt-action (or Harris M-96 semi-auto)

If it needs to be solved by rifle fire, one of these can do it.

What about making do with only *one* rifle?

❷ In a world of *perfect* caliber availability, if I had to have only *one* rifle and was more concerned with bad guys than game, I'd have a sub-MOA AR10 in .264 Boston. This would be 83-95% as powerful as the .308, yet ammo'd weigh 25% less.

❸ If bad guys were few, then I'd have a tack-driving stainless .284 with a 3-12x BDC Mil-Dot scope. This would give me excellent .280 ballistics from a lighter short-action.

How about getting by with just *two* rifles?

❷-❹ They would be an AR10 in my .264 Boston (6.5x48) and the LOD Marksman .300DM.

❷-❺ If you're *very* concerned about *very* hard and *very* far targets, then bypass the .300DM and get a .338 Lapua.

O.K., what if you could have only *three* rifles?

❶-❷-❸ If you weren't concerned with 400yd elk, 1000yd bad guys, bears or armored vehicles, then the .22LR, .264 Boston AR10, and .284 would handle your needs--however, I'd still rather have a .338 Lapua over a .22LR. Therefore,...

❷-❸-❺ You could skip the .300DM since the .284 would serve out to 700yds with a 175/2700 BT spitzer.

❷-❹-❺ If the .284 isn't enough for those situations between the AR10 and the .338 Lapua, then choose the LOD Marksman in .300DM. For deer, the .300DM shoots reduced loads well. (I'd miss having, however, a lightweight .284 to pack around in the high country. It's a very capable caliber which doesn't weigh near as much as the .300DM.)

If you need a .50BMG as one of your only three rifles, then you're in a nasty paradox: high threat and meager funds.

Which rifles for a battery of only *four*?

The three you've chosen above, and a Harris .50BMG.

Which *five* rifles?

Add the missing centerfire (.284 or .300DM).

The last rifle would be a suppressed, accurized stainless AMT 10/22 (with suppressor). Gee, now you're all set.

Getting *realistic*

The point of my six page theoretical discussion and list is to contemplate the *ideal* and thus illustrate the standard against which our *real-world* choices must be measured.

Since the .264 Boston lives only in my mind, we'll have to settle for the .223 and .308. In a similar vein, even though the .260 and .280 Rem., 7mmSTW, and .30-378 Weatherby *are* factory calibers (and superior to the .308, .30-06, 7mmRM, and .300WM respectively), they're *still* funky enough to cause supply problems, especially if you need a box from Buford's General Store-n-Things.

Thus, *for sheer off-the-shelf availability*, the .223, the .308, and .300WM are the best choices for efficient overlapping. As military calibers, there's a wealth of ballistic dope on them, which *really* tilts the scale to their favor. With these cartridges plus the .22LR you can take *any* American game. Add a .338 Lapua and a .50BMG for the *really* bad guys.

So, the real-world *core* rifles should be an AMT 10/22, an AR15, an FAL (or H&K91, AR10, Galil), and scoped bolt-actions in .308, .300WM, .338 Lapua, and .50BMG. **These seven rifles can do *everything*.** One could *theoretically* skip the .223 battle rifle, but I personally would not. One could even skip the bolt .308, relying on the AR15 out to 400yds and using the .300WM for all longer shots--but I wouldn't be without a bolt .308 unless I just couldn't afford one.

So, *my* ideal *real-world* rifle battery would grow like this:

1: **FAL**, (or H&K91, AR10, Galil)
2: FAL, **bolt .300WM**
3: **AR15**, FAL, *bolt:* .300WM
4: AR15, FAL, *bolts:* .300WM, **.50BMG**
5: AR15, FAL, *bolts:* **.308**, .300WM, .50BMG
6: AR15, FAL, *bolts:* .308, .300WM, **.338LM**, .50BMG
7: above, plus an **AMT 10/22**
8: above, plus a *quality* AK47 (for training)
9: above, plus a Steyr Scout Rifle (.308 or 7-08)
10: above, plus a Marlin lever action (.30-30, .44 Mag, .45/70)

You can have fun and enjoy rifles 11 to infinity, but get *the first 8, **especially the first 3**.* (You could do without *both* the .338 Lapua *and* the .50BMG, but get at least *one*. Bad times are coming, and you'll need a heavy. I'd love a Browning M2 .50, a 20mm Solothurn, etc., but we're not talking *NFA34* stuff here.)

Two 1998 SHOT Show rifles I've just *got* to try out

From SO Precision Weapons of Germany is the "Shorty"--a Ø1,795-2,420 bullpup with a revolutionary slide-action operated from the pistol grip. This action is extremely fast and strong. The rifle is 8.2lbs, 31" long with a *24*"bbl. The quality is superb. Available in target and hunting models in calibers from .243 to .416RM, the Shorty even has a 5-10rd detach mag. *Wow!* Call Wilcox at 603-431-1331 for a color catalog.

From Professional Ordnance is the carbon fiber AR15 weighing only *4¾*lbs. It felt as light as a walking cane. Since the BATF forbids new folding and telescoping stocks, this rifle comes with a *detachable* stock. *Heh!* Gotta have one of these.

Getting *really* realistic

Don't let my list get you all upset if you can't afford all those rifles. Joe Trailer Park with a .22LR, an AK mag SKS and a good scoped .308 (or .270, .280, .30-06, etc.) has a *solid* rifle battery. He can easily carry these in his trunk and be ready for 95% of *all* rifle-solved problems.

Assuming an Ø80 Marlin 60, a Ø175 SKS, and a Ø450 Ruger M77II with Tasco 3-9x, plus Ø300 of gear and ammo, he's got a very decent rifle battery for only Ø1,005. **People spend more than this each year on *beer and cigarettes*.** A man who cannot (*will* not) acquire this in a year is pretty worthless.

The other 4 core rifles fill in the remaining 5%. The only thing Joe T.P. *perhaps* needs is an LOD Marksman .300WM for those truly *long* shots, but this is more *nice* to have than vital.

If you can afford only the above 3 rifles, fine--*but don't skimp on quality!* Don't get some crappy .22LR, an SKS and a beat-up .30-30 and think that you're all set. Granted, they're better than *no* rifles at all, but save money *elsewhere!*

Anyway, get to a gun show and start shopping. Remember to buy reloading equipment and supplies for at least 1,000rds per bolt gun, and at least 5,000rds per battle rifle. Don't forget three sets of spare parts and two barrels per rifle. An extra scope and pair of rings wouldn't hurt, either.

All this stuff will soon be either purchase tracked through computer and ID card--or outlawed altogether--so buy now what you and your family need for a *lifetime*.

Then, act like a free American and *give 'em hell* someday, because they've had it coming since 1933 when they outlawed gold! If you need any convincing on this point read (or *reread*) John Ross's *Unintended Consequences*.

I hope my books have been helpful and inspiring, and I look forward to seeing you someday on the *other* side of this looming, awful mess. Good luck, and God bless!

❖ 10

WOMEN & GUNS

Statistically, women have a *50%* chance of being a victim of violent crime by age thirty. This predatory environment is the result of too many men abdicating their duty to protect women against society's nastier elements. I don't mean that women *cannot* protect themselves. My point is this: **Why should they *have* to?** They shouldn't *have* to any more than they should have to change their own oil. **Yes, they *can* do it-- but they shouldn't *have* to, and there's a *difference*.**

Ladies, you are *much* finer creatures than us. You are too precious and lovely for such crude tasks. Let *us* change the flats, put out the forest fires, and defend the borders.

Rabid "feminists" (e.g., the men-hating kind) are no doubt shrieking at this point. *"We're liberated!"* they exclaim. *"We don't need men to protect us!"* Technically, they're right--they don't. But that's not the issue, and they've missed it.

"Women who seek equality with men lack ambition." Be careful what you ask for. In Russia, men and women *are* equal. The Socialist State recognizes only *"citizens"* and women join men in *all* the grimy chores. Women fix sewer pipes and change truck transmissions along with the men. And they *look* like men because of it. Civilization, random beauty and elegance has died there--and *that's* the vital issue here. Women *can* do a man's job, but men *can't* do a woman's job. It's just not in us.

Jeff Cooper said, *"Men are here to protect women, and women are here to civilize men."* When women are consumed with a myriad of coarse chores which men would rather bear, they have no time or energy (or inclination, it seems) to civilize men. My other point is this: **Women can more easily protect themselves than men can self-civilize.**

So? Well, when men are *not* civilized, society becomes a beer-swilling trailer-park. Left to our own canine devices, men will regress to the raunchy raconteurs and methane dispensers we are at heart. While often dissatisfied with men, women don't realize that *they themselves* are the solution. **Men don't make men, *women* do. Women determine the quality of men** As Louise told Thelma, *"You get what you settle for."* If women would quit having the children of oafs and morons, then they'd die off. Women are the *lifeguards* of the gene pool, and they should start choosing *quality* mates, as the animal kingdom does. (Women have been debased so as to give oafs better odds. The question is, *why* have women *allowed* their debasement?)

Ladies! Do not speak to, date, sleep with, or marry a hopelessly substandard male. Above all, do *not* have his children! Do not feel sorry for him. He deserves no pity. Don't encourage him with the slightest of smiles. He shouldn't exist, so treat him that way. If he can't catch an introspective clue, then let him die alone; let his shoddy genes be lost forever. **This is not cruelty--this is *quality control*.** *You're* responsible because *we'll* sleep with almost *anybody*. We're the seed-sowers and it's not in us to be *picky*. You're the child-bearers, so you *have* to be.

When women refuse to civilize men, men become Al Bundy from *Married With Children*. Why? Because inside *every* man is a *potential* Al Bundy, and it's women's duty to ensure that he never sees the light of day. Although men *can*, with rare and great effort, singlehandedly keep their own "Al" locked up, what's the *point* if women no longer seem to *care*?

Believe me, we can *tell* if women care. They don't, and they're reaping the cruel justice of getting the lazy, irresponsible men they deserve. Scoff at genuine courtesy, honor and responsibility in men and women get prissy, whining, amoral cowards. Fill up a nation with such males, a country is left with only women (male and female), and the predators begin to take over. Courting Darth Vader, the feminized society then cries for a hyper-masculine police state to restore order. When gentlemen are gone, government thugs fill the vacuum. This has been accelerating in America since the late 1960s.

> There was a time even in my remembrance when American men were manly, heads of their houses, and respected by their wives and children. They were rugged and hard-nosed and not swamped in a soft pink jello. A thief was a thief to them, and not a "disadvantaged, underprivileged, culturally deprived" weakling. I've seen men

beat up other men who attempted to snatch a woman's purse on the public streets, or who kicked a dog or punched a child....
When men are unmanned, spiritually if not physically, then a country becomes depraved, weak, degenerate, feeble of spirit, dependent, guideless, sick. **Such a country can never resist authoritarian despots, tyrannies, the men on horseback, Communism.**
Our Presidents are always talking about our image abroad. I have news for them. Our "image" is a surrogate Mama, in an apron, with a baby's bottle in his hand. Surrogate Mama to a laughing and contemptuous world! Bottle-feeder to ravenous "infants" to proclaim themselves heads of some obscure state in some backyard continent!
That is our image abroad. Does it make a nice picture to you? Then do something about it. Start in your own house, and then with your own local government. Unseat your emasculators in Washington. Drive them from your schools and your courts. Proclaim to the world again--and again--that you will stand for no more nonsense, and that our flag is to be honored wherever it flies over any embassy; that you have power and are quite willing to use it, in the name of freedom and justice, tempered only slightly by masculine mercy.
Then, perhaps, America will be honorably feared and respected, and peace might really come to a mad and disordered world. The center that "cannot hold" might tighten and become iron and invincible, and Doomsday thus averted. (p.100-101)
Remember this: The strongest sign of decay of a nation is the feminization of men and the masculinization of women....The decay and ruin of a nation always has lain in the hands of its women. *So does its life and strength, its reverence for beauty, its mercy and kindness. And above all, its men.* (p.116-117)
-- Taylor Caldwell; *On Growing Up Tough* (1971)

Men *will* be responsible, honorable, and even heroic--*if* women encourage and respect us for it. We *need* it, for we cannot forever run on our own meager batteries. (Granted, no man is emasculated without his consent, but we cannot fight the relentless onslaught on manhood without women's help.) A dime's worth of love, respect and approval from women gets a *dollar's* worth of effort from us. Men are the draft animals of the human race, and we work cheaply. (We're built that way and don't mind shouldering the yoke of human existence.) But we *do* need at least that dime, and we're getting pennies.

Ladies are not silly froth. Gentlemen are not brainless brutes. There's a complementing role for each of us. But, until American men are respected for their manhood so they clean up our streets, American women, sadly, should carry a handgun.

HANDGUNS

A high-quality, reliable, concealable, and powerful handgun is essential for women. Without it (and the training to use it) women are at the mercy of random chance.

Which *kind* of handgun--a pistol or a revolver?

Semi-autos are pistols, revolvers are revolvers. **Pistols** are usually more powerful, hold more rounds, are quicker to reload, and are more concealable. They do, however, require a bit more training and practice.

If a woman cannot or will not spend the extra time and money for an auto, then a good **revolver** (e.g., a S&W .38 Special or Taurus .44 Special) will suffice. Have a handgun.

Pistols

Again, my rule: **Carry the *largest* pistol you can conceal, in the *most powerful* caliber you can *handle*.** When I mean "handle" I mean *comfortably and confidently so.* Unless you *enjoy* shooting your pistol, you won't train with it often enough (if at all), and regular training is vital. If you're not well-trained with it, you won't carry it, and your pistol must be with you to do its job.

Yeah, I *did* say to skip the 9mm for the .40S&W, but if the .40 is just a little *too* stout for you, then go 9x19 (or even 9x18 Makarov, or .380). **Any caliber is better than *none* at all.** (Besides, with practice you'll be able to go up to the .40 or .45 later.) First rule of any gunfight: **Have A Gun.**

Any good indoor gunrange will have various pistols to rent. Go with a teacher friend (preferably one who has attended Thunder Ranch, etc.) and try out different pistols. Among the models below, choose one that feels *best* to you, as personal affinity is very important.

Which caliber?

In **.45**, the Glock 30, the Para-Ord 10, Springfield V-10, Colt Officer's ACP, and AMT Backup.

In **.40**, the Glock 23 and 27, SIG P-229, H&K USP40 Compact, Astra A70 (SA) and A75 (DA).

In **.357 SIG**, the Glock 32 and 33, and the SIG P-229.

In **9x19**, the Glock 19 and 26, SIG P-228 and P-239, AMT Backup, H&K USP9 Compact, Astra A70 (SA) and A75 (DA).

In **9x18**, the East German, Bulgarian, or Russian Makarov (they're identical except for the polishing), and the CZ. In .380, the stainless SIG P-230, the Walthers, AMT Backup, Sphinx AT-380M, the Makarov, and CZ83. In **.32ACP**, the NAA .32 Guardian, or Beretta Tomcat. In **.22LR**, the Beretta 21A, or *German* Walther TPH. Choose a stainless steel model over blue, if possible (the steel resists corrosion better). If it *feels* junky, then it probably *is*. Don't stray from my recommendations, as they're all fine guns, and there's something there to please any lady.

If you want a quick recommendation, go for the micro Glock in .40S&W (the Model 27), or .357 SIG (Model 33), or 9mm (Model 26). Get a 27 as the .40 is common and effective. If that's too powerful, then get the 9mm 26. Glocks work, *period*.

Revolvers

The choices are much simpler: a S&W or Taurus snubnose (.38 Special, .357 Magnum, or .44 Special) with a shrouded or concealed hammer, preferably in stainless steel.

How to daily carry your handgun

Experiment with many different carry methods. The better the concealment, the slower the draw. You'll have to decide on the right compromise between concealment vs. speed. A good gun purse is probably your best choice for off-body carry.

conceal holsters

I like ISW (inside waistband) holsters. They are very quick to draw from, but need to be covered by an untucked blouse, vest, sweater, or jacket.

ThunderWear or the PagerPal (from CTD, 817-625-7557) are *not* quick draw rigs, but provide *great* concealment. They require loose fitting slacks or skirt.

An inside-the-thigh holster under a dress will work fine for the smaller handguns. Buxom women can bra-conceal, though this is quite slow on the draw.

on-body conceal gear

These are items you wear vs. carry. Many common articles are now made for handguns, such as fanny packs, and even *faux* pagers (for the .32 Seecamp). The ActionPac (Ø54ppd; 800-472-2388; www.action-direct.com) under a T-shirt is great for jogging, etc.

off-body conceal gear
These are items you carry. There are many choices: purses, daytimers, soft attachés, and cell phone cases. Or, a simple jacket pocket will work. The downside to off-body carry is that you and your gun can become more easily separated.

So, which is *best*?
There is no "best." It all depends on your situation, which is dynamic. You will need two or three methods in order to carry all the time. I'd recommend on *and* off-body carry methods: An ActionPac (or fanny pack) and ISW holster for on-body, and a purse or daytimer for off-body.

Don't forget a *belt* holster and mag pouch for shooting school and open-carry opportunities (e.g., being in the country). Mad Dog Tactical gear (520-772-3021) is the best.

Handgun defensive ammo
This is expensive stuff at Ø1-3 per *round*. So what? Isn't your life *worth* that? **The best is MagSafe.** Glaser Silver (or Blue) Safety Slugs are a close second, followed by CorBon. MagSafe and Glaser come in 6rd packs; CorBon in a 20rd box. Less expensive but still very good are Remington Golden Saber, Starfire, Federal Hydra-Shok and Speer Gold Dot.

Handgun practice ammo
Any quality FMJ (full metal jacket, which means a copper shell without a hollowpoint). At gun shows you should buy it 500-1,000rds at a time for 12-17¢/rd, versus 50-70¢/rd at the store in the 20rd box. If you can't get to a gun show, then pick up a copy of the *Shotgun News* and have some shipped to you UPS. This bargain ammo is called "factory reloads" which means professionally reloaded from once-fired brass. Don't worry--this ammo is quite safe and reliable. (I let my girlfriend and my mother use it, if that comforts you.)

Training with your handgun
If you can't get to Thunder Ranch, etc., then at least go through a local concealed-carry course. These are at gunranges for Ø80-100 over a weekend, and will teach the basics of safe and effective gun handling. (You don't have to get the CCW permit afterwards, if you don't want to.)

Or, you might be fortunate enough to know a shooting academy alumnus who can teach you. It's not difficult or grueling stuff; just a few hours and 200rds will give you the basics.

Regarding husbands and boyfriends as instructors, that depends on his own weapons expertise, *and* how well you two do in the Teacher/Student scenario. Many men turn into their fathers and get too bossy. Many women turn into daughters and get too sensitive. If a session is not working out with your man, then politely say so and find a professional instructor.

Practicing with your handgun

Any unpracticed skill *will* erode over time. Get good training to imprint your short-term athletic memory, and then *practice* a lot in your first six months to imprint your *long*-term athletic memory. Find a gunrange you like (outdoors is better), and go there at least twice a month. Dryfire practice several times a week, if not every night. Keep your presentation, front sight acquisition, and trigger press crisp and second nature.

SHOTGUNS

Chapter Five applies equally to women. You might, however, prefer the lighter recoiling 20 gauge (which is nearly as effective as the 12ga), although most women can master the 12 gauge with proper training. The Remington 870 and Winchester 1300 Defender pump shotguns are excellent for home defense. Take an Awerbuck Yavapai Firearms Academy course.

Skeet, clays, and trap shooting are fun sports, with many women involved. The over/under barrel shotguns are rather expensive, but what can one expect from the "polo" of shooting.

RIFLES

In my experience, women naturally shoot rifles better than pistols. They just seem to "resonate" better with them. As long as you don't start out with a too powerful caliber with scary recoil, you'll enjoy shooting rifles. Start with a .22LR to learn the technique and bolster your confidence, then go to a .223 AR15. Handling the bigger calibers is merely something to work up to, and one simply stops where one feels comfortable. Again, with proper training, most women can enjoy the .308/.30-06 class of rifle power, and this suffices for most needs.

Defensive rifles

For indoor defense, a shotgun (with #2 birdshot) or a handgun is better choice given a rifle's penetration through walls. For a *rural* environment, however, a rifle is king.

The semi-auto AR15

Yeah, a .308 FAL is marvelous, but a lightweight, easy recoiling AR15 is a better choice for most women. It's better to hit with a BB gun than miss with a cannon, and the .223 is no BB gun. Besides, the AR15 is easy to work with, and after women struggle with the stupid controls of the AKs, they kiss the AR15. (So do the men.) For a semi-auto rifle, go with the AR15.

The lever-actions

If a Ø750-900 AR15 is too expensive, or you don't want a semi-auto, then the "mere" lever-action .30-30 will usually solve your problem. Most women like the western look and feel of lever-actions. Being more rugged and easier to load, the Marlin is a better choice than the Winchester 94. A used .30-30 Marlin goes for Ø150-190. This is a good deer hunting rifle, a good car rifle, and a good ranch rifle. Since the .30-30 is only a 250yd round, no scope is necessary on your Marlin. I'd simply replace the original rear sight with a Williams peep sight for Ø40.

A *real* sweetheart Marlin is the Model 1894 in .44 Magnum (which recoils less than the .30-30). The 1894 is a bit smaller and handier rifle than the .30-30, and you'll pay about Ø275 for a decent used one. With a 20" barrel it holds 10+1 (versus 6+1 in the .30-30). The rare 16"bbl "Limited" holds 7+1 and is as handy as an umbrella. I absolutely *love* mine.

If you want a lever-action in a more powerful caliber than the .30-30, then get a Browning BLR in .308. The BLR is very accurate, has a 4rd detachable mag, and scopes well. This is an excellent and handy 400yd rifle for hunting and defense.

The scoped bolt-action

First, let's talk about caliber. You want something powerful, accurate, and *common*. The .308 is ideal. It's quite effective, yet not a beast to shoot. Some women will think so and want a less powerful caliber, such as the .243 or .223. Since cartridges can be handloaded to more docile velocities, there's no reason to prefer a .243 over a .308. Get a .308, have some lighter ammo loaded for you, and it'll recoil as easy as a .243. Then, after practice, you can shoot the full power loads and enjoy what a .308 can accomplish. My point is this: A .308 can be downloaded to the recoil of a .243, but a .223 or .243 cannot be upped to .308 power.

Which bolt-action rifle in .308? The stainless steel Remington Model 7 is probably my favorite, but just about *any* Sako, Winchester, Ruger, or Remington will be fine. You might need an inch or so removed from the stock. (As a test, put the butt in the crook of your arm. You should be able to easily reach the trigger.) Don't skimp on the scope--get a nice 3-9X Burris or Leupold. Quality guns are a lifetime purchase, so expect to pay for that quality. Guns are *not* the things to save money on.

Hunting rifles

The .30-30 (use the 170gr bullets) is fine for 200yd deer and 75yd elk, but is too weak for longer shots. The .44 Magnum is *positively* limited to 100yd deer and 50yd elk--don't exceed!

The .308 is great for 400yd deer/250yd elk. If you want *more* power than a .308 (though such is necessary only for 250+yd elk), then the .30-06 or 7mmRM is probably the most you'll want to shoot. Author Ragnar Benson's wife shoots 1MOA groups at 800yds with a .300WM, so there *are* exceptions. If you can handle *and enjoy* the big Magnums, then you're beyond needing *my* advice on the matter. Safari in Alaska or Africa and bag some big game.

DEFENSIVE TACTICS--*BRIEFLY*

Stay alert and aware--Condition Yellow

Most assaults (and car "accidents") could have been *avoided* if the victim was in Condition Yellow at the time. A potential threat anticipated is a threat halved. When a lethal emergency arrives, you'll have *at most* only 3 seconds to draw and fire your handgun, and that's *not* enough time to go from Condition White directly to Red. Start from Yellow.

During a specific threat go to Condition Orange

When some creep is following you on the street, don't be shy. Immediately grip your handgun, and draw it, discreetly if you can. If the situation is *beyond* discretion, then draw it openly. Don't be shy--your *life* is at stake.

Never let any Condition Orange focus get within two car lengths of you. An athletic man can cover 20' in only 1½ seconds. Distance equals time, and you want as much time--therefore distance--as possible. If he *advances* on you, back up and maintain distance while drawing your handgun. **If he's a good guy,** *he will stop.* **If he** *doesn't* **stop, he's a** *bad* **guy.**

Conditions Red and Black

If he *continues* to advance on you even though he sees that you're armed, then he is not "lost." He doesn't need a quarter for the phone. A *fight* is imminent. He *will* harm you if you *let* him. He will rape you and throw your dead, disgraced body in the nearest dumpster. *Shoot* **him. Shoot him until he** *drops.* Do not listen to what he says. Heed not the innocent smile. Anybody advancing on an obviously scared and armed woman is a perp who should be shot *immediately.* If there's time for a verbal warning and you remember to give it, fine. If not, fine. His seeing your handgun should be warning enough.

A word about "warning shots"--*Don't.* A warning shot is a *purposeful miss,* and you *didn't* get trained to *miss.* Anytime you contradict your imprinted muscle memory, your *conscious* mind has to orchestrate the contradiction--before, during, and after. **There's** *no time.* The conscious mind is *too slow* and you *won't* be able to engage your subconscious training quickly enough to get your hits. Regardless of that, a warning shot wastes a round, and sends that bullet who knows where. Finally, legally speaking, you may not brandish or point a gun at a nonthreat. Conversely, if he's perceived to be a lethal threat, then why aren't you *stopping* him? The choice is clear: You *don't* shoot him, or you *do.* Tactically and legally, warning shots are a *big* mistake.

"What about just wounding him in the leg?" First of all, neither you or I are that good a shot to reliably hit a thin, moving target as the leg. And even if we *were,* a leg shot is not a reliable stopper. Studies of police shootings have proven this. No shooting academy trains for "mercy" shots. *Listen to me:* this dirtbag is about to mug/rape/kill you, you're scared shitless, and you need to stop his actions *immediately.* Body and head-shots only! Don't get fancy. **Have no mercy but for** *yourself.* Somebody should have dropped this sick creep in his socks years ago, but didn't. Now it's up to *you.* Shoot him and *live.*

Get this book

Armed & Female by Paxton Quigley is a great introduction to gun ownership for women. An ex-liberal and gun-control advocate, Ms. Quigley is one of women's champions. Then, join the Gunowners of America and get involved as a woman.

❖ 11

ODDS & ENDS

SO, *WHAT* GUNS SHOULD I HAVE?

Everybody's needs and tastes differ. Here's a guide:

Urbanites

Your weapon needs will be much different from those of us in the country. Your primary need is to repel nearby boarders.

Dirt poor (only Ø80-165)

At the *very* least, get an Ø80 Marlin Model 60 .22LR rifle. Better yet is a Ø110 S&W Model 10 .38 Special, or a more concealable Ø165 Makarov 9x18 pistol.

Rather poor (above, plus Ø200)

Get a Winchester Defender 12ga. Birdshot #2 is fine.

Lower middle-class (above, plus Ø80-175)

The above pistol and shotgun, plus a rifle. Find a Ø80 Lee-Enfield No.4 Mk.I, a Ø100 SKS, a Ø175 SKS/AK mag, or a Ø175 Marlin .30-30. Also, get the Ø80 Marlin .22LR, if you can.

Middle-class (above, plus Ø1,500 on)

A Glock 27. An AMT 10/22. An AR15. Perhaps a backup handgun. Training and ammo.

Upper middle-class (above, plus Ø1,500 on)

The immediate above, plus two more rifles: a battle .308 and a Level 1 scoped .308 bolt-action.

Filthy rich

Buy a ranch and leave the city. The metros don't deserve you. At least have a helicopter on the roof with a full tank of gas to fly you out when the cities implode.

Rural folks
More emphasis on working and long-range weapons.

Dirt poor (only Ø160)
A Lee-Enfield No.4 Mk.I for Ø80. With this you can hunt and/or defend yourself. Cut it down to carbine length. Also get a Marlin 60 .22LR rifle for Ø80.

Rather poor (above, plus Ø110-200)
An inexpensive handgun (Makarov, S&W 10, CZ52).

Lower middle-class (above, plus Ø365)
An SKS, Marlin .30-30, and Ruger .22LR pistol.

Middle-class (above, plus Ø2,000 on)
A Level 1 scoped, bolt-action .308. A battle .223. A Glock (23, 27, 21, 30). An AMT 10/22 rifle. Training and *lots* of ammo.

Upper middle-class (above, plus Ø2,000 on)
A Remington 870. A .308 FAL. A Level 3 sniper rifle. Some backup handguns. More training. *If you can afford it*, then also get a .44 Mag revolver, a Level 4 sniper rifle, and a duplicate arsenal for offsite storage.

Filthy rich
Have fun. Build a shooting range. Get a Level 5 .338L and a .50BMG. Night vision goggles and scopes. Radios. Ghillie suits. Get *all* the training. Invite me over for a visit.

PURCHASING YOUR GUNS

Here's a half page from Chapter 14 *Privacy & Your Guns* in my book *Bulletproof Privacy*, which you should already have.

Buying privately
In 24 states Americans can still privately buy and sell firearms without any forms, paperwork or registration. In many cities there is a classified ad section for guns (under "Guns" or "Firearms" or "Sporting Goods"). Call from a pay phone and pay cash.

Or, go to a gun show and seek out the private sale tables (they'll usually advertise this with a little sign). At gun shows, beware of anybody suggesting that you participate in any unlawful activity, such as "straw sales" (buying a gun for somebody forbidden to buy it themselves). If this happens, it's probably a BATF agent trying to set you up. Threaten to alert the police if he persists. BATman or not, he'll leave at once.

The FFL
If you buy or sell through a federal firearm licensee (FFL), then you must fill out a Form 4473. These forms are, illegally, being photocopied or scanned by BATF agents for the growing national database. Avoid FFLs if at all possible. A friend will often do this for you, claiming later that he sold it at a show.

Record keeping
I'd record all of your guns and their serial numbers in an encrypted file (PGP is fine), and hide the diskette off site. This way, you can report any guns being stolen, if necessary. Do *not* keep a "master list" of your guns on paper--*ever*!

TRAINING
Gun school-- *"learning, then forgetting"*
Until you've been to a good shooting academy, you can't appreciate what you *don't* know about defensive firearm handling. Long-term muscle memory of these techniques requires *3,000* repetitions, which is infeasible from any course, but these schools *can* imprint your *short-term* athletic memory (which takes only 300 repetitions). The remaining 2,700 repetitions you'll be able to practice at home on your own--and that's the *goal* of gun school; teaching quality skills to the point of mature self-sufficiency. Learn the techniques and ingrain them forever so that you can "forget" (consciously). Do you have to remember how to catch a ball? No, you've learned and "forgotten" it. You just *do* it. Defensive gun handling must be *just* as ingrained, or else you'll *lose* the fight, and maybe your *life*. **In any crisis you'll only do what's already been *imprinted* on your *subconscious*.** No imprint means a "nothing" response.

While there are now a couple of dozen schools, I recommend the following as the best currently available.

Thunder Ranch
HCR 1, Box 53, Mountain Home, **Texas** 78058
830-640-3138/3183fax
Founded/operated by Clint Smith (of the ITC road shows), Thunder Ranch offers extensive courses in all small arms on a 900ac. ranch in the Texas Hill Country (NW of Kerrville). Facil-

ities and instructors are excellent. I recommend starting with Pistol 1 and Urban Rifle 1. Each are 5-day courses costing Ø900. The five on-site cabins at Ø70/day are convenient and well-equipped. Fly to San Antonio or Austin and rent a car. Ship your ammo to TR ahead of time (include 200 extra rounds).

If some nosy guy asks about your Thunder Ranch T-shirt or ball cap, reply that it's a summer camp for weathermen.

Chuck Taylor's American Small Arms Academy
P.O. Box 12111, Prescott, **Arizona** 86304
520-778-5623 phone/fax

In January 1997, the Swiss Army and Air Force formally adopted Taylor's techniques and training system, making him the only individual trainer in the world whose methods have been adopted by a major military power. That's quite a recommendation! Offering courses in defensive handgun (4-day; Ø750), precision rifle (7-day; Ø1,200), and submachine gun (2-day; Ø650), Chuck Taylor's courses are a bargain.

Fly to Phoenix and rent a car for the 90 mile drive to Prescott. Hotels and motels abound.

Yavapai Firearms Academy
P.O. Box 27290, Prescott Valley, **Arizona** 86312
520-772-8262

You'll like no-nonsense Louis Awerbuck, renowned for his excellent shotgun courses. Louis teaches by doing, unlike many instructors. Paladin Press sells his video and book.

Bill Rogers School of Weaponcraft
Rog-Con, 1736 St. John's Bluff Rd., Jacksonville, Florida 32246
904-641-5404

A champion pistol shooter, holster designer for Safariland, and inventor of the Rogers Sure-Fire Flashlight Technique, Bill is a relaxed, easygoing instructor who personally demonstrates every drill. Catering primarily to the military, he fortunately offers four pistol classes each year to civilians.

His Ellijay, **Georgia** range is quite innovative--all head shots. Each shooting lane has seven pneumatically-operated/computer-controlled steel plates at ranges from 7 to 25 yards. They pop up at random and remain for as little as ½ second. Speedy, exciting stuff! You *will* learn your front sight. Unless you've gone through other intermediate-level courses at TR, etc., and have done *lots* of dryfire practice, start with the basic class.

I recommend the Ø700 class with room-and-board deal. Fly to Atlanta and rent a car to Ellijay. Send ammo prior class.

What about Gunsite Training Center?

Originally founded by Jeff Cooper as the American Pistol Institute, it has been under new ownership since 1993. Depending on whom you talk to, the quality of instruction and facilities is not the same. It certainly is not the equal of Thunder Ranch. GTC seems to cater more to the feds, unfortunately.

Jeff and Janelle still live on-site at the Sconce and graciously welcome old "Family Members" and friends. *If,* however, you are taking a GTC course, don't expect much warmth from the Coopers (who will chide you for supporting *"Brand X."*) It's a long story, with one best remaining uninvolved.

Training videos

Paladin Press and GunVideo (800-942-8273) offer many of these, which are good for those who can't get to a school. Go in with some shooting buddies and get the collection. Then, go out and *train.*

GEAR

This subject deserves an entire book, so I'll just hit the highlights. First of all, you shouldn't shoot what you can't identify, so get a Laser Products Sure-Fire flashlight (from CTD). Every pistol needs holsters (Mad Dog Taylor ThunderBolt for belt; ISW; Bagmaster fanny pack, PagerPal or ThunderWear for deep concealment), mag and Sure-Fire pouch (from Mad Dog). Every long gun needs a sling (1¼" heavy web is fine). Get a multitool by Leatherman, SOG, or Gerber. Eye protection (shatterproof, 99% UV blockage--sunglasses, and yellow lens for night). Ear protection (orange foam earplugs for rifle work, muffs for pistol; Walker's Tact'l-Ear for tactical work, 800-424-1069). For tactical vests, go Eagle or London Bridge. Steiner 7x50 binoculars. Leupold spotting scope with Mil-Dots.

SIGHTING IN

Your zeros will change with different bullet weights, powder loads, case brand, and even primers. Every rifle is an enigma regarding its optimal load. You'll have to experiment with handloads to find the tastiest combination. Start with the proven winners in the reloading guides, and work from there.

Battle rifles

For military-style rifles with adjustable rear sights, the front sight is usually adjustable for basic elevation. An AR15 is adjustable with a bullet tip, whereas the FAL, SKS and AK all need an AK front sight tool (only Ø10). Using the most reliable feeding and consistently accurate ammo available for your rifle, set the rear sight at 100 and adjust the front sight if necessary.

Rule: Move the front sight *opposite* to how you want the bullet to move. (If impact is too high, then front sight is too low.) Move the rear sight in the *direction* of desired bullet impact.

If you might use different ammo (e.g., 55 *and* 62gr .223), then test them against your primary ammo and make notes for field use. Tape a card to your rifle's buttstock.

Scoped rifles

If your scope has a BDC cam, then set at 100 and test with the necessary ammo. Once zeroed at 100, test at all other cam distances. Know for sure how precise the compensation is.

If your scope does not have a BDC, then you should zero for MPBR (which is usually 225-300yds--check the reloading manuals), or for 200 or 300yds and have holdovers marked on a taped card. (Holdovers more than 36" are very difficult to make. You'll need a Mil-Dot reticle past 400yds.) I also recommend the temperature-calculated Ballisticard Systems from Schwiebert Precision (805-461-3954) for only Ø15.

If your scope has Mil-Dots, then zero at 300yds and know your comeups. Mark them on a taped card. (Premier Reticle can add Mil-Dots to any quality scope for Ø100. A "must.")

For .308/.30-06 hunting rifles, I'd create three loads: deer, bad guy, and elk. The deer bullet will be a 150gr Nosler Ballistic Tip or Sierra GameKing, the bad guy bullet a 168-180gr Sierra HPBT MatchKing, and the elk bullet a 150+gr Barnes X. Zero for each. The lighter bullets will print higher. (If I could have only *one* .308/.30-06 load for *everything,* then I'd go with a 180gr Sierra GameKing at 2600/2750fps.)

AMMO

You *must* test your ammo in its gun. You must have reliable, *firsthand* knowledge that it fits in your mag, feeds perfectly, chambers easily, fires accurately, and extracts cleanly. If using any defensive pistol ammo other than hardball, then test it thoroughly. If you've chosen MagSafe or CorBon, spend the Ø on three test boxes. Don't trust your life to any assumptions!

In a pinch you should at least rack test several mags (with the safety on, if possible), but live fire is the only way to make *absolutely* sure. I learned this on an SKS which dry-racked perfectly but jammed at the range.

Buy only reputable ammo. Saving 2¢/round with Earl's Ammo is *not* the place to be economical. I once bought 100rds of generic 62gr .223 at a bargain price, only to learn that 3" groups at 50yds were the norm.

Save your brass. Even if you don't reload, somebody else does. One day, brass will be like gold.

Reloading

While I don't bother handloading my practice pistol and rifle ball (I get it by the case), I do handload my bolt and lever action ammo. For this, a simple single-stage press is fine. With scale, Redding powder measure, case trimmers, priming tool, dies, tumbler, caliper, kinetic bullet puller, screwdrivers, punches, etc. you can get started for under Ø300. If you need a progressive reloader, then go Dillon Press (800-762-3845; www.dillonprecision.com). I like the RL650.

Buy some good basic reloading manuals and apprentice under a buddy who has the experience. If you're reloading for only a few calibers, then the cartridge specific manuals by Loadbooks USA (Ø8; 800-676-8920) are a bargain. You'll see them often at gun shows.

Brass

Buy new brass and chamber fire-form for each rifle (don't mix them up). Use a neck-sizer die instead of the full-length die for more consistent brass with less stretching. Keep track of how many times each case has been reloaded. Brass varies significantly with different manufacturers. Military brass is usually heavier (less case volume, thus more pressure) than civilian brass. Research and test thoroughly. For near-max loads, pay *strict* attention to the make of brass.

Powder

While powder drops are pretty accurate, I prefer to *individually* weigh by digital scale all sniper and near-max loads.

The Finnish VihtaVuouri powders are excellent, providing the highest velocities and best accuracy. It gives a .308 the extra 100fps velocity of a .30-06. VV is a dollar more per pound, but in .308 that works out to only ½¢/rd.

Primers

These are more critical than you might think. For best accuracy, Federal Bench Rest primers are king. For everything else, I like CCI, but Winchester, Remington are fine, too.

CLEANING

Since modern American primers are no longer corrosive, immediate and thorough bore cleaning is not vital. Unless I'm putting away my semi-autos for storage, I generally clean them only every 200rds. Bolt-actions I clean after every session. My Glocks easily go past 500rds without needing attention, but I keep them spotless, nonetheless.

Cleaning products

For bore cleaner, Shooter's Choice or Sweet's. For wet lubricant, BreakFree or Prolix. Sentry Solutions (800-546-8049) makes superb *dry* lubricants. Use Dewey nylon-coated cleaning rods and guides. You'll need brass jags and brushes. Dillon Press has it all if your local gunshop doesn't. Also, get an aerosol can of Gunscrubber to loosen caked powder residue.

Cleaning technique

For greasy military stuff, use a disposable paint brush, plastic pan, and a gallon of low odor mineral spirits (Ø2.50). Soak the parts to cheaply and easily loosen and melt the gunk, then clean as usual and lubricate.

Rule: If possible, clean from chamber towards muzzle, the direction the bullet goes. (Some rifles don't allow this.)

Apply bore solvent onto your brass brush (do *not* dip the brush in the bottle, contaminating all), and one-way scrub the bore, detaching the brush at the muzzle. Spray off the brush. Next, attach the jag and push wet patches through one pass each until *clean*. (This'll take 10-20 patches. Be patient.) When clean, send a wet brush through the bore again, and repeat with patches. When clean, *lightly* coat bore with BreakFree patch.

Clean and lubricate your slide/bolt and its rails. Any rust spots should *immediately* be removed with oil and 0000 steel wool. (Flitz metal polish also works well, and without wool. It's safe on all finishes.) Wipe exposed surfaces with a *light* coat of BreakFree. Occasionally, you should remove the stock and clean out all the accumulated gunk. If the gun is to be stored, cover the muzzle with a piece of tape or stick in a foam earplug. (You can safely shoot through such if you forget to remove it.)

Yeah, all this is a pain, but accuracy and reliability aren't convenient. (Beats throwing rocks.) Spend the time and money your guns deserve, and they won't let you down.

SPARE PARTS

Gun parts *will* break and wear out. Expect it. Also, count on availability of spare parts to evaporate in the future because of the increasingly hostile regulatory environment. If the feds locked up the Gun Parts Corp., thousands of gunowners would have paperweights overnight. Get the parts you'll need, *now*.

Firing pins, extractors, and small internal springs are the most universally needed parts. Hi-cap mag springs will weaken from lengthy loadings. Finally, every gun has its "Achille's heal" or two, so find out now and stock up. You should also have exploded parts diagrams for each weapon.

THINGS TO BUY *NOW!*

First of all, get your unpapered handguns and battle rifles. Then, buy plenty of ammo, spare parts, mags, etc. for each. Next, get trained at a quality shooting academy.

The following list is based on my view of what will be outlawed *sooner* versus later. **Bold items you should get *first*.**

Rifles

Get a .50BMG while you *can*. With some diligence, you can actually find them for private sale in your local paper.

Mag-fed semi-autos (FALs and AR15s). Stick with .223 and .308 rifles, as 7.62x39 ammo will dry up quickly.

Handguns

Unpapered quality guns. Pick up every 9mm/.40/.45 Glock you can afford, as they work perfectly right out of the box, rarely break, and are easiest to train with. Unpapered 26s and

27s you should immediately snap up, as well as the 21s and 30s. The 17/19s and 22/23s are secondary to the micros and the .45s. The 10mm 20/29s are too caliber uncommon, sadly.

Stock up on bargain trading *wampum* guns (S&W 10, Makarov, FEG, CZ, etc.). Finally, highly concealable pistols will be *very* desirable in the coming years.

Shotguns

Rifled slug barrels and mag tube extensions are soon to be *cosas non grata*. Specialty ammo (slugs, Dragonsbreath, flechettes, etc.) should be acquired now.

Ammo

I forecast that **.50BMG ammo** will be outlawed soon. Have 500rds of *very* accurate handloads, and 1,000rds of ball. Dial in and practice with this rifle while you can.

Stock up on defensive handgun bullets, match rifle bullets (Sierra HPBT MatchKing), primers, and the powder you need.

Parts and accessories

High-capacity mags. Soon, you'll wish you bought even some of those cheesy 10rd mags.

Spare parts for all your guns. Scopes and rings.

Miscellaneous gear

Night vision devices and infrared lasers. Great high-tech stuff which offers a huge tactical edge to the user. We soon won't have access to this. Expensive, but worth it. Sell your jet ski if you have to. **Bulletproof vests** from Second Chance.

Reloading equipment. Dump your weird calibers and concentrate on the common stuff.

YOUR SPARE WEAPONS

It's just plain foolish to keep *all* your guns in one place. At home, have only what is needed to defend yourself and, if necessary, fight your way out. *Everything else* should be stored someplace away from your home or business.

Storing spare weapons

A storage unit, rented under an alias or by a friend, is a decent option. Long-term food (if the unit stays cool enough), extra ammo, documents, etc. should also be stored.

In my *Bulletproof Privacy* I discuss the RV-in-the-country idea, which is very practical. Buy a Ø3-8,000 RV and park it on some old rancher's property for Ø50/month. Keep your mouth shut about it. You'll have a cheap, self-sufficient retreat site.

Caching (burying) weapons

All illegal weapons (unregistered Title II stuff, full-auto parts and plans, silencers, reverted post-ban guns, etc.) should be *buried*. Don't store any such items at home.

What to cache

Include ammo, mags, mag pouches, spare parts, cleaning and loading supplies, tools, and latex gloves with each gun so that every cache is self-sufficient. Every rifle cache should also include a spare pistol and holster. Try to imagine under what situations you'd have to retrieve your cache, and what your physical condition might be. Will you be tired, hungry, cold, or broke? Some cash, gold coins, food bars, flashlight (lithium batteries only), etc. might be handy. Remember, retrieving a cache is a last-resort, *Oh, shit!* option, so think it through well.

Guns should be lightly coated with BreakFree and sealed in waterproof plastic gun bags with desiccant. Ammo should be separately packed. Use disposable latex gloves to leave no fingerprints on the contents or the pipe.

Caching materials

PVC 8-10" sewer pipe with silicone-sealed watertight caps and internal desiccant is the best thing for caching. Buy this pipe out of town with cash; multiple, traceable purchases are a red flag to caching activity. Burn the receipts.

Where to cache

If cached stuff is found on private property, the land could be seized. Use National Forest or BLM land. Pick a spot *far* from any hiking trail or inviting campsite, where runoff is not a problem. Besides making a detailed map, I'd GPS notate the location and encrypt it. Trees and rocks are *not* utterly permanent landmarks, so don't rely too heavily on them. Use a posthole digger, and dig deeply enough to have at least 2' of earth on top of your container. A nylon rope or strap looped underneath with an extra 3' on top will assist in pulling out the pipe when you retrieve it (use a notched 2x4 to lever up the thing). Cover the container with a small tarp to deflect water.

Visually check every year that the site is undisturbed. Obviously, make certain that you're not followed.

WHEN THE RAIDS COME

First, they'll visit the homes on their gun registration lists. If you're on the list, prepare yourself for a knock at the door. **Do *not* let them in under *any* circumstance!** Speak to them through a closed door, and reply, *"If I were a gunowner, you can be sure that I would comply with all applicable laws. Beyond that, I've got nothing else to say. Good day, officers."*

Later, they'll get around to List #2--the problem children. By then, you should have *moved*, or at least hidden your prohibited guns out of town/state. If you haven't, then the choice of "Pass or Play" will be forced upon you. Know in advance what you'll do, and make necessary preparations.

The raids *will* come. The freedom-haters are far too committed to back down on the gun issue. If only to save face, the raids will be ordered. When that happens, the gloves are off, folks. Give up your guns and expect the camps a few years later. Do not be "declawed"! Get tough *now*, because you'll need to be tough later--and toughness (like a callus) is built up over years, not created in the moment. Steel yourself for all this now, as it'll be too late to grow a penis later.

❖ 12

WEALTH VS. LIBERTY

Here's how the 2nd Amendment was *supposed* to work:

> The Second Amendment is a recognition of the danger of standing armies. Its purpose is to recognize that every citizen has the right to keep and bear the same type of basic arms as a soldier in the modern military. A militia embodies all able-bodied men over the age of sixteen. **Therefore, a militia will always outnumber a standing army by at least twenty to one.** If this militia is armed with weapons similar to those used by the individuals comprising the standing army, **it will be impossible for that standing army to inflict the will of a tyrannical government upon the people.** The Second Amendment is the guarantee behind all the other articles in the Bill of Rights. It is the ultimate guarantee that citizens in the United States [of America] will remain free.
>
> -- John Ross; *Unintended Consequences* (1996), p. 47

Well, what *happened*? **If we're so armed, why aren't we free?** Because too many Americans are *wimps*.

Arms are one thing; the *will* to use them is another. Tools without users are worthless. So, the 2nd Amendment doesn't actually assure freedom for it can neither guarantee the citizens' *dedication* to freedom nor their *courage* to maintain it at all costs. No constitutional amendment can do that. As Judge Learned Hand so eloquently explained it for the ages:

> I often wonder whether we do not rest our hopes too much upon constitutions, upon laws and upon courts. These are false hopes, believe me, these are false hopes. **Liberty lies in the hearts of men and women;** when it dies there, no constitution, no law, no court can even do much to help it. **While it lies there it needs no constitution, no law, no court to save it.**

We have grown to love comfort, ease and convenience more than liberty. Today, we can hardly be roused over *anything*.

Yes, we did produce a near perfect Republic. But will they keep it, or will they, in the enjoyment of plenty, lose the memory of freedom. Material abundance without character is the surest way to destruction.
  -- Thomas Jefferson

What is lacking in this country is a climate of unrest. A certain air of mewling discontent does exist, but it is too similar to the affectionate bickering young lovers indulge in as they jockey for the role identities that will endure between them for the rest of their married lives. Except for your criminal elements, who through circumstances or choice are the pariahs of any society, I defy you to find nowadays any of the implacable ferocity that must have been extant in the Jacobin, Cromwellian, pre-Revolutionary American, and Czarist-ruled societies.
  -- Oliver Lange, *Defiance* (1971), p. 417

Based on my past six years of attending Patriot meetings, I can say with sad certainty that we will not be roused until we suffer a few more atrocities. Collectively, Americans have much more pain to endure before we wake up. We'll need another Pearl Harbor. The next Waco-type massacre might do it.

We scaled the mountain but have grown fat, dumb and lazy on the peak. Now, we're sliding back down. It's a human cycle, and we simply went through it faster than any other civilization, that's all. We're not *quite* through, but very close.

Part of any serious program of economic and political survival is that of mental and psychological conditioning. It is not sufficient to stock up on your supplies of dehydrated fruits and gold coins. The rifle you bought is no better than your determination to use it and your ability to use it. This means that you have to have some sort of guideline when and under what circumstances to use it. In a time of true terror, which I hope never comes, but which cannot be dismissed lightly, each man must have a mental line drawn, over which his opponent cannot step at zero risk. The drawing of that line is probably more important than other physical preparations. Where a man's treasure is, there is his heart. What am I getting at? Simple: all of your preparations should be aimed at preserving your freedom first, and only secondarily aimed at protecting your wealth. Your wealth is simply a tool for expanding your productivity under freedom. Your wealth must not be allowed to capture you, to chain you to the ground while the wolves plan your demise. Get this into your mind early: your wealth is your tool to utilize freedom, not your enemy's tool of dominion over you. The soft underbelly of America is here: our inability to understand the proper use of wealth. We cling to our wealth as if it could save us in a major crisis.

We have confused means with ends, and we have worshipped means.
-- Dr. Gary North; *The Pirate Economy,* pp. 180-1

Alexander Solzhenitsyn in his profound *The Gulag Archipelago* discussed the necessity of an *early* resistance to tyranny:

...At what exact point, then, should one resist the communists?...How we burned in the prison camps later thinking: what would have things been like if every security operative, when he went out at night to make an arrest, had been uncertain whether he would return alive and had to say good-bye to his family?

Or if during periods of mass arrests people had not simply sat there in their lairs, paling with terror at every step on the staircase, **but had understood they had nothing to lose** and had boldly set up in the downstairs hall an ambush of half a dozen people with axes, hammers, pokers, or whatever else was at hand... **The** [police] **would have quickly suffered a shortage of officers...and notwithstanding all of Stalin's thirst, the cursed machine would have ground to a halt.**

If...If... **We didn't love freedom enough.** And even more--we had no awareness of the real situation. We spent ourselves in one unrestrained outburst in 1917, and then we hurried to submit. We submitted with pleasure! ...We purely and simply deserved everything that happened afterward.

Americans, we ultimately have *nothing* to *lose*. Quit worrying about your precious stuff--they don't put luggage racks on hearses. **Our vast material wealth is Delilah's shears to our strength.**

Better a sovereign in squalor than a slave in splendor.
-- Dresden James

A slave with weekends off is not 2/7ths free.
-- Boston T. Party

I've given a lot of thought to exactly *how* our wealth buys off our independent spirit, and I've come up with a few ideas on resetting our priorities. (No, we don't have to live in a cave with one set of homespun clothing.)

HAVING WEALTH *AND* FREEDOM
Long-term *liberty*, not comfort, is the goal
Modern slaves are comfortable. They don't even have to think for themselves; they only have to do as they're told. If,

however, *you* want to deliberately live an "examined life" of your own, then freedom-of-action will supercede comfort. (For now, at least.) Liberty and comfort are *somewhat* mutually exclusive, so choose *now* and quit bitching. Besides, there's a peculiar comfort to liberty, so if you focus on liberty, comfort will follow. In fact, only in liberty lies *true* comfort.

Wealth is *expendable*
Wealth is not an end, but a *means* for Liberty

Get this through your head *now* if you've chosen Liberty. Regardless of what happens to us after we're dead, it seems fairly well settled that we *don't* get to use our earthly stuff. Our wealth is here while *we're* here, and moot when we're gone.

We don't actually get to own *anything* down here. We just get to *use* it for a few years. Everything is "rented" including our bodies, so treat "your" stuff like that rental car--pedal to the floor. If the tires aren't smoking when you turn it in, then you didn't get your daily Ø39.95's worth. Use wealth to maximize liberty for yourself and for your children. Wealth is *expendable*.

Maintain income, lower your living standard

My income could drop by half and I wouldn't know the difference. Why not? Because I live *beneath* my means. I do not "live for today." I forsake much of the comfort I *could* enjoy today for future value.

Don't waste your disposable income on transitory entertainment and luxuries. Don't put your investment capital in stocks, bonds, or mutuals. Invest in yourself--knowledge, training, and tools--things which will increase your chances of future survival and prosperity.

Your biggest expense is probably for shelter. Living beneath your means requires shelter less than you "deserve." Trade down your 5/4 for a 3/2, or your 3/2 for a 2/1 mobile home. After a bit of adjustment, you won't miss your fancy digs. As long as your home is sufficiently spacious, warm, dry, and cheery--what else *really* matters? It's all *attitude,* folks.

For example, if you save Ø300 per month in rent or mortage for just one year, then you can buy a .308 FAL battle rifle *and* send yourself to Thunder Ranch for training. In only one year, you will have acquired something priceless--especially since you will not be *allowed* to buy such a tool or its training for too much longer. Do this for *two* years and you can include 12 months of excellent food storage, a good handgun and some gold coins. Do this for *three* years, and you can go back to Thunder Ranch for Pistol 1 and Rifle 2. Do this for *four* years, and you can buy a small used RV and store it on somebody's country property. Do this for *five* years, and you can buy a few acres yourself to eventually build on.

Actually, this could be done in just *two* years with deeper cutbacks and harder work. *Backwood Homes* had a story of an Oregon *waitress* who bought some country acreage and built her own log home in just a few years from tips and salary. If you want it badly enough, *anything* can be accomplished. What's *your* excuse--you're not some single waitress in rural Oregon?

You all would be surprised if you knew how modestly I live. Conversely, you all would also be shocked if you knew how much I had salted away. I tallied it up recently, and was shocked myself. This is not to brag, but to reassure you that Boston T. Party "walks the walk." Most Patriot authors *don't*. I know of one who can't find his Mini14 right now. (Hint: It's either under the entertainment center or behind the waterbed.)

Fractionalize your assets
Have 2x50%, or 3x33%--not 1x100%

Remember our goal: Liberty, not comfort. Americans don't rock the boat because they basically don't want to lose their precious stuff. Their precious stuff is all in one big, pretty basket--and this is tactical leverage against the owner. One simple raid can clean out the unprepared dissident. He can go from fat and comfy to hungry and cold in an afternoon. The IRS has done this to *thousands* of Americans already.

The solution? Have smaller eggs in several baskets. I recommend living on 50% and having 2 other 25% places. Having ½ your assets elsewhere does two vital things for you:

❶   You won't be as likely to make some tactically futile stand for 50% as you might for the whole 100%.

❷   It gives you someplace else of your own to go to if your public/primary pad gets raided or seized.

What goes in your private hide-outs

Most of your guns, food storage, how-to books, "subversive" materials, tools, cash and gold. These are your "Mr. Hyde" places. Keep your "Dr. Jekyll" home squeaky clean.

What remains in your public/primary home

Guns: only enough to fight your way *out*. This means at most per person: two handguns and one long gun. Long guns for a family of four (assuming the children are of rifle bearing age) might be a scoped bolt, two battle rifles and a shotgun. You won't be able to lug anything more than that with you, much less wield it in your two busy hands. Extra guns should be stored at locations 2 and 3. If battle rifles are forbidden in your city/state and you don't want to be at risk, then have instead bolt-action Lee-Enfields or Mausers, or lever-action .30-30s. *Any* decent .30 caliber rifle will do if *you* will do.

Food storage for a month. If a crisis lasts longer than *that*, then you don't want to remain in the city, anyway. Don't prepare to outlast some siege. Get out when (preferably *before*) it looks ugly--you can always go back home later.

Bugout packs for every member. One should already be in every car (including rifle, though maybe not semi-auto). Notarized copies of all important documents. Passports. Spare eyeglasses. Medicines. Ø1,000+/person. Gold coins (¼s and ½s).

Vehicles: A 4x4 with trailer (already packed with "camping" gear, etc.). Gasoline for at least 600 miles per vehicle (1,000 is much better). Radios. Spare parts. Tools. Tires. Enough gear to get you out, but not so much to bog you down.

Now, get *rugged*

You've removed much of the negative tactical leverage of wealth and assets. You are the master of your stuff, not vice-versa. Now, you need to toughen up yourself.

I know many great Patriots and Libertarians who have all the right gear, but no calluses. Gear alone won't do it. **It's the *man*, not the gun. The *man* is the weapon system--the gun is just a tool.** Get to every shooting school you can afford. Take up martial arts, preferably at a *dojo* where there's *lots* of sparring. Shun modern comfort and camp out for a week or two at a time. Go the gym regularly, lose that gut and *get in shape*. Backpack with your rifle--become "as one" with it. Get *rugged*!

❖ 13

PREPARING
FOR THE WORST

The strongest reason for the people to retain the right to keep (own)
and bear (carry) *arms is, as a last resort,* **to protect themselves**
against tyranny in government.
-- Thomas Jefferson

We are fast arriving at our point of no return--if we're not there
already. I see little chance of successful reforms. The Freedom
Movement began too late, and we probably *won't* acquire the
necessary mass influence for political change. We're almost
assuredly past political solutions, anyway, so let's now focus on
what we've probably been forced to resolve ourselves to--a
resistance movement.

I estimate that there are about 500,000 hard-core, "damn-
the-torpedos," liberty-loving Americans who will *never* give in
to tyranny. Maybe it's 100,000, or only 36,000 (the IRA's per
capita numbers extrapolated here). Although 36,000 is only one
in every 2,083 gunowners, it's still a lot of people, numerically.
Percentage wise, we're negligible, but that's merely a *political*
disadvantage.

There are 200 million guns in 75 million private American
hands. **Even if *99%* of the guns could be collected, *there***
would still be 2 million left. The only guns *successfully*
confiscated will be from those owners *who know in advance* that
they will never resist--those who value sandwiches over
freedom, temporary comfort over indelible honor.

The rest of us (and I devoutly hope this includes you) will
not--will *never*--give up our arms. If liberty-loving Americans

are treated so shabbily *when we have guns,* then how much *more* brutal will the treatment be if we are *disarmed?* If the fedgoons are *this* bold, when they can be easily shot at, imagine their savagery if we give up our tools for self-defense.

> *...Guard with jealous attention the public liberty. Suspect every one who approaches that jewel.* **Unfortunately, nothing will preserve it but downright force. Whenever you give up that force, you are inevitably ruined.**
> -- Patrick Henry, 5 June 1788

> **No slave shall keep any arms whatever,...**
> -- A Bill Concerning Slaves, Virginia Assembly (1779)

No, we will never allow ourselves to be defanged. Well, then, what are our chances? What odds do only 100,000 recalcitrant gun owners have? An historical example offers a clue:

> *"Let me summarize: Ireland is an island* [about the size of Arkansas].   *Residents there have to store their weapons at government-sanctioned gun clubs. Anyone with a relative even suspected of belonging to the IRA cannot own a gun, cannot belong to such a club, and must go outside the country if he wants to shoot at paper targets.   The Special Air Service has quite a bit more...latitude in dealing with terrorists that we have here, and the SAS is one of the finest fighting units in the world. It is fully the equal of our own Special Forces.* **And for decades, the SAS has been held at bay by a group...similar in number to the spectators at an average American Little League baseball game. Is that about right?"** *"Spot on," the SAS Major said...*
> -- John Ross; *Unintended Consequences* (1996), p. 730

Some thoughts on the bureaucrats

> *The bureaucrats and politicians do not fear armed criminals or armed political zealots as much as they fear peaceful Americans who will probably never use their* [so-called] *assault rifles, but whose mental toughness may be enhanced by possession of military weapons.*
> *The gun controllers are not deterred by the facts about guns and crime,* **because their primary fear is not of criminals. They fear ordinary Americans whose lives and freedom their policies are destroying. In this fear and in their world, they are on target.**
> -- Arthur B. Robinson, Ph.D.; *Access to Energy,* Vol. 21, #11

The front cover of Dr. Gary North's excellent book *Government By Emergency* beautifully illustrates this point: a bald, wimpy bureaucrat with a clipboard flanked by two thug cops brandishing shotguns to enforce his edicts.

Bureaucrats are *weenies*. I learned this firsthand in 1991 when I was writing *Good-Bye April 15th!* and had to get some sample IRS forms at their district HQ. Having picked up forms months earlier, I knew in which building they were kept, but what I *didn't* know was that "customer service" had been moved into *another building* entirely. I was in the wrong place. I casually walked past the newly placed security guard and entered. Although no forms were displayed as before and the office had been rearranged, I nonetheless pleasantly and confidently requested to be supplied with the forms on my list. The drones seemed quite confused and asked if I was with the EEOC ("Equal Employment Opportunity Commission"), which confused me. When they finally realized that I was a mere member of the *public*, they all but panicked and called for security. I was escorted outside by the same guy who had let me walk right in (wearing "Mad Max" motorcycle garb, no less). You see, they felt all warm and safe and fuzzy because of their "security"--until my visit. I have often savored the memory of their faces flooding with terror, *over nothing*.

Congressmen, judges, bureaucrats--they're all *weenies*. Without their black-suited ninja thugs, they're nothing. If the government pushes things much further, these thugs will have their hands full. **Even if American revolutionaries number to only the IRA's per capita, it still equates to 36,000.** The feds simply simply don't have enough trained people to handle 36,000 righteously pissed off Americans. That averages to 720 revolutionaires per state. So relax, but stay alert.

The federal ninja are preparing...
Honed. Honed to a fine edge. Honed to kill!
       -- a Kansas City FBI agent at Waco, waiting for action

The fedgoons take all this seriously. Long before the OKBombings the FBI ordered almost 2,000 suppressed .308 sniper rifles with night vision scopes. These rifles were made by Brown Precision with AWC suppressors and STANO image tubes. These rifles will be used to assassinate members of the Patriot Movement and gun culture. (The feds hope to "decapitate" the Freedom Movement by simultaneously arresting and/or eliminating and several hundred key people.)

This purchase order was placed at the same time the FBI was saying their sniper Lon Horiuchi maybe *shouldn't* have murdered Vicki Weaver, and they would keep tighter control on their "Rules of Engagement." *Wink, wink.* The BATF now has Bradleys. (They *almost* got OV-10D gunships, but *tooo bad!*)

> *It is my belief that we now have reached the point of diminishing returns in our battle to restore the Constitution.* **We would serve each other better to spend our time and energy learning how to survive in a country devoid of freedom,** *which is, I believe, the unstated goal of powerful interests who are now running our nation.*
> -- Colorado state senator Charles Duke

In 1994 the Pentagon's deputy chief of staff for intelligence, a Major Ralph Peters, wrote a position paper called *Warrior Class*:

> **The desire for patriotism is considered an enemy doctrine.** *The U.S. armed forces must be prepared to fight against all those who oppose the New World Order and who are holding out for nationalism... This new warrior class is most dangerous because they consist of those who fight out of strong religious beliefs... There is a worldwide class of patriots* (meaning terrorists) *who number in the millions, and if the current trend continues, there may be more of these who...love freedom and are now the target of the New World Order... You cannot bargain and compromise with these warriors... We, as the military, need to commit more training to counter these warrior threats. We must have an active campaign to win over the populace.* **This must be coupled with irresistible violence.**
> -- from the *McAlvany Intelligence Advisor*, May / June 1994

There you have it. Patriotic American gunowners are the #1 Enemy of the New World Order. Since we can't be bargained or compromised with, prepare for *"irresistible violence."*

DON'T GET SKITTISH!

> *You will never know how much it cost...[us] to preserve your freedom.* **I hope you will make good use of it.**
> -- John Quincy Adams

If we are left alone, either by truce or by inefficiency, so be it. However, *if,* despite our best efforts for peaceful privacy and gun ownership, we be hounded unmercifully, if we be raided for our guns--**then give 'em tooth and claw.**

I will not compromise, I will not grovel, I will not toady at the feet of mammon. I will give every man his due. I will honor my word even to my own hurt, and if these be insufficient grounds to be left alone, then somebody will have a seething problem on their hands.

I *will* be left alone to cause no harm. I hereby pledge to you my life, my fortune, and my sacred honor that I will die on my feet before I ever live on my knees. What about *you*?

The final, simple, human truth

Today, we need a nation of Minute Men, citizens who are not only prepared to take up arms, but citizens who regard the preservation of freedom to be the basic purpose of their daily life and who are willing to consciously work and sacrifice for that freedom.
-- John F. Kennedy, in defense of citizen militias (1961)

As the total subjection of a people arises generally from gradual encroachments, it will be our indispensable duty manfully to oppose every invasion of our rights in the beginning.
-- Silks Downer; *A Discourse at the Dedication of the Tree of Liberty* from *American Political Writing during the Founding Era, 1760-1805*, p. 1071

It all boils down to this: you *have* no rights unless you are willing to *fight* for them.

*The price of freedom is the **willingness** to do sudden battle, anywhere, anytime, and with utter recklessness.*
-- Robert A. Heinlein

I *don't* mean to say that you have no rights *unless* you fight--I mean you must only be *willing* to fight, if necessary. The mere *will* to fight often avoids the fight itself. (Observe your neighborhood dogs on this point.) Obviously, the feds scoff at our will. Guns without the resolve to use them is perhaps worse than resolve without guns, for it creates a false confidence.

And yet no weapons, no matter how powerful, can help the West **until it overcomes its loss of will power.** *In a state of psychological weakness weapons become a burden for the capitulating side.* **To defend oneself one must be ready to die, and there is little such readiness in a society raised in the cult of material well-being.**
-- Solzhenitsyn; *Warning To The West*

Never was anything great achieved without danger.
-- Niccolò Machiavelli

Most gun owners will wet their pants when the raids come, and the feds *know* it. However, many Americans *do* have the will *and* the guns, and the feds know *this*, too.

I don't *want* to shoot *anybody*--not even fedgoons.
All I'm saying is that it's a real possibility that peaceable folks

will be backed into an ugly corner by government--and we should mentally and physically prepare ourselves for this, while we can. Let's have no more illusions. I'd much rather that awful day never came, but *if* it comes, *fire*.

> *Fight, and you may die. Run...and you'll live. At least a while. Many years from now, would you be willing to trade all the days, from this day 'till that, for one chance--just one chance to come back here and tell our enemies that they may take our lives, but that they'll never take...our freedom!*
> -- William Wallace before the battle at Stirling, *Braveheart*

I pray for the Lord's wisdom and courage. **We need *heroism* above all else.** Freedom cannot survive without it, no matter how brilliant a nation's constitution. Freedom *clearly* cannot survive under *our* Constitution. It wasn't written tightly enough, as I proved in *Hologram of Liberty*. The feds always have a way out of their constitutional "straightjacket."

> *Keep your overall goal in mind above all. Those who swerve to avoid a few cuts and bruises defeat themselves. Understand from the very minute the fight begins that you're going to take damage. **Accept it.** You'll suffer far worse from the idiots and cowards on your own side.*
> -- L. Neil Smith; *Pallas*

> *I do believe that where there is a choice only between cowardice and* [defensive] *violence, **I would advise violence**.*
> -- Gandhi

> *Strike back when you're strong, and still have your wits about you, and the enemy isn't expecting it. **Give them your teeth, not your belly.***
> -- John Ross; *Unintended Consequences* (1996), p. 618

> *The history of liberty is a history of resistance.*
> -- Woodrow Wilson

> **Live Free or Die.**
> -- New Hampshire state motto

Hey, there's no immunity from historical constants just because we're *Americans*.

❖ 14

THE PATRIOT *LIGHT!*

That, too, was another self-deception,...on the part of those who thought they could get by without toeing the line. I mean the idiocy of the guerrilla business. **That's all it turned out to be: business** *--big business American-style, with endless promotion on all the junk, ranging from Geiger counters and do-it-yourself fallout shelters with revolving periscopes to James Bond folding rifles. Distilled water, fancy food concentrates, snakebite kits, vitamins, machetes, sunglasses. Goosedown sleeping bags, alpine rucksacks, Anzac campaign hats, with accompanying literature on how to assemble your own neighborhood* Maquis. *Batman in the Boondocks. To listen to some, if the day ever came, five hundred thousand citizens, all appropriately* Rogue Male *types, would melt into the hills, and when they weren't creating havoc among the brutal Occupation forces, they would be practicing the fine art of survival.*

Why, if a survival-and-guerrilla nut brought all the stuff the sporting-goods stores and catalogs said he needed, it would have taken a twenty-five-foot long U-Haul trailer and two weeks of packing to get him out of his damned carport....

There were gadgets...to keep...many men alive and operational, but there was one thing nobody considered--or maybe it was too grim to contemplate and so we conveniently wiped it out of our minds--one thing that had simply gone away from us.

What I'm referring to was the actual collective climate of temperament that existed at any given moment in this country: the real, as opposed to the fancied, state of mind.

Barring a few million in the armed forces who were coerced into at least perfunctorily practicing bravery in order to gain peergroup approval, **Americans, as it turned out were not tough.** *For us to leave comfortable homes and camp outdoors for longer than a week was a major adventure planned far in advance, and then the idea was to make wilderness camp as much like home as possible -- tents, portable generators, folding chairs, tables, collapsible crappers, radio, television, the works.* **Ché would have flipped.**

-- Oliver Lange, *Defiance*, p.83

A third less courage than the regular Patriot!
The spineless, sellout "conservatives"

[The Nazis]...*came for the Jews, but I wasn't a Jew, so I didn't speak out. They came for the trade unionists, but I wasn't a trade unionist, so I didn't speak out. They came for the Catholics, but I wasn't a Catholic, so I didn't speak out. **Then they came for me, and there was no one left to speak out!***

    -- Reverend Niemuller

...*between freedom and sandwiches, they will choose sandwiches.*

    -- Lord Boyd-Orr

When men reduce their virtues to the approximate, then evil acquires the force of an absolute; *when loyalty to an unyielding purpose is dropped by the virtuous, it's picked up by scoundrels-- and you get the indecent spectacle of a cringing, bargaining traitorous good and a self-righteously uncompromising evil.*

    -- Ayn Rand; *Atlas Shrugged*

A society of sheep must in time beget a government of wolves.

    -- Betrand de Juvenal

Do you know *why* conservatives and Patriots get *so* upset at the passage of each new oppressive measure? Why do they become so utterly livid at the "assault-weapons" ban, at the *Exclusionary Rule Reform Act of 1995* (H.R. 666), at the "Crime" and the "Anti-Terrorism" bills? Granted, these acts *are* outrageous on their very face, but there's another reason. **They already know that they will likely *comply*.** Present outrage stems from the imagined pain of their future obedience. They already *know* that they'll redraw their line in the sand.

    Folks, draw the line *somewhere* and keep things in perspective. If Congress passed a bill demanding that you throw your children off a cliff, would you comply--even if the fedgoons tried to enforce it? Of course not! So why is everybody so unhinged about some future gun ban? **Why should we even *care*, much less get our blood pressure up?** Draw your line in advance, firmly commit to your principles, make plans, and quit howling about what Congress does!

    Quit playing Patriot or Libertarian or Republican or free-market advocate. Quit the NRA and sell your guns, assuming you had the nerve to ever own any. **Quit fooling yourself-- *wimp*.** Tear up your von Mises Fan Club Card. Cancel your subscription to the *National Review*.

The country that draws a broad line between its fighting men and its thinking men **will find its fighting done by fools and its thinking done by cowards.**
-- Sir William F. Butler

This is the Conservative Movement today--cuddled up in the American flag. All most folks have ever done is pay smarmy lip service to liberty and play "American" if it's not risky. Example: A man selling a mint AR15 at a gun show for just Ø600 was asked *why.* He replied, *"My son wants a jet-ski."* (Gosh, at least it wasn't for something *frivolous...*)

If ye love wealth greater than liberty,
the tranquility of servitude greater
than the animating contest for freedom,
go home from us in peace.

We seek not your counsel, nor your arms,
Crouch down and lick the hand that feeds you;
and may posterity forget that ye were our countrymen.
-- Samuel Adams

If you penny-loafer conservatives--you slaves in splendor--ever had the courage of a housecat, we'd have a free America today. But, no, you chirped for the gilded cage. And you got it--*for all of us.* Our vile "leaders" are not the *real* enemy. *You* are.

The only man who makes slavery possible is the slave.
-- John W. Campbell, Jr.

I will not, under the guise of politics, initiate force or steal, and I will resist those who do. I despise thieves, liars, and bullies--*especially* when they sanctimoniously couch their immoral actions under "legal" government authority.

There are whole *families* out there--right now--striving for honest government and responsible leadership while you prance around in your Stars and Stripes costume. Quit playing "American" and step into the ring!

To rebel in season (when victory is sure) **is not to rebel.**
-- Greek proverb

The Eastern Bloc "demonstrations" of 1989 were totally *"in season"* because the Communist regimes *allowed* the people to "rebel" in preparation for the politically timed demise of the Soviet satellite governments. I know--I was *there.* They rebelled without risk. It wasn't like the *real* uprisings of 1953 East Berlin or 1989 Tiananmen Square where people were shot and killed for throwing rocks at tanks. Remember the photo of that lone courageous soul who stopped a column of Chinese tanks? Now *that's* desperation. That's *courage!* (The tanks didn't stop for long. They ran him down--made hamburger of him--because he stood his ground. We're not "there" yet.)

There were no "Patriot *Lights*" on 4 July 1776

The price paid by many signers of the Declaration of Independence was truly staggering:

Francis Lewis had his home burned and his wife tortured by the British for two years. She died shortly after her release.

John Hart's home was looted and burned, his ailing wife died and his 13 children were scattered. He eluded capture by sleeping in caves.

The 1,000 acre estate of **Lewis Morris** was ransacked and burned. His home was destroyed, his cattle butchered, and his family driven off.

Richard Stockton was imprisoned and repeatedly beaten at the brink of starvation. His home was destroyed, his papers burned.

Carter Braxton saw virtually every merchant ship he owned sunk or captured. He was forced to sell off his land.

Thomas McKean *"was hunted like a fox"* and once *"compelled to move my family five times in a few months."*

Thomas Nelson, Jr. led 3,000 Virginia militia against the British. Redcoats took refuge in his own home, so he turned a cannon on it.

Your assets have already been conscripted by the State. The UN bureaucrats are drooling over your children. **It's 1998 and we're in the calm before the stormtroopers.** Liberty has no friend but the simple, brave American. Rebel with me, with *us*, because it's *not* fashionable. Rebel "out of season" when it's truly necessary and truly risky. Get involved *now* so that we perhaps don't *have* to give 'em our teeth later.

> On too many occasions in the history of civilization, people have accepted authority without subjecting that authority to rational examination. A complacent population leaves itself wide open to control. Eventually the abusive bureaucracy demands too much. The end is either revolt or subjugation. Perhaps the problem is not with the power of the abuser; perhaps the problem is with the individual who is willing to submit. Free men and women need not apologize for being enraged by arrogance in government.
>
> **Look into your soul. Corner apathy. Root it out. The darkest hours of human history are marked by muted minutes of indifference.** (p. 108)

I think I know what real courage is. **Real courage is to leave that nice chair and walk into the flame of history.** *Real courage is to fight when there are so many places to hide, so many excuses. The halls of forever are long. Somewhere, far from this time, you may have to look into the eyes of your children once again. Somewhere, far from this time, you may have to look into the eyes of patriots. Somewhere, far from this time, you may have to look into the eyes of the young soldier who never got to hold the tiny hand of his firstborn;* **who took the hit for you because he knew that somewhere, somehow, in all the confusion of his youth, freedom mattered.** (p. 207)
-- Bill Branon; *Let Us Prey* (1994)

Get involved *now* so that *you* won't crumple and give 'em your *belly* later. We're all going to die some day. What counts, and what will count, is how you lived your life. How are *you* living *your* life right now? For honor and decency, courageously? Or for comfort, cowardly and shamefully?

These are the times that try men's souls. *The summer soldier and sunshine patriot will, in this crisis, shrink from the service of his country; but he that stands now deserves the love and thanks of man and woman. Heaven knows how to put a proper price upon its goods;* **and it would be strange indeed if so celestial an article as Freedom should not be highly rated.**
--Thomas Paine, *The Crisis,* 23 December 1776

How are *you* living *your* life right *now*? As Jefferson said:

What country can preserve its liberties if their rulers are not warned from time to time that their people preserve the spirit of resistance?

In the dark days of 1941, Winston Churchill admonished:

...this is the lesson: never give in, never give in, never, never, never, never--in nothing, great or small, large or petty--never give in except to convictions of honour and good sense.

If my talk of armed resistance is getting you squeamish--*good.* **It's better to discover your lack of mettle *now* than later.** Example: A Patriot was shopping for a lever-action .30-30 so he'll still have *some* kind of politically-correct, unbanned rifle after they take away his H&K93. I told him to also shop for a BB gun so he'll have something after they confiscate his .30-30. (Skewered, he saw my point, though I probably should have open-handed him across the face just to make it stick.)

Folks, when they come for your "assault rifles" either give 'em up and admit that you were just a wimpy hobbyist--or use 'em for their true purpose.

Oh, and by the way, decide *now*, please.

Every oppressed people in history was, at some point, forced to resort to arms. *We* were forced to 223 years ago, and it's almost certain to be our "turn" again very soon. Big deal. That's life. And death is part of life. It goes something like this:

We weren't here.
We *were* here.
We left.

We are here for 76 orbits around the sun and then we check out. The world spun before our arrival, and it will spin after our exit.

What will *you* have accomplished during the interval? Don't let this scenario be your own:

*The feds came for the White Separatists, but I wasn't a White Separatist, so I didn't speak out. They came for the Branch Davidians, but I wasn't a Branch Davidian, so I didn't speak out. They came for the militias, but I wasn't a militia member, so I didn't speak out. They came for the "assault weapons" owners, but I didn't own any "assault weapons," so I didn't speak out. They came for the rest of the gunowners, but I wasn't a gunowner, so I didn't speak out. They came for the holistic health practioners, the home-schoolers, the ranchers, the Libertarians, the Buchanan Republicans, the Christians, but I wasn't one of them, so I didn't speak out. **Then they came for me, and there was no one left to speak out!***

-- any non-Socialist American, a few years from now...

It's *not* how comfortable did you make yourself, or how much money did you earn, but *what* did *you* do to stand against evil?

OUTRAGE,
THEN COURAGE

If you want a picture of the future, imagine a boot stamping on a human face--forever.
      -- George Orwell; *1984*

*We are trying to reinforce to them (the Branch Davidians) that we (the FBI) are in charge of the situation, that the compound (sic) is under the complete control of the Government. It is in fact no longer their compound (sic); that we have the ability to exercise whatever control we want over that compound (sic), and we will do that at various times to demonstrate to them the fact **they are impotent in their ability to control their everyday lives.***
      -- Bob Ricks, FBI spokesman at Waco, April 1993

*These, muh, uh, pieces of equipment (the CS-injecting tanks from Ft. Hood, Texas) were unarmed, as I understand it, and were contracted...**I mean, it was like a good rental car.** Uh, they were...*
                      (Attorney General Janet "For The Kids" Reno)
Ah, a good...a good rental car? A tank going into a building?
                            (Congressman Bill Zeliff; R-NH)
Uh, ah, ah...   (Attorney General Janet "For The Kids" Reno)
      -- from the House hearings on Waco

Men that are above all fear, soon grow above all shame.
      -- Trenchard and Gordon, *Cato's Letters* (1755), vol. I, p. 255

A *2nd* AMERICAN REVOLUTION?

The Clinton era has spawned an armed militia movement involving tens of thousands of people. The last time anything like this occurred was in the 1850's with the emergence of the southern gun *clubs. It is easy to dismiss the militia as right-wing nuts: it is much harder to read the complex sociology of civic revolt. **At the very least, the militias reveal the hatred building up against the irksome yuppies who run the country.***

It is under this president that domestic terrorism has become a feature of life in America, culminated with the destruction of the Oklahoma Federal Building on April 19, 1995. What set the deadly spiral in motion was the Waco assault two years before, and the coverup that followed.

    -- Ambrose Evans-Pritchard, 1997 letter to America

Look, I am *not* advocating an armed rebellion or the lynching of public officials. What I *am* saying is *this:* **Do not cherish your own life or property *so much* as to be bought at the price of *slavery.*** Quit worrying about your precious skin! As William Wallace said in *Braveheart, "**Every man dies. Not every man really lives.**"*

What country can preserve its liberties if their rulers are not warned from time to time that their people preserve the spirit of resistance? ***Let them take arms...*** *What signify a few lives lost in a century or two? The tree of liberty must be refreshed from time to time with the blood of patriots and tyrants. It is its natural manure.*

    -- Thomas Jefferson; 13 November 1787, *Papers* (12:356)

You are a sovereign human being, created by God with unalienable rights as much a part of you as your lungs. **It is *not wrong* to *defend* these rights, force against force.**

*A strict observance of the laws is doubtless one of the highest duties of a good citizen, **but it is not the highest. The laws of necessity, of self-preservation, of saving our country when in danger, are of higher obligation.*** *To lose our country by a scrupulous adherence of written law, **would be to lose the law itself,** with life, liberty, property and all those who are enjoying them with us...*

    -- Thomas Jefferson; 20 September 1810, *Human Events*

Our lives are not blank checks for government. Our backs were not made to be saddled nor our mouths to be bridled! **We are the sovereigns--*they* are the *servants.* When government is afraid of the people, it's Liberty. When people are afraid of the government, it's *Tyranny.*** What our "last straw" will be, I do not know. Perhaps the new "Anti-Terrorism" Act with its suspension of *habeas corpus* and its new death penalties will snap the camel's back.

Those who profess to favor freedom, and yet depreciate agitation, are men who want crops without plowing up the ground. They want rain without thunder or lightning. They want the ocean without the *awful roar of its waters. This struggle may be a moral one; or it may be a physical one; or it may be both moral and physical; **but it must be a struggle. Power concedes nothing without demand. Find out just what people will submit to, and you have found out the exact amount of injustice and wrong which will be imposed upon them;** and these will continue until they are resisted with either words or blows, or with both.*

The limits of tyrants are prescribed by the endurance of those whom they oppress.

-- Frederick Douglass, a self-freed black slave, in 1857

I do not *seek* an armed rebellion, but I will *not* live as a *slave*. Not in *America*. Nor will I run off to Costa Rica in silly hopes of freedom, as if tyranny won't become global. (Besides, they wouldn't let me in with my guns...)

*Individuals obtained recognition of their freedom by fighting and bargaining, or--failing in this--they could run away. This running was possible **because they had somewhere to go.***

-- L. Neil Smith; *Pallas*

Folks, America is truly the last stand. There's nowhere else *to* go. I will stay here and *work* for freedom.

*If a nation values anything more than freedom, it will lose that freedom; and the irony of it is that if it is comfort that it values more, **it will lose that too.***

-- W. Somerset Maugham

Liberty is always unfinished business.

-- anonymous

*If you will not fight for right when you can easily win without bloodshed; if you will not fight when your victory will be sure and not too costly; you may come to the moment when you will have to fight with all the odds against you and only a precarious chance of survival. There may be even a worse case. You may have to fight when there is no hope of victory, **because it is better to perish** [free] **than to live as slaves.*** (As did Jews on 19 April 1943 in the Warsaw Ghetto uprising. They killed 80 Nazi troops! KWR)

-- Winston Churchill

We're probably already at that *"worse case."* In *Hologram of Liberty* I described how our constitutional system has allowed a federal stranglehold on America. But the *real* culprit *hasn't* been the Constitution. **We've only *ourselves* to blame.**

We *should* have resisted in 1798 when Congress criminalized political dissent. We *should* have strung up Congress for handing monetary control to a private consortium of bankers and then dragging us into WWI in 1917. We *should* have resisted in the 1930s during FDR's atrocious "social" programs and the confiscation of our gold. We *should* have shouted down the 1945 U.N. We *should* have pushed through the righteous tax revolt of the late 1970s instead of accepting the sop presidency of Ronald Reagan. We *should* have hounded out the Clintonistas after their murder of the Branch Davidians.

Etc. Etc. Etc.

The only times when Americans stood up to the Federal Government were in 1794 (Whiskey Rebellion) and 1860 (the secession of the South over economic autonomy--not slavery). Other than that, we have *chickened out* on a dozen crucial opportunities to rein in Washington. Evil has triumphed, because good men have done *nothing*. We have become a paper tiger, and Congress is no longer afraid of us. The servant now scoffs at his master, and the servant's bulldog routinely sinks his teeth in our legs.

All they need is some long-overdue fear and they'll run.

The French could have nipped WWII in the bud by calling Hitler's 1936 Rhineland bluff. We could have easily pushed the Soviets out of Germany, Poland, Austria, etc. in 1945, kept our military strong, and avoided the Cold War. We certainly could have rolled into East Berlin in August 1961 and smashed the barbed-wire wall with righteous impunity. What starts out as mere barbed-wire eventually is replaced with *concrete*.

If there's one constant to bullies it's that they're *bluff*. Knock their teeth in suddenly and they crumple every time. It's only hard to do the *first* time.

Prepare for that day, because it's coming.

Jefferson spoke of occasional mild rebellions for a America's health. Rebellions are sort of like vomiting. The *prospect* is very unpleasant, but you feel so much better *afterwards*. Only the first heave is scary. We've been so queasy with political poisoning for so long, but we won't hug the toilet and stick a finger down our national throat. **We're *so* afraid of vomiting that we'd rather stay queasy.** Well, by the time we vomit on the *poison's* timetable, we'll probably be too weak and ill to recover.

You chew on *that* thought for a while.

✦ **16**

THIS AUTHOR IS *NUTS!*

I want to give you Liberals, Social Democrats and other coercive collectivists a final chance to understand the Freedom Movement's mindset. Your political agenda, enforced by government thugs, *created* the Freedom Movement in the mid-1970s. We did not create you. You created *us.*

Had you modern Tories been content to let peaceable folks alone to raise their own children, control their own schools, attend church unmolested, use their own property, shoot their own guns, pay *reasonable* taxes and keep their own wages, and generally live their own lives--there wouldn't *be* a Freedom Movement. Such is superfluous in free countries. Thanks to you, America is now Land of the Fee, Home of the Slave.

As *Kulaks* we have never injured you, but our independent spirit has offended your controlling nature. Since you Know Best, since it horrifies you that Americans actually have the *nerve* to live without your license, you have nearly bridled this glorious mustang of a people. We will never, however, take your saddle. You will never be our jockey. *Never.*

You're probably too committed to hear reason. You're probably too confident to believe the tremors. Nonetheless, for the sake of fairness and conscience, I offer you this warning:

[Liberty minded people are] *all the same. And the kicker is, every single one of us believes that as honest adult citizens, we have the absolute right to own any and all small arms and shoot them just as often as we want.* **We have a specific culture.** *Guns and shooting are very important to us, just like...hunting buffalo was important to the Indians....*

Our culture is important, and we're willing to pay for it. We have above-average educations, above-average incomes, and almost nonexistent criminal involvement. We pay far more taxes and re-

ceive virtually no subsidy payments. You'd think Washington would be happy, but instead they are doing everything they can to destroy our culture.

In the '20s, soldiers sat on their bunks in the cold at Camp Perry, cleaning the handmade .22 target rifles they would compete with the next day. When the President proudly announces that today, seventy years later, he is ordering these same guns thrown into a blast furnace, we in the gun culture feel powerful emotions. **They are the same emotions a Native American would feel if the President proudly ordered the destruction of war clubs and other sacred tribal artifacts. They are the same emotions that the Jews felt watching...Nazi** *Sturmtroopen* **gleefully burning intricate copies of the Torah.**

We offer to buy the government's surplus guns, and instead they pay to have them cut up. We offer to buy their surplus military ammo, shoot it, sell the brass to a smelter, and give the government the proceeds, and instead they pay to have it burned.

These government slugs ban our guns and they ban our magazines and they ban our ammo. They ban suppressors that make our guns quieter and then they ban our outdoor shooting ranges because our guns are too loud. They ban steel-core ammunition because it's "armor piercing", then they close down our indoor ranges where people shoot lead-core bullets because they say we might get lead poisoning.

The people in the gun culture have a better safety record than any police department in the nation, but several states actually prohibit us from using guns for self-protection, and in all the other states except [Vermont] they make us buy a license. They tax us so we can have more cops, and when crime still goes up, they tax us more and ban more...guns.

[We] endure waiting periods that no other group would stand for. We undergo background checks that no legislator, judge, doctor, or police officer has to tolerate, and we submit to it not once, or once a year, but over and over again. Then, after we yield to this outrage, they smile and forbid us from buying more than one gun in a 30-day period.

If we sell one gun we own that's gone up in value, they can charge us with dealing in firearms without a federal dealer's license, which is a felony. If we get a dealer's license, they say we are not really in business, and report us to our local authorities for violating zoning ordinances by running a commercial venture out of a residence.

If the steel or the wood on our guns is too long or too short, they make us pay $200 taxes and get fingerprinted and photographed. They make us get a law enforcement certification from the local police chief. If he refuses to sign we have no recourse. If he takes the forms in the next room and brings them back out, signed, he can *later claim the signature is not his, and the feds will charge us with a felony.*

We in the gun culture have played all their stupid games on [National Firearms Act of 1934 licensed fully-automatic] weapons for over half a century, without a single violent crime being committed by any person in the system. So when a bill comes up to keep travelers with guns locked in the trunk of their cars out of jail, what happens? A scumbucket from New Jersey,...puts an amendment on it that closes down the whole NFA process.

Then, if they even suspect we've ignored the $200 tax process altogether, on the guns where the wood and steel is too long or too short, they'll spend over a million dollars watching us for months, then they'll shoot our wives and children or burn us all alive. When the public gets outraged by these actions, the government issues letters of reprimand and sends the guys who did the killing on paid leave. In the decades that the feds have been raiding and killing people in the gun culture over suspected non-payment of $200 taxes, not one federal agent has been fined a single dollar or spent even one night in jail.

And you know something else that's never happened? To this day, not a single person in the gun culture has ever dropped the hammer on one of these feds. Not once.

Then, after these statist bastards have done all these things, they grin and tell us how they like to hunt ducks, and how the only laws they want to pass are "reasonable ones."

***One of two things** [is going to happen]. One of the political parties is going to have to wake up, smell the coffee, and start restoring all the articles in the Bill of Rights--the Second, Fourth, Fifth, and Tenth Amendments.*

[And if that doesn't happen], then we're going to have a civil war. (at pp. 555-6)

Stripping a motivated people of their dignity and rubbing their noses in it is a very bad idea. (at p. 9)

-- John Ross; *Unintended Consequences* (1996)

In no time in history has an oppressive government been *so* thoroughly and fairly warned *to back off*. Not even the English in the 1770s. When you weren't playing deaf to our pleas, you scoffed at them. We have not resorted to violence. We have only rarely resorted to righteous self-defense. No oppressed people, with the arms to resist, have ever been more patient. Your greed for Power and Control has nearly dried up our tolerance.

Americans will *not* take much more. Don't expect us to merely whine about the tune you fiddle while Rome burns. We won't let you strike the match. Your goons fight only for their next paycheck. *We* will be fighting for our culture, our rights, and our lives. Many in your military will defect.

You will *lose*. America is the greatest potential guerrilla base in history. You have transformed thousands of normal Americans into Patriots who spend every waking hour planning for your rout. We have been preparing for your Soviet Amerika since the 1970s. Many of us are combat veterans, or have military experience. We have land, food, tools, guns, friends and an unquenchable fire for Liberty.

You are making guerrillas out of whole families, counties and states--*that's* how serious this civil war will be, if you continue your oppression. *"Stripping a motivated people of their dignity and rubbing their noses in it is a very bad idea."* Keep squeezing us, and we'll make Afghanistan look like a spitwad fight. You don't believe this, of course, and that's good. Because of our patience and long suffering, you continue to underestimate your opponents. You're in for a rude shock.

Again, it is under Clinton that an armed militia movement involving tens of thousands of people has mushroomed out of the plain, an expression of dissent that is unparalleled since the southern gun clubs before the Civil War. People do not spend their weekends with an SKS rifle, drilling for guerilla warfare against federal forces, in a country that is at ease with itself. **It takes very bad behavior to provoke the first simmerings or armed insurgency, and the militias are unmistakably Clinton's offspring.** *Would they have happened if America were governed by a President Tsongas or a President Bush? Of course not.*

Which compels the question: What is it about the combustible chemistry of Bill Clinton that causes such a reaction? What has he been doing to America?

The original sin, I believe, was the FBI assault on the Branch Davidian community in Waco, Texas, on April 19, 1993. At least 76 people were incinerated, most of them women and children, after FBI tanks went smashing through the walls of Mount Carmel. The death toll adds up to the worst tragedy precipitated by government on American soil in this century. You have to go back to the slaughter of 200 Sioux Indians at Wounded Knee in 1890 to find an abuse of power on this scale. Just like Waco, Wounded Knee was designated a "battle" by officials; and just like Waco, the victims were demonized as sexual deviants. Some methods never change.

-- Ambrose Evans-Pritchard, *The Secret Life of Bill Clinton-- The Unreported Stories,* p.xiv (1997)

You politicians have broken your American pact with us. Government was to be a means to an end, *not an end in itself.* We merely delegated our sovereignty to federal officials for courts,

Congress, and national defense--*not* to be viciously ruled within our own homes, schools, businesses, and churches.

> The United States owes its existence to the Bill of Rights. Were it not for the Bill of Rights' explicit promise to limit government power over the citizenry, the U.S. Constitution would never have been ratified. Americans in the Revolutionary Era would only permit a national government to come into existence if...that government would solemnly pledge to limit their power in perpetuity. But this sacred compact is now violated by thousands of officials at all levels of government. **If the government will not keep its pact with the people, what do the people owe the government?**
>
> -- James Bovard; *Lost Rights*, p. 333

You have broken your sacred trust, and you will pay a price far higher than that of tyrants. You will pay the *traitor*'s price.

Even if you *do* successfully disarm the people, materially and spiritually, you will still lose. The more responsibility you take away from people, the less responsible they will become. At some point, you will reap the inverse of *"People have the government they deserve"*--you governors will have the *people* you deserve (and I suspect this has *already* begun to occur). In *On Liberty*, John Stuart Mill put it well:

> A State which dwarfs its men, in order that they may be more docile instruments in its hands even for beneficial purposes will find that **with small men no great things can really be accomplished;** and that the perfection of machinery to which it has sacrificed everything will avail nothing.

Either way, you *will* lose, and that's the lovely irony of it all. Whether you eliminate or tolerate this independent mustang of the American people, you will lose. Either way, our presence *or* our absence will destroy you. (Irony's a bitch, ain't it?)

Back off. Back off, *now*, before you step into the abyss.

Back off, *now*, while you are *allowed* to.

❖ 17

SOURCES

BOOKS

Unintended Consequences, John Ross
    A fantastic novel about American gunowners pushed too far by the feds. Unnecessarily risqué in parts and totally dismissive of any possible conspiracies, it's still "must" reading. Available from Paladin Press for Ø28.95.

Civil War 2, Thomas Chittum
    A Vietnam vet and professional mercenary makes a compelling case for America cracking at her ethnic seams in about 20 years. Not at all a racist book, but wholly logical. A very timely and unique title. From Loompanics.

101 Things To Do 'Til The Revolution, Claire Wolfe
    A fun, zippy book full of practical ideas and morsels of hilarious wisdom. Wish *I* had written it! From Laissez-Faire.

Lost Rights, James Bovard
    An excellent, sweeping overview of mindless federal tyranny. Not a Patriot work, but it might as well have been. Infuriating reading. At any bookstore.

Defiance, Oliver Lange
    Originally titled *Vandenberg*, this utterly absorbing novel describes Amerikan life in the U.S.S.A. and what a handful of average folks do about it. A must. At any used bookstore.

The Moon Is A Harsh Mistress, Robert A. Heinlein
    The best novel I've ever read about a successful rebellion. A lunar penal colony in 2075 revolts from is Earthly masters. A marvelous story deserving to be a movie! At any used bookstore.

The Probability Broach, L. Neil Smith
A real romp of a novel in which tandem-dimensional Americas exist--one Jeffersonian, one Hamiltonian--and battle each other. Great fun! From Laissez-Faire Books.
Followed by *The Gallatin Convergence*.

Safeguarding Liberty--The Constitution & Citizen Militias, edited by Larry Pratt of Gun Owners of America
A superb collection of essays on the 2nd Amendment. Visit GOA's Web Site at www. gunowners.org.

To Ride, Shoot Straight, and Speak the Truth, Jeff Cooper
A collection of fascinating essays on guns, travel, hunting, and philosophy from the Professor of the Modern Shooting Technique. I recommend all of Jeff's books. From Paladin Press.

Art of the Rifle, Jeff Cooper
An excellent book on a long-overlooked subject, the Queen of weapons, by one of the Masters. From Paladin Press.

Life Without Fear, Mike Dalton and Mickey Fowler
An excellent beginner's book on the use of defensive handguns. Written by staff of the International Shootist Institute, it has dozens of superb pictures to complement its thorough coverage of lethal confrontations. Ø14.95 ppd. Call 818-891-1723.

Street Stoppers, Marshall and Sanow
A sequel to their *Handgun Stopping Power*, it gives the latest results of hundreds of shootings in every major caliber. Includes the seminal Strasbourg Goat Tests and a chapter on MagSafe Ammo. From Paladin Press.

The Ayoob Files: The Book, Massad Ayoob
Good cross-section of 30 shooting incidents.

MOVIES AND VIDEOS

Red Dawn
A modern classic. Alpine high-schoolers fight the Communist invasion of America. An utterly unique film.

Amerika
Powerful mini-series on the Soviet takeover of the U.S.A.

misc. videos

Militia of Montana (406-847-2735)
Ask for the video with official footage of *Operation Cooperative Nugget* at Ft. Polk, Louisiana where 4,000 soldiers of 14 Eastern European countries learned how to shoot American flag T-shirted *civilians*, many of whom are women and children. Also shows footage of the "nonexistent" American detention camps for us dissidents. M.O.M. also carries my books. Great folks.

Waco--The Rules of Engagement

This is the new documentary film, 136 minutes long, which has been sweeping the country at film festivals. It is *so* good, *so* convincing, that even California liberals are upset at the feds. It's now out on video. Get a copy and invite a crowd over to see it. Infrared footage of machine-gun firing executioners of trapped Davidians, feds caught lying through their teeth, a charred child bowed backwards from the hydrogen cyanide gas poisoning, *60 Minutes* refusing to touch the issue--*wow!* If this is ever aired on national TV, there will be a revolution the next morning. *Run*--don't walk--and get this video. From Laissez-Faire Books.

Braveheart

Mel Gibson portrays William Wallace, the George Washington of 14th century Scotland. Outstanding!

Michael Collins

Liam Neeson portrays the 1920s founder of the IRA and its guerilla resistance to the British occupation.

The Parallax View

An older film with Warren Beaty. A corporations seeks out unstable, budding sociopaths to be groomed for assassination duty. An eerie, disturbing film. A similar scenario is probably used today to create these mass murdering gunmen (many of whom, it's rumored, were on *Prozac®*--"delayed violence").

The Manchurian Candidate

A 1963 feature film starring Frank Sinatra. An American soldier from the Korean War is brainwashed and molded into a sleeper assassin of a presidential nominee. *Way* beyond its time. Frank personally had it suppressed for years, claiming that showing the film after JFK's assassination was distasteful. (Yeah, *right*. Whaddaya bet Frank got a little visit?)

Executive Action
A 1973 feature film on how JFK was likely assassinated. As a rifleman and mystery buff, I've been to Dealey Plaza and read many books. This film dramatizes a highly credible theory. If the Insiders succeeded in *1963*, just imagine how much better they are at it *today.*

Conspiracy Theory
A backhanded spoof on us nutty folks, yet with enough plausibility to remain interesting and thought-provoking. There *are* scheming Bad Guys, after all. *Gee, who'da thunk it?*

MAIL ORDER BOOKS
Underlined companies carry my books.

Laissez-Faire Books   800-326-0996   www.laissezfaire.org
A Libertarian/Objectivist oriented, highly intellectual catalog company. Top quality "food for thought."

Liberty Tree   800-927-8733   www.independent.org
The book catalog by the Libertarian think-tank *The Independent Institute*. A good selection of erudite material.

Loompanics   800-380-2230   www.loompanics.com
With over 700 titles carried in its 190+ page catalog, if it's unusual, they'll have it. *Really* eccentric stuff. Not only do they have books you didn't know existed, they've got books on *subjects* you didn't know existed.

Eden Press   800-338-8484   www.edenpress.com
A smaller, but more personal, alternative book catalog company. A good source for privacy and ID material.

Paladin Press   800-392-2400   www.paladin-press.com
They carry a bit on everything, especially weapons and tactics. They are the target of an insipid, vicious lawsuit because a hired hit man used one of their books to commit murder. A federal judge (grudgingly) granted summary dismissal, but an appellate court reversed. This is *the* First Amendment battle.

Knowledge = Freedom   702-329-5968
This is the Freedom Movement's "Yellow Pages." With over 2,000 listings (alphabetized and cross-referenced by subject matter and state/city), this continually updated compendium is a labor of love by Dennis Grover. A must.

Delta Press   800-852-4445   www.deltapress.com
Primarily military and weapons oriented.

CPA Book Publishers   503-668-4941
They carry nearly *every* Patriot/Freedom book.

Information Exchange   800-346-6205
Good selection on a variety of topics.

Freedom Bound   888-385-3723
Your "untax" connection. Solid, hard-working folks.

The Free American   **505-423-3250**
Great news magazine from New Mexico.

The Resource Center   800-922-1771
Mostly books on financial privacy, trusts, foreign banking, passports, etc.

Bohica Concepts   360-497-7075
Good selection on freedom-oriented subjects.

Militia of Montana   406-847-2735
Good selection of anti-NWO and survival books, gear, etc.

NEWSLETTERS & MAGAZINES

Shotgun News
Published thrice monthly, the FFLs source list. A "must."

Gun List
National classified ad gun paper. Excellent resource. *GL* and *SN* are available at gun shops, gun shows, and newsstands.

The Anti-Shyster   **214-418-8993**
Highly original legal contrarian magazine.

American Survival Guide
A quality magazine. Highly recommended. I'm grateful for their reviews of my last three books.

Backwoods Home Magazine
A must for rural types. An excellent, groundbreaking zine.

Aid & Abet   **602-237-2533**
Put out by *Police Against the New World Order* ministry.

Media Bypass Magazine
Highly informative.

The *McAlvany Intelligence Advisor*
A great monthly Christian newsletter on politics, economics and police state updates. For a free sample *MIA* newsletter, gold/silver IRA investment information/portfolio consultation, call **Dave Saleh at 800-525-9556 ext. 134.**

SHOOTING GEAR

BlackHawk 800-694-5263 www.blackhawkindustries.com
Tactical Nylon gear of all description.

BlackStar Barrel Accurizing   218-721-6040
Electro-polishing of rifle bores to increase accuracy.

Brigade Quartermasters   800-338-4327
A competitor of the above.

Brownells   515-623-5401
Fantastic catalog of parts and accessories.

Cheaper Than Dirt 817-625-7557 www.cheaperthandirt.com
America's leading sports discounter. Great folks.

Cryo Precision   888-310-CRYO
Blackjack Cryo   217-347-7700
Cryogenic Tempering, Seville, Ohio
300 Below, Inc.   800-550-CRYO
Cryogenic treatment of rifle barrels to relieve stress.

Delta Force   800-852-4445
Color catalog of shooting equipment.

Firing Pin Enterprises   602-275-1623 (Tu, Wed, Th)
Sells many books, parts, and gun show items.

Mad Dog Tactical, Inc.   520-772-3021/3022fax
Best knives and Kydex gun gear, hands down.

Major Surplus & Survival   800-441-8855
Good selection of outdoor survival gear.

Midway   800-243-3220
Reloading equipment and shooting accessories.

Premier Reticles   540-722-0601
Installs the Mil-Dot reticle on scopes.

Robar, Inc.   602-581-2648/582-0059fax
Corrosion-resistant finishes. Grip reduction for Glocks.
M1A mags in bolt guns. "Snout" (scout/sniper) .308 rifles.

Shomer-Tec   360-733-6214
Fascinating selection of police and spy stuff.

Sierra Supply   970-259-1822
Good value and service since 1978.

Tapco   800-554-1445   www.tapco.com
Lots of gun parts and accessories.

The Survival Center   800-321-2900
Interesting survival gear.

U.S. Cavalry   800-777-7732
Great color catalog. Tactical Heaven.

GUN AND PARTS DISTRIBUTORS

They run ads in *Shotgun News* and *Gun List*. While you
must order their guns and receivers through your local FFL,
sometimes it's the only way to acquire something too new or uncommon to be found in the unpapered used market.

Bandet   915-698-0409   www.bandet.com
Burns Bros.   516-234-7676
Bushmaster   800-998-7928   www.bushmaster.com
CDNN   800-588-9500
Century Arms Intl.   800-527-1252   www.CenturyArms.com
CFI   817-595-2485   www.cfiarms.com
Cheaper Than Dirt   817-625-7557 www.cheaperthandirt.com
Classic Arms   800-383-8011
DPMS   800-578-3767
DSA Inc.   847-223-4770   www.dsarms.com
Entréprise Arms   818-962-8712   www.entreprise.com
Fulton Armory   www.fulton-armory.com
Gun Parts Corp.   914-679-2417   www.gunpartscorp.com
J&G   520-445-9650   www.jgsales.com
MarStar   www.marstar.com.ca/
Northridge   800-678-3931   www.northridge.com
Samco   800-554-1618

Sarco   908-647-3800   www.sarcoinc.com
Shomer-Tec   360-733-6214
SOG   800-944-GUNS
Springfield Armory   www.springfield-armory.com
Tapco   800-554-1445   www.tapco.com
World Wide Gun Parts   www.gun-parts.com

WEB SITES

Gun Rights organizations
www.gunowners.org   Gun Owners of America
"No Compromise!" gun lobby. Fantastic links.

www.nra.org   National Rifle Association

www.saf.org/   Second Amendment Foundation

www.ccrkba.org/
Citizens Committee for the Right to Keep and Bear Arms.

Miscellaneous
www.i2i.org
The Independence Institute. Great stuff, with great links.

www.laissezfaire.org
Great links.

www.shooters.com
The most complete source of shooting info on the Net.

www.law.cornell.edu/uscode
Search within the entire U.S. Code

www.findlaw.com/scripts
Search for any legal case.

❶ The FAL. (Also, the Bushmaster M17S, but I hadn't told you.)
❷ The AR15 and H&K. (Also, the FA-MAS and the AG42B.)
❸ AK, H&K, FAL, M1A, SKS, AR
❹ AR, FAL, H&K, M1A, SKS, AK
❺ AR, H&K, AK, SKS, M1A, FAL
❻ SKS, AK, FAL, AR, M1A, H&K

HOW TO ORDER FROM US

Good-Bye April 15th!

We are out-of-stock until further notice on our Web Site.

You & The Police!

5½"x8½", 128 pages. Published January 1996. Prices each: *1-5* copies are Ø15; *6-31* copies are Ø9; *32-91* copies are Ø8.40; a case of *92* or more copies are Ø7.50 each.

Bulletproof Privacy

5½"x8½", 160 pages. Published January 1997. Prices each: *1-5* copies are Ø16; *6-31* copies are Ø10; *32-79* copies are Ø9; a case of *80* or more copies are Ø8 each.

Hologram of Liberty

5½"x8½", 262 pages. Published August 1997. Prices each: *1-5* copies are Ø20; *6-15* copies are Ø12; *16-39* copies are Ø11.20; a case of *40* or more copies are Ø10 each.

Boston on Guns & Courage

5½"x8½", 192 pages. Published March 1998. Prices each: *1-5* copies are Ø17; *6-31* copies are Ø10.20; *32-59* copies are Ø9.50; see Web Site for case discounts.

Shipping and Handling are *not* included. Book Rate add: Ø3 for the first copy and Ø0.25 for each additional copy. First Class Mail add: Ø4 for the first copy and Ø0.50 for each additional copy.

These forms of payment *only:*

Cash. (Preferred. Cash orders get autographed copies.)
ecash. Accepted soon. Check Web Site for details.
payee blank M.O.s. (which makes them freely negotiable).
Unless prior agreement has been made, we do not accept (*and will return*) checks, C.O.D.s, filled-in M.O.s, or any other form of tender.

NOTE: The Ø symbol denotes "Federal Reserve Notes" which are no longer redeemable in, and masquerade as, real $ gold or silver money. Prices and terms are subject to change without notice. Send orders to:

JAVELIN PRESS
c/o 504 West 24th St., #73E; Austin, Texas.
(Non-Domestic. Near "78705." All Rights Reserved.)
www.javelinpress.com